HOME-GROWN
HARVEST

HOME-GROWN HARVEST

THE GROW-YOUR-OWN GUIDE TO SUSTAINABILITY AND SELF-SUFFICIENCY

Eve McLaughlin &
Terence McLaughlin

DAVID & CHARLES

www.davidandcharles.com

Contents

Introduction

I learnt gardening seventy-five years ago from my grandfather, who grew the finest vegetables in Hampshire. From him I picked up all the tips that he probably inherited from his grandfather – like planting carrots next to onions so that they could frighten off each others' pests; and never throwing anything away until you had considered carefully what else it could be used for.

Even in our first house – which had very restricted growing space – I scandalised the neighbours by planting cauliflowers in the tiny front garden, and building a 'roof' garden on top of the air raid shelter which filled the back space. Of our progressively larger gardens, I recall with affection the raspberry plantation in Twickenham and the rhubarb so vigorous that it beat its way through paths.

I also learnt that you can have far too much of a good thing unless you plan ahead and arrange to sell or barter. I remember a glut of asparagus and pumpkins and the ingenuity exercised in finding new recipes (asparagus and pumpkin cake, anyone?).

My husband had never laid fork to earth in his youth, but as a practical scientist, he took up the challenge of self-sufficiency and invented various labour saving devices. Harnessing the power of nature to horticulture was something rather new and strange then. Rain, wind and sun come free, so he fixed water butts on all the downpipes, made a Savonius rotor mill from an oil drum and salvaged car parts, and solar panels from recycled beer cans at first, and then second hand radiators.

When we wrote the original version of this book in 1978 it was around the same time as the popular comedy show, *The Good Life*, was being broadcast. The series did set some people thinking 'we could do that, and better!' however, despite this we were widely regarded as cranks and in hindsight the book was well ahead of its time.

Now, 40 years on, homeowners are realising that they are in possession of a valuable asset, whatever the fluctuations of the property market. They understand that better use can be made of their gardens: rather than covering them with expensive paving and slippery decking they can grow fruit and vegetables, free of unwanted and untested additives.

People are discovering the mind-blowing flavours of produce picked fresh from the garden half an hour ago, compared to the often dull-tasting produce from supermarkets, as well as the other benefits: saving money; energy; replacing fossil fuels; and generally going green; even if they only have a small plot of land.

I am delighted that this book has been reissued, with a sympathetic and comprehensive update by Diane Millis. Although almost all of the gadgets mentioned in the book are now readily available in shops and online, we have kept to the spirit of the original book and included information on how to construct some of your own equipment using recycled materials. We have also added a guide to the most helpful self-sufficiency websites for more information.

I hope new generations of householders will read it, decide to make the most of their assets and enjoy a truly good life.

Before you begin

1. Getting away from it all

Are you tired of the rat race? Do you long to get away from it all – to sell up everything and buy a farm somewhere? Do you want to buck the money system and escape the throwaway consumer economy? Do you sincerely want to be thrifty?

Climate change, peak oil, deforestation, industrial farming systems reliant on chemicals, food-linked health scares, rising food prices and fears for food security – there are many reasons driving people like you towards self-sufficiency and back to the land. Just consider the fact that our consumption of food in this country accounts for 19 per cent of all the greenhouse gas emissions generated from what we consume. If you take the deforestation and other changes in land use overseas that happen as a direct consequence of our food purchasing decisions then this figure rises to 30 per cent.

Even the Government wants you to 'grow your own' – already one in three of us grows fruit and vegetables, but as a nation we grow only around 60 per cent of the food we eat, so the country's self-sufficiency is also on the line.

But consider the realities of starting a farm. Good, undeveloped farming land is expensive, and if it isn't there's a reason: it is too poor to support vegetable or animal life to any extent. Add in the cost of a new tractor, a dear little pink pig for fattening, and your lowing herd winding slowly o'er the lea, and it could take the whole of most people's life savings. You could pool your resources with a group of like-minded folk and form a commune, but when you think how difficult it is for just two people to live together in complete harmony, it may be a step too far attempting it with 12.

However, there is a compromise between remaining a discontented cog in the business machine and sinking your savings into a sea of mud. Stay put and develop your own patch. Make your garden – whether it is an estate or a backyard – into a productive asset, instead of a recurring expense. Rather than working overtime to earn the money to buy convenience foods that are convenient only to the manufacturer, resign yourself to working less hard for other people, and start working for yourself. At least you have more chance of being appreciated.

Don't try to be entirely self-sufficient at first just for the sake of foolish consistency. If your friends point out that you are still dependent on the wicked commercial world for your clothes, cars or carpets, agree with them, and go on saving money on the things you can produce for yourself. As you get more adaptable, the range of these will widen all the time. Concentrate on food production first – this is, after all, the heaviest item of expenditure for most families – then on the saving of fuel and energy, or even home-production through solar or windpower. If you can provide these essentials for yourself, you will find that a relatively small amount of paid work will keep you in clothes, transport, entertainment and other home comforts.

Of course, you may have to change some other aspects of your life. We have concentrated in this book on the use of land to grow the widest possible variety of vegetables because these will provide a perfectly adequate diet with little (or no) added meat and with the best utilisation of the space available. Rearing animals for meat is a dreadfully wasteful use of land in terms of costs and a diet rich in meat won't help climate change either – global meat production is estimated to contribute around 18 per cent of the gases thought to cause man-made global warming. If your family's criterion of a proper meal is a large slab of meat with anaemic 'two veg' so subordinate as to go almost unnoticed, try to re-educate them.

We have only one motto for this book – 'Think thrift'. Don't be seduced by books or articles that tell you about gardening, wine-making or utilising solar energy, as if these are hobbies – a nice respectable way for the middle classes to use their spare time and a lot of their spare money. Don't buy gadgets that are really only toys. This is an unconventional book, blatantly concerned with saving money, a parsimonious book that, we are pleased to say, grudges every penny.

> Resign yourself to working less hard for other people, and start working for yourself

2. Making the most of what you've got

Using what you have already means you can start right away. It doesn't involve moving house; you can go at your own pace and, if you get fed up with the whole idea, then at least you haven't burnt your bridges behind you. In fact, in this way, you are much less likely to get fed up.

Britain has around 15 million back gardens – making up an estimated 3 per cent of all land – and the vast majority of these could be productive. Yet most gardens, even in rural areas, seem to consist of a scruffy lawn and a few measly herbaceous borders. If they, or even part of them, were used to grow vegetables, they could produce more, in proportion to size, than our arable farmers do on their vast acreages.

Farm and commercial horticultural planting is done at distances which allow for the ultimate height and spread of the various plants – you will often see this spacing quoted as correct for ordinary gardens. But, at home you do not plant a mass of carrots 8 in (20cm) apart and harvest the lot at once. You could plant at quarter of that distance, and take every other one at intervals as young carrots when you want them, and let the rest mature. A commercial grower couldn't do that, so they lose half the potential of the planting space available.

In a garden, too, you can plant quick-growing crops in the gap between slow growers – which is called catch-cropping – and fill in any small spaces with a handful of lettuces, or similar fast growers. The commercial grower has to wait for a decent bit of space to be clear, if they don't double-crop, since they can't sell half a dozen of anything separately.

So it is very difficult to say what size of garden you need to be self-sufficient. Unless you're a vegan, you will have to keep and perhaps kill some sort of animal, and these need much more space than crops. You can't really do much with grazing animals with less than about 1 acre (0.5ha) of garden, since some of it will have to be fenced off for stock. Even then, you will have to buy in feed at times. Small animals or chickens need less space, but they can present certain problems in a suburb. If they are near the house, then they are probably near the neighbours' houses too, and there could be complaints about noise/smells.

If you intend to live vegetarian, or to buy in any meat you want, then a much smaller space will do. The average family of four is reckoned to get a year's vegetables off a plot which measures 30 x 60ft (9 x 18m). But who is 'average'?

If your available land is less than this, don't despair because your own requirements may be less too. The great beauty of domestic gardening is that the producer is also the consumer and can forecast very precisely what the family's needs are. If your growing family eats around half a hundredweight of potatoes a week, and there is a reasonably cheap source of supply locally, are you going to fill the plot with potatoes, or buy them and grow yourself the pricier, fancy vegetables? One thing to remember is that vegetables straight from the garden taste nicer, so more and more varieties get eaten.

Even if you scarcely have a garden at all, it is possible to grow quite a lot in containers and odd corners. If you want to do better than that, are you keen enough to move to another house with a larger garden in the same area? And don't forget your front garden – hopefully you or previous occupants will have resisted the temptation to concrete over any space you have out front. Do all you can to hold onto your front garden and make it pay by creating an edible herbaceous border or even a vegetable patch, although you might need to consider how secure and free from pollution your patch is.

> Small animals or chickens need less space, but they can present certain problems in a suburb

Finally, if you really have no outdoor space to call your own, then remember the increasing number of other growing options out there. Community gardens, allotments, local garden sharing schemes and even national services that match growers with available land are springing up all over the country. There are even plans for a Government initiative to allow landowners and voluntary groups to set up temporary allotments on land awaiting development.

These suggestions and many other practical, money-saving ideas are examined in more detail in the following pages.

Getting started

3. Basic equipment

You will probably need a lot less than some would have you think. Many an armchair economist would consider the home grower to be seriously under-capitalised. Get some machinery, runs the argument. Install specialised buildings and automatic controls with flashing lights. Invest in elaborate watering systems and high-power spray equipment. And, if there is any room left in the garden after all this, get those undisciplined crops into neat lines, a metre apart, so that the machines can plant, tend, water, weed, spray, pick, wash, and finally pop them into polythene bags so that they look almost as good as the shop varieties.

The machinery manufacturers are, as you might imagine, all in favour of this approach. You can buy machines to dig, furrow, plough, trench, rake, hoe and earth-up – all reduced in size to garden proportions – and even such aids to gracious living as powered wheelbarrows, ride-on mowers, and automatic lawn-spikers that trundle around like some awful medieval weapon.

No doubt, if you have all these, you can afford the time to go around the golf-course on your battery-powered trolley – and, after your heart attack from lack of exercise, live the rest of your life with a battery-powered pacemaker. The fact is that most of these devices are merely toys for people who want to play farmers at the weekend, while others are useful but for such a limited time that their cost cannot be justified in any real economic terms.

There is also the carbon footprint of your home-growing operation to consider. Self-sufficiency means providing for yourself as much as possible, and plugging in a leaf blower when a leaf rake will do the job just as well doesn't square with this. Reducing your energy needs, and not adding to them, should be the home growers mantra. This will cut down the carbon costs of your kit and reduce the emissions that your activities generate.

In general, don't imagine that machines can be a substitute for care and thought. Use them only when you have no other option but hire them if possible and don't expect them to take over your responsibility for deciding exactly what has to be done.

When it comes to anything other than basic tools we would recommend the following:

2.5 acres (1ha) or more of arable land (not just pasture):
You will need a small tractor, not only for planting
and cultivating but for all the other jobs that go with
this sort of area of land: ditching, hedging, bulldozing
piles of compost around, and so on. If you want to use
it for general carrying, even from your plot to your
neighbour and back, you will need to license it before
taking it on a public road.

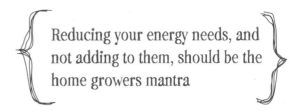

Reducing your energy needs, and
not adding to them, should be the
home growers mantra

Less than 2.5 acres (1ha) of arable land:
If you still need help, the answer may be a cultivator, which certainly takes a lot
of the backache out of preparing the soil each year, although some believe they
actually damage soil structure and they can certainly inadvertently spread weeds.
They are also expensive. As one cultivator advertisement puts it: 'One weekend
can turn an overgrown wilderness into a mini market garden,' which is true
enough in its way but the problem comes in deciding what your expensive pet is
going to do for the other fifty-one weekends in the year.

The advertisements talk glibly about furrowing, weeding, raking, and earthing-up potatoes ... but wait until you try to do all these things with a machine that often feels like Boadicea's chariot with the steering gone. You can't weed by machine unless you leave room for it between rows, which entails a tremendous loss of productive ground. You can't earth up potatoes by machine – at least, we have never met anyone who could – without losing large numbers of tubers from the edge of the rows, unless again you have your rows uneconomically wide apart. You usually end up by buying a rotary mower attachment for your cultivator, and using it to cut the grass for the rest of the year – employing a really pricey machine to do the job of a cheap mower.

The best answer to this problem is to hire a cultivator for a week at the beginning of the season if you can't do without it. This way you get the work done for less than the interest on the capital cost of a cultivator, and someone else has the costs of housing and servicing the machine. You can even get a small cultivator into the back of a small hatch-back car, so saving delivery costs.

Depending on the size of your plot, you might even be able to share a week's hire with a neighbour – as you can't depend on it not to rain on the day you have chosen, a week is a sensible period.

Of course, if you can buy a second-hand cultivator cheaply this makes economic sense, because it will probably struggle on for another four years, possibly more. The feasibility of this idea will probably depend on your skill in reviving them, as most people sell such machines cheap when they 'won't go'.

> If you want to cultivate a vegetable garden, there are a certain number of basic tools you will need

OTHER MACHINES

We quite like another garden machine, the compost shredder, but they are expensive. They shred organic waste, such as tree prunings, to ensure they are composted quickly and easily – saving time and making your compost heap more efficient. Finer shreddings produced by micro-shredders can also be used as a mulch.

Again, if you can acquire such a thing second-hand, or build it from scrap parts, it is useful. Ours was made from an old hammer-mill of doubtful parentage, and is driven by a home-made windmill.

TOOLS

If you want to cultivate a vegetable garden, there are a certain number of basic tools you will need and the rule with all of them is: if you are buying them new, the cheapest will not always pay off in the long term. Keep your tools shopping list to a minimum but get the best quality you can afford. If you are starting from scratch, your outlay on tools can be cut dramatically by buying second-hand. Look out for car boot sales, jumble sales, and local auctions, especially where the contents of big houses are being cleared. A full set of garden tools of good quality, with years of life in them, will often go cheap.

Or ask your neighbours – there are bound to be some who are happy to share those bits of kit that are less regularly in use and others who have perhaps lost the gardening bug. Offer some of your produce or rake up their autumn leaves in return and you could save pounds when it comes to tools.

While buying online may be a good way to knock some pennies off your purchasing it may be best to buy in person giving you the chance to test the tools for size, weight and balance – you will be working together for many hours to come.

Traditional tools were tough, with smooth ash shafts which lasted a lifetime. Some more modern tools use inferior wood, so either seek out good quality wooden tools – car boot sales are worth a visit for these – or go for a good strong metal tool. If going for metal, choose forged steel, not stamped or tubular steel. Polished stainless steel is a good choice for garden tools but will typically cost 40 per cent more than inferior metals although it will look smarter longer with less effort as it is corrosion resistant. Avoid tools made from cheap thin metal that has been epoxy powder coated as this will not add any strength to the metal and rust will set in if it breaks or bends.

Don't be led astray by pretty paintwork, which wears off in no time and covers up low quality wood, or plastic handles which snap at the first pressure. Whatever the material, pick a nice rounded handle, either D-shaped or T-shaped, it's up to you (avoid trendy garden tools with over-designed handles and opt for traditionally designed ones that have stood the test of time), but make sure the one you choose is big enough for you to grip comfortably even when you're wearing gloves.

> Select a tool which feels comfortable to your own hands when you hold it in a digging motion

Spade and fork

The spade – the one with the flat blade, not the curved-blade shovel used for muck-shifting – cuts edges, rough digs and scoops out trenches. The fork probes into the ground and breaks it into a workable tilth, letting nourishment down to the roots of plants. Both implements should be as solid and strong as possible, since they are in constant use in tough situations.

Select a tool which feels comfortable to your own hands when you hold it in a digging motion. Check, cautiously, that there are no sharp or rough edges on the handle or shaft which could lacerate your skin.

Also consider a long-shafted spade – the extra leverage when you dig and lift soil can save back ache and they were the spade of choice in years gone by for this very reason.

As for the fork, if you are very small, you may find a fork with short tines easier to handle than a full-sized model. Any size of person will find one useful for top-forking bits of the ground in confined situations between growing crops. These border forks are almost as expensive as the big ones, though. Whichever size fork, the tines should be forged from a single piece of steel to maximise strength.

Trowel, rake, hoe, and dibber

You will need a strong hand trowel for planting out, and a rake for taming the dug soil into smooth earth. Again, pick what feels comfortable and tough to you and check for sharp projections.

A hoe for weeding is also necessary. No two gardeners will ever agree about which kind is better – a push hoe or a draw hoe. A draw hoe has a curved neck and a blade roughly at right angles to the handle. It is used by bringing it down from above on to the weeds and chopping them vertically. The big danger is that the upstroke will clout any tallish plants adjacent and the down stroke can miss and slice into root vegetables or cut seedlings off in their prime.

The push or Dutch hoe, which has a flat blade in line with the handle, is moved forward to cut off weeds below the surface. If your angle is too shallow or the pressure too feeble, part of the weed may be left in to grow again. However, it takes very little practise to become expert with it.

We think the push hoe is a far more precise instrument and allows planting much closer than is safe with the draw hoe. On the other hand, the draw hoe is more adapted to earthing-up potatoes. But you're paying for them so you make your choice.

The other basic tool is a dibber – a piece of wood for prodding tidy holes in the ground in which to plant potatoes, beans, small plants, etc. You can make it yourself from the handle of an old fork or spade, with a comfortable D-shaped grip and tapered end – the abandoned corpse of a rusty tool would do. Or you can use a walking stick, a child's beach-spade handle, a garden cane or a strong stick with no spiky ends to jag your hand. But you will find it useful to burn inch/centimetre-divisions on the business end of the dibber.

OTHER USEFUL KIT

A pair of shears, plus sharpening stone, helps with hedges and tough weeds, as well as awkward grass outcrops and edges. It even does crude pruning.

Secateurs are the correct thing for pruning anything you value, like fruit trees and bushes, but it is worth waiting before buying. They are very often given away by gardening magazines as prizes for handy hints of the simplest sort and they are sure to appear on a list of birthday presents for anyone known to be taking an interest in gardening. Choose between the parrot-beak (bypass) variety or the anvil type – it's a matter of personal preference – but only use on stems ¾in (15-20mm) thick. Larger stems could damage your secateurs, the plant and your hands – try to borrow a long-handled lopper for these jobs instead.

Wood prunings from old trees, broom handles or scrap wood can be adapted for the purpose, but when these run out wood or bamboo canes must be bought

If you possess trees, a wire rake with spring tines will remove the autumn leaves from the lawn and beds without ripping holes in them, as the ordinary rake does. Leaves should not be wasted (see 'Leafmould', page 36), and the right tool makes it easy to collect them from the street and other people's gardens (with permission).

If you grow peas, beans or any other tall, weak-stemmed crops, you will need stakes. Wood prunings from old trees, broom handles or scrap wood can be adapted for the purpose, but when these run out wood or bamboo canes must be bought. Wood in roofing-batten thickness, sometimes available second-hand, makes strong stakes and frames. Smooth canes are less rough on delicate plants, but string ties tend to slip down them more easily.

If you foresee much use of canes – for runner beans, say – then study the prices online for bulk purchases that work out much cheaper than some of the mainstream shops; Ebay, for example, has some good deals from a variety of online stores. For shorter canes, consider buying long canes and cutting them in half yourself – cutting near a joint on the cane.

If you grow many beans or raspberries, or any tall plant, a quantity of strong twine will be needed. Look for twine made from sustainably-sourced natural fibres, such as jute or hemp, which can be composted after use and avoid synthetic fibres.

For minor tying-up jobs, you will need very soft twine for stringing-up plants without cutting through the stems. The hairy string recovered from parcels will do as a substitute, but not thin, hard cord with a sharp cutting edge. Torn-up rag, old bits of bandage or plaited wool scraps are better.

Finally, you might need wheels. There is no denying that a strong metal wheelbarrow is handy for shifting heavy loads or loose earth as well as allowing small children to participate harmlessly in the work. If storage space is short then

consider a folding barrow and be aware that there are plenty made from recycled plastics. Alternatively, you can adapt an old pram or go-cart, or fix wheels to a box from the greengrocer, lined with plastic for carrying soggy stuff. If you only have a small plot with short distances between it and the compost heap, consider instead plastic tubs on wheels and two handled trugs – both of which are long lasting and can be found made from recycled materials including old car tyres.

PLANTING KIT

Plastic trays for germinating seeds are valuable. Similar trays can be improvised from the following:
- shallow wooden boxes, or cardboard ones covered in polythene with drainage holes pierced
- polystyrene packaging, thrown away by shops, which has the added advantage of keeping the soil warm
- a washing-up bowl with a hole in it
- rusty baking tins
- waxed cartons

Some of these will have a limited life span, but they will have given some extra service.

CANNY POTS

Turn your tin cans into plant pots by removing the tops completely and hammering any jagged bits flat. Then turn upside down and make four or six holes in the base with one of those triangular can piercers, leaving the points sticking up inside. Drop the lid in on top of these, which will give space for drainage. Fill with earth and plant up. When you want to get the plant out again, stick a skewer or knitting needle through the base holes and push the plant up on the lid.

Buying plant pots in bulk and online is probably going to be one of the cheapest options but ask neighbours, family and friends as some people have hundreds of them accumulated over the years following trips to the garden centre. Use what you've got as well – every household has a lot of plastic containers, holding liquid detergent, shampoo, squash, yoghurt, soft margarine and so on, which can be washed and re-used for tender plants. Egg boxes can be filled with earth for germinating seeds and even tin cans are re-usable.

One of the best homemade solutions is to make your pots from old newspapers – you can buy small wooden devices to help you shape them correctly if you like, but it's easy enough to do without once you've done it a few times. These biodegrade once planted out and so save you moving seedlings/small plants and possibly damaging the roots.

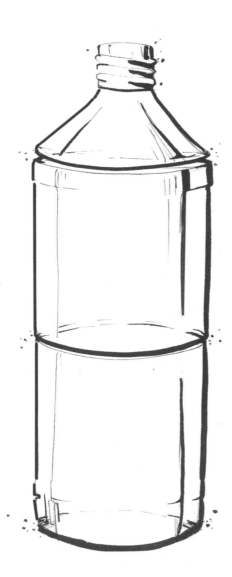

Biodegradeable pots are also available to buy – they are often made from coir fibre, the unused husks of coconuts.

Larger purpose-made pots or planters, for tomatoes say, are costly. Large squash containers, with the tops cut off, take quite a large plant and – if it is going to continue growing in a container – a plastic household bucket can be used; this is easily pierced with a hot skewer to make drainage holes at the base.

A garden line is useful to keep your planting rows straight. It isn't the aesthetic appeal so much as knowing where it is safe to hoe before the seedlings are up. You can buy a commercial one, or make your own from strong twine or string and sticks.

Any sowing of seeds in protected boxes and pots will necessitate a sieve. You might be able to make one from a wooden frame and wire netting, but the difficult bit is tucking all the sharp ends of wire safely out of the way.

BOTTLE POTS

Detergent bottles should be cut in two places (see illustration). The bottom makes a pot, with pierced drainage holes. The middle section, placed on a lid or saucer and filled with earth, becomes a ring planter. The top makes a 'dark cover' for early germination and then a funnel for local watering. Transparent bottles, cut and upturned, become mini-greenhouses for delicate seedlings. The thinner sorts of plastic usually disintegrate in the sun after one season, but this doesn't matter, since they were free in the first place.

Create a bottle pot using an old detergent bottle. Cut the bottle in two places as shown above with drainage holes in the bottom

WATERING EQUIPMENT

A watering can with a fine rose is a help with seed planting. But just as important is a water butt or several to collect and store rainwater – you can connect a couple together to collect water from house gutters, and have another collecting water from gutters installed on your shed or greenhouse. Gardeners use about two-thirds of the domestic water supply during dry spells, which is why you can often buy water butts at a discount from your local authority or water companies.

Look out for those made from recycled plastic or recycle yourself. Old plastic dustbins, fruit barrels, old baths, discarded water tanks and cisterns will also do the job nicely but be sure to cover them with a tight fitting lid to prevent small children falling in and stop evaporation during hot weather.

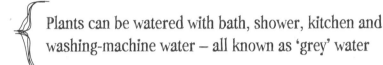

Plants can be watered with bath, shower, kitchen and washing-machine water – all known as 'grey' water

Saving other types of water can also help the self sufficient gardener. Plants can be watered with bath, shower, kitchen and washing-machine water – all known as 'grey' water. It usually contains some degree of contamination from soaps and detergents, but soil and potting compost act as a filter and the short-term use of grey water can help tide plants over during a summer drought. (Avoid using water containing bleaches, disinfectants, dishwasher salt and stronger cleaning products as they can harm plants and avoid using grey water on salads and other produce to be used without cooking.) You can spend a fortune on a bespoke grey water storage and filtration system, or start small-scale by diverting bath water through a pipe to a container/butt but make sure you use it quickly as if left, potentially harmful organisms might multiply and it will start to smell at the very least.

There are many other ways to spend a lot of money on watering kit but if your water is metered it can pay off in the long run.

The following should be considered when choosing what to invest in:
- drip irrigation systems ensure that up to 90 per cent of the water reaches the roots of the plants as opposed to sprinklers which are only 40–50 per cent efficient
- a sprinkler can use as much water in an hour as the average family of four uses in a day
- hosepipes can suck up to 220 gallons (1,000 litres) of water an hour but one with a trigger nozzle allows you to direct the flow of water more accurately to where the plant needs it most – the base and not the leaves

4. Protection

Certain items can make a big difference both in speeding up the growing process and ensuring survival rates of your precious plants. This applies equally to the early stages of germination and growth and when plants are in the ground. Even the minimum of protection for your plants against the dire effects of the weather will extend the growing season and markedly increase productivity.

PROPAGATORS

Permanently shaped propagators, which act like small greenhouses, consist of a clear, hard plastic cover over a double-sized seed tray, and can cost under £5. You can make a similar propagating cover from the very thick, glass-clear plastic used in double glazing. Tape the cut corners or, if you have a very steady hand, try heat-sealing them. The material is not particularly expensive and can be sourced online from suppliers of glazing plastics although cheaper offcuts are often available in DIY shops

An even simpler solution is to cover a seedling in a pot with a transparent bag – the wrapper in which tights are sold, for example – propped up on a couple of lolly sticks, to make a mini-greenhouse. For a box of seedlings use a shirt-size bag and four to six lolly sticks.

For the more ambitious, a heated propagator will ensure that, even in the north, early crops can be raised. The standard unit comprises an electrically-heated base, with thermostatic control, over which the seed trays or pots are balanced. This is often topped with a shaped plastic cover to keep in the heated air. They are not cheap but they certainly work; however, when the seedlings have outgrown them, more spacious protected accommodation will be needed.

You could make your own propagator in various ways. Tubular heaters – giving 60 watts and obtainable from an electrical wholesaler – could be clipped to brackets under the staging which holds your trays and boxes. A soil cable kit could be used to make a heated base unit, taking six trays: lay a bed of sand or pea gravel in a large flat tray, set out the cable in a grid pattern, with no part touching another, cover with more sand and sit the trays on top. You could connect a thermostat, if you want one. Study the small ads or look online before buying, as any equipment like this can be a lot more expensive in a local store.

The advantages of protected growing are:

• the opportunity to extend the normal cropping season by at least two months and probably more; tender plants can be grown which are not normally practical for outdoor sowings because these leave too little development time before the frost;

• it is possible with a cold greenhouse, and with careful management with lesser protection, to have something fresh growing all the year round;

• a greenhouse is somewhere sheltered to work in when the outdoor temperature is uninviting;

• early cash crops can be raised for market; and

• the more you can grow in the colder times of the year, the less you have to buy at top prices.

However, any form of protected sowing means extra work, since rain cannot easily reach the growing crops, even in the so-called self-watering cloches. The actual equipment costs more than plain sowing in the garden, and this reduces the apparent return in the first year, so it is all the more important to choose durable materials, which will last long enough for the initial costs to be absorbed.

Plus, remember that cloches unused in mid-winter and mid-summer have to be stored somewhere out of harm's way, while frames and greenhouses are a permanent feature of the garden.

Longer soil cables can be used directly in the earth either in greenhouse beds or in the open garden. The cables are set out in grids or long rows, up and down, in freshly dug soil. It is important not to forget just where they run, or adjacent digging may spear them. Obviously, the heat so generated should not be allowed to dissipate – cover the area with a line of cloches or a cold frame.

All these heated propagators have to be powered by electricity, which is far too expensive to be used casually.

An upturned half of a plastic bottle can protect delicate seedlings from from pests and cold winds

CLOCHES AND COVERS

For protecting plants from pests and keeping newly planted-out plants warm early in the year cloches are useful and easily made. The top half of a transparent plastic drinks bottle will do the job nicely while milk cartons can be used as protective cloches at night but will let less direct light in through the day. Glasses with chipped rims or wine glasses with snapped stems can be upturned over potted plants as mini-greenhouses. Obviously, you should put them somewhere in full view, so that no one tending the plants puts a hand down on the broken spike – preferably bind it with tape or cover with a blob of blue tack. Jam jars can be used the same way, but should be removed before the plant grows wider than the neck opening.

A length of polythene sheeting can be used to construct an outdoor tunnel cloche or polytunnel. The sheet is propped up on sticks and supported at intervals by wire hoops stuck into the ground. Pull the ends of the sheet tight and anchor them with heavy stones. A second set of hoops over the top may be necessary to prevent the tunnel being blown away by the wind. You can buy the sheet in rolls and hoops in multiple packs quite cheaply from garden suppliers online.

All types of plastic cloches are on sale, some of which seem to be remarkably cheap. But be sure to buy plastic stated to be 'UVI' (ultra violet inhibited) or it will disintegrate after the first summer, due to the action of the sun. Some cloches are made in semi-translucent, doubled-walled plastic. In our experience, these do not let through enough light for the plants to grow, and they are flimsy.

Thin polythene isn't very durable or stable, and high winds may strip it off. Rigid plastic is pre-formed into a sheet or shaped as a cloche, but some of it isn't all that rigid – vacuum formed, like the old transparent egg boxes in shops – it is about as flimsy. This is useless out of doors, because it blows away with the slightest breeze; but it can be used in a greenhouse to cover a seed tray without the need to prop up the plastic.

> Glasses with chipped rims or wine glasses with snapped stems can be upturned over potted plants as mini-greenhouses

Thicker plastics may be had in a semi-rigid sheet, which can be bent to a curve, or a ridge-tent shape, or shaped permanently as a cloche or tray cover. The thicker the plastic, the more expensive it is, but the better the protection given and the longer the article lasts. A good home-made cloche option is to use a sheet of the clear plastic corrugated material sold for roofing carports – a 6ft (1.8m) sheet would make two cloches, with wire or metal pegs needed to hold the sides in place.

No sort of plastic gives as much protection as glass, which is still used by traditional gardeners because of its greater thermal insulation and as it's less likely to blow away. Wired or plate glass is tougher, but it costs an astronomical amount, even compared with ordinary glass. If you do use glass cloches, remember to ask for horticultural glass, which is cheaper than window glass and normally comes in standard sizes to fit greenhouses.

A cloche can be simply two panes of glass held together by a wire or rubber clip at right angles. This gives excellent protection to growing seeds for the first few weeks of their lives. This kind of cloche is stable against the wind, but awkward to move aside for weeding or watering. However, if you have weeded the spot first, it should stay reasonably clear for a short time, and glass cloches will stand being hosed over or under better than plastic ones..

A plastic tunnel cloche made from plastic bird netting stretched

Where protection is needed for growing tender plants to an advanced stage, a tall, barn cloche is necessary. This has high sides and a mansard roof, held by a complicated system of wire hooks and clips. It is quite heavy and very awkward to move – the roof section tends to slide off if the clips are at all loose. An old method of correcting this was to fill in the top section with wire netting, from which the roof glass could be lifted for watering.

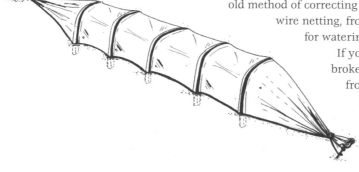

If you have glass cloches, you soon acquire broken glass, either from careless moving or from stones flung by mowers or cultivators. Dogs and argumentative cats take their toll too. If you have children, glass is not ideal for cloches: babies might fall on them, older children could kick things through them – neither cloche nor child does the other any good. Glass is also risky for elderly people with unsteady balance or arthritic hands.

As well as having structures placed over them, tender plants can be covered to reduce or avoid frost damage. Horticultural fleece is a popular option and is permeable and light enough to cover young tender stems. You can buy it in bulk and cut to fit. For plants in containers you can buy fleece jackets or even biodegradable jute frost jackets.

NETS AND GUARDS

There's another kind of protection you might need to consider – protection from wildlife. Protective netting will be a must if your garden is plagued by birds – and they come from miles around at the first rumour of free food being provided. Your seedlings must be protected from them; this particularly applies to peas. If you have the money, you can buy plastic bird netting or make protective cages from chicken wire – look online for the cheapest bulk purchase deals. You can also improvise by protecting peas with a barricade of twigs, covering fruit with old lace curtains and so on.

A variety of other netting and wire guards are also available online for protection against other predators – rabbits, deer, etc.

COLD FRAMES

The next stage up from a cloche is a cold frame. This is basically a bottomless box, higher at one end than the other, and covered with a glass or plastic framework; the lid lifts off, slides back or hinges open for ventilation. Glass or plastic sides allow more light to enter, avoiding spindly stems, but they do not hold the heat as well overnight as the wooden-sided coldframe. It can be used to hold boxes or trays of seeds for later planting out, but mostly it serves to protect tender crops growing in soil.

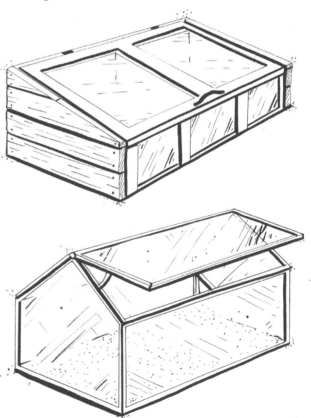

The base of the frame is filled with fine potting soil – sterilised to remove weed seeds, which saves a lot of trouble later on. Plants are usually started under closed cover; then, as it gets warmer, the top is opened up or taken off, and replaced when cooler weather comes. A small, portable frame can be stood over a crop in the open ground and moved along to shelter a later one.

You can make your own frame from scrap wood and an old window-frame which will determine the size, or design one to your own specification, tailored to the size of plant you mean to grow, and incorporating glass panels in the sides as well for extra light (see right). For a more temporary solution you could also use straw bales with an old window or even a car windscreen balanced on top, or a cardboard box or old crate, using clear plastic sheeting on top and black plastic lining the walls to maximise heat absorption.

Top: A cold frame made using an old window frame and scrap wood. Above: A lightweight plastic frame with hinged sides

There are also many commercial versions available with wooden or aluminium frames and glazed with either glass or twin-walled polycarbonate. The polycarbonate does not allow as much light through as glass but is far better as an insulator than glass and not as fragile or dangerous if broken. Because the light is diffused by the material, the risk of scorching in sunny weather is also reduced.

The 'barn' shape is probably best for these lightweight frames, with both sides hinged, since you have to lean on and over them to tend the plants.

Vertical cold frames, or wall greenhouses, are popular for growing tender, tall plants – like tomatoes – against the wall of the house. Generally a metal framework, about 5ft (1.5m) square and under 2ft (60cm) deep, it is hooked to the wall and covered with plastic. In this frame, you can start seeds in trays or pots and grow about two levels of bushy plants, like peppers, or shelves on staging, or around four tall plants, like tomatoes, in pots or bags on the ground. A house wall will act as a radiator and plastic covers are quite adequate for wind shelter; the frames are pretty stable, with the house to steady them.

GREENHOUSES

Greenhouses come in all shapes and sizes, from the small lean-to, which is a walk-in version of the vertical cold frame, to a free-standing palace. The minimum width is 4ft (1.2m) which allows one thin person to tend one line of plants or shelf of pots; 6ft (1.8m) – two sets of shelves (staging); while 8ft (2.4m) plus is best for serious greenhouse work, leaving room for double rows in beds on either side and space to manoeuvre in the middle.

In old-style greenhouses, the bottom half or third of the walls was generally panelled in cedar, with only the top part glazed. They were intended to be heated by large-diameter pipes along those walls, which is far too expensive for amateurs these days. In a cold greenhouse, that obscured area is not much use, except for forcing rhubarb, storing pots and sheltering families of toads. In the modern 'Dutch light' greenhouse, with glass to ground level, plants can be grown directly in the borders or in pots on the three-deck staging.

Traditional greenhouses, made of wood or aluminium with glass, are best from the point of view of temperature, stability and durability. They are usually sold in kit form which you erect yourself. Aluminium ones mostly bolt together, with patent clips for the glass, which makes glazing and replacement a much simpler and less messy business than using putty.

Sometimes a second-hand greenhouse is advertised locally, but allow yourself most of the weekend to take it down and re-erect it.

NATURAL GREENHOUSE WARMING

Try these tips for a cosy greenhouse:

• keep your greenhouse glass clean, especially where panes overlap; even normal grime will dramatically reduce light levels and cut down on free heating from sunlight;

• place your greenhouse in a bright spot that gets sun all day and isn't shaded by evergreen trees or walls;

• a lean-to greenhouse against the back wall of your house will need less heating;

• free-standing greenhouses with the lower part made of brick or timber conserve heat better than all-glass houses;

• seal gaps around poorly-fitting panes or doors to stop heat escaping; and

• consider moving less hardy plants indoors for the winter instead of heating the whole greenhouse for them.

Plastic greenhouses – aluminium frameworks with covers of various plastics – are much cheaper. The polythene is UV, but any plastic sheeting used in a greenhouse is fearfully easy to rip and tends to take off in a high wind, leaving your plants naked to the elements. You must reckon on replacing the cover every third year, unless you are unlucky from the outset. This cover often forms a very high proportion of the total cost, so over the years you will pay as much for a plastic house as for a glass one, and with more trouble attached. Rigid or semi-rigid plastic is better, but obviously costs more.

With any plastic house, make sure that adequate ventilators are provided. A greenhouse is like an oven in summer and plants must have plenty of moving air to survive. It is simple to put windows in a glass house,

> Traditional greenhouses, made of wood or aluminium with glass, are best from the point of view of temperature, stability and durability

> Trays are usually placed on top of the staging (or integrated in the staging you buy). These are filled with sand or gravel on which the pots stand

but not nearly as easy in plastic. The rigid house has no roof ventilator to let the hot air out; it has doors at both ends, but these complicate planting across the back as well as the sides, so reducing the productive area.

We would vote for a glass greenhouse, if you can possibly afford it, with a rigid plastic one as second choice. Although its maintenance problems are infinitely less, a glass greenhouse probably counts as a fixture, should you have to move in a year or two; it is certainly more trouble to dismantle than a plastic one, which is rather like a frame tent.

There's a huge variety of aluminium staging available that can be adapted to suit the needs of your plants as they grow. You can also buy aluminium wall-mounted shelf brackets that will enable you to fit your own shelf. Any old, narrow table can be used in the greenhouse, but first paint or varnish the wood and wrap polythene bags around the feet where they touch the earth. The standard width for staging along the sides is a maximum 2ft (60cm) and across the back about 3ft (90cm) – or your own convenient stretch. If you use a table wider than the door, a clear area will be needed nearby to shift it in and out.

Trays are usually placed on top of the staging (or integrated in the staging you buy). These are filled with sand or gravel on which the pots stand. If the sand is kept wet, the plant roots can draw up moisture and the air in the greenhouse is kept humid. The trays can also be used for ring culture of tomatoes (see page 107). On ordinary staging, cheap plastic tea-trays will serve the same purpose, but painted metal ones will rust in a season in the damp atmosphere.

In high summer, the roof will need shading; this can be done by painting it with a thin whitewash or cheap emulsion, which can be scraped off again in autumn (fairly cheap but nasty to remove); by rigging up old curtains or nylon shading net inside or out (costing little or nothing); or by fitting automatic blinds which raise and lower themselves according to the amount of light (very efficient, very smart and very expensive).

In winter and early spring some people heat their greenhouses but an entirely heated greenhouse is probably out of the question for anyone but the commercial grower or the wealthy. A lot of the heat from a glass-walled house, and practically all the heat from a plastic greenhouse, would escape into the air, which might improve the local temperature but is hardly economic or good for the planet. You might be

THE BEST SPOT FOR YOUR GREENHOUSE

Because you will want to work in your greenhouse when the weather is bad, and attend to it possibly late at night if conditions suddenly change for the worse, it should be sited near the house – not at the bottom of the garden, as indicated in so many landscape plans. Set it just beyond the area shaded by the house and run a path to it, so you do not have to wade through wet grass to reach it. The nearer it is, the easier it will be to connect electricity or carry water.

Try not to let the door opening face the prevailing wind, so the plants are not assaulted every time you go in. Leave room outside the door for getting staging in and out, if you want to plant into the greenhouse borders in summer, and for bringing up the wheelbarrow when you need to change the soil.

If the site faces south or west, the greenhouse may get too much sun in high summer, which would wilt the plants. A deciduous tree, carefully sited to serve as a screen, will put on foliage in summer to give dappled shade, while in winter the bare branches do not obstruct light at all.

able to set up a solar panel for greenhouse use (see page 235); or, in the few cases where it is practical, tap the resources of a methane digester or a wood/rubbish-burning stove.

To prevent some heat loss, it may be possible to 'double-glaze' the greenhouse with bubble plastic, or line it with polythene sheeting; in wooden houses, this can be pinned on, but for aluminium you will need plastic 'suckers' of double-sided tape. You could curtain off one end of the greenhouse, or drape plastic over the staging to make a small tent. Place a small heater underneath, taking great care that the plastic cannot flap on to it. The lining will reduce the amount of available light, possibly to unacceptable levels, and watering must be very cautiously done. Too little and the plants will dry out; too much and mould will develop.

5. A compost

Alongside your basic tools and a water butt, a compost bin is an essential item for any keen grower. It not only provides a home for all those prunings and grass clippings, it converts them into something that will go back into your soil, improving its structure and fertility.

All crops remove vital raw materials from the soil and these have to be replaced to ensure fertility for further produce. While the cost of buying these raw materials as commercial fertiliser chemicals is not excessive, it obviously makes sound economic and environmental sense to recycle as much of your surplus raw materials as possible.

This not only saves money; it improves the texture of the soil and the future yield from it and saves you or your rubbish men endless trips to the tip with your green waste (around 45 per cent of most households' rubbish could actually go straight into a compost bin).

MAKING A COMPOST HEAP

The simplest method is just to create a pile of all your vegetable waste as well as plenty of fibrous material like straw or long grass to aerate the softer and closer vegetation. Keep the pile damp but not soaking wet. With luck you will have reasonable compost in the middle of such a heap after six to nine months but the outsides should be cut away and used as the basis for the next heap, as they will not have become warm enough to be thoroughly composted.

A minor improvement that costs very little is to cover each heap, when completed, with a sheet of black agricultural polythene held down by pegs or heavy stones. Water the heap really thoroughly before you cover it, as it may be inconvenient to moisten it afterwards. The plastic will not only keep moisture in, and flies away, but will also absorb heat from the sun and thus keep the compost warmer. Again, you will probably have to cut away the sides and top for further composting and if you make your heap against a wooden fence, protect it with a thick sheet of polythene, otherwise it may rot with the compost.

COMPOST CONTAINERS

If you want good compost in a relatively short time, build a compost box in some shaded part of the plot. A 3ft (90cm) cube box will hold enough compost to prevent the mass cooling down quickly, without stopping aeration – the problem with very large boxes. You will need one compost box for every 300 sq yd (250 sq m) under cultivation or grass, or more if you add other wastes to your home-grown compost. While you are at it, you might as well build two boxes – one for collecting current waste while the other is maturing.

The boxes can be made from any old timber; they should not be close-boarded, so battered second-hand floor boards would do. Alternatively you can set up strong corner posts and make the sides of wire netting, in which case you must provide insulation to keep the working heap warm. The whole secret of constructing a good compost box is to maintain this balance between aeration and over-cooling. Make the front of your wooden box as a sliding panel – a discarded sheet of steel shelving would be ideal.

SOME LIKE IT HOT

Having a hot compost can speed things up a lot – your compost can be ready in 12 weeks – and can give you peace of mind when it comes to killing off any weed seeds that end up in there. Tips for a hot compost include: filling the compost up in layers but all in one go and keeping a lid on it, turning the heap every few weeks, shredding tough and bulky material, and insulating your compost bin. You can also buy a hot composter that includes an insulating jacket.

Pile the vegetation directly on to the ground so that worms can get in, and keep the lid on, especially in wet weather, so that the heap does not get too wet or cold. In autumn and winter you may have to provide some extra insulation – a length of roof insulation can be tied around the box with string to form a sort of overcoat. Alternatively, you could get panels of polystyrene foam insulation about ½in (12.5mm) thick and tie these against the outside. If you paint them black or dark green they will absorb more heat on sunny days. If you use polystyrene, make extra sure that your heap does not get to smouldering temperatures, or your insulation may go up in a cloud of black smoke!

You can, of course, buy ready-made compost containers, the commonest being barrel-shaped bins often made from recycled plastic. Check with your local council, as many offer these compost bins at heavy discounts in an effort to encourage more composting.

These will make perfectly good compost and look tidy in a very small garden or patio. But you may need quite a few if you have a big plot whereas, for a fraction of the cost, you could build a highly efficient compost 'production line' of several second-hand timber boxes for successive heaps.

LEAFMOULD

Composted leaves can make a good soil improver. As leaves are slower to break down than other compost items, taking a year or two, they are best recycled separately. You can use all sorts of leaves but avoid evergreen leaves such as holly, laurel or Leyland cypress and other conifers. As well as your own, try asking your local authority for leaves that have been collected from parks and cemeteries (never from woodland where they are a vital part of the ecosystem) or arrange a leaf-gathering event at your local school. But avoid those collected from roads, which may contain unwanted contaminants. Keep them in tied, black plastic sacks (with a few holes in the side), build a simple wire-mesh leafmould bin, or you can buy jute sacks which will biodegrade as well over time.

COMPOSTING METHODS

The aims of any composting system are that it should:
- produce plenty of humus;
- not lose excessive amounts of soluble minerals;
- kill weed seeds, so that these cannot germinate when the compost is spread;
- kill insect pests and their eggs or larvae, so that they are not perpetuated from one season to another.

In addition, most people would vote for a method that does not involve backbreaking amounts of work, produce smells or attract insects. Fortunately, all these requirements can be met by a number of composting systems.

Despite all the fuss made by the proponents of rival methods, there are really only three essentials for good composting: bacteria, air and warmth. Any method which provides all three will be effective.

1. BACTERIA

The actual work of breaking down vegetable material, from the lumps in which it usually appears to the even texture of fibrous humus, is performed by bacteria, so you must encourage them as much as possible. You can increase the numbers of active bacteria right away by mixing farmyard manure, such as chicken manure, into the compost heap about once every two weeks – alternately layering the vegetable waste with the manure and so on. Some recommend making a pit or channel at the top of the heap and pouring liquid farmyard manure into this. The layer system seems to work just as well though and is a lot less messy. But checking the provenance of the manure is a good idea – manure from a nonorganic farm is likely to be polluted with residues of veterinary products, such as antibiotics which are fed to most intensively-reared farm animals on a daily basis, or the remains of toxic worming products. So consider getting your manure from an organic farm or a local source who can provide guarantees regarding its purity.

> If you can manage it in some fairly hygienic way, and without scandalising the neighbours, urine has quite a useful speeding-up effect on compost – the Chinese used to call it Chairman Mao's secret ingredient in the fight for improved agriculture

If you can manage it in some fairly hygienic way, and without scandalising the neighbours, urine has quite a useful speeding-up effect on compost – the Chinese used to call it Chairman Mao's secret ingredient in the fight for improved agriculture.

Do not despair if you have no ready source of manure. The bacteria that cling to particles of earth on weeds, etc, will multiply quite rapidly given the right conditions.

There are branded 'compost accelerators' on the market which contain microorganisms especially cultured for composting, but you can help things along without them by increasing the nitrogen and decreasing the acidity in your compost. Try adding nettles to the heap before they have flowered, use washed seaweed or seaweed extract or add comfrey to the pile.

2. AIR
To ensure that the right kinds of bacteria develop, air is essential. The aerobic bacteria are the goodies, taking in oxygen and breaking down vegetation without producing any unpleasant by-products – a well-made compost heap has hardly any odour, apart from a slight and rather pleasant mushroomy smell – and they produce compost with a fine, springy texture like shredded peat, very useful for lightening heavy soil.

If the heap is too dense or wet, and the supply of air is cut off, aerobic bacteria cannot thrive, and their disreputable relations, the anaerobic bacteria take over. These produce evil-smelling gases and tend to give the compost a slimy texture which is quite unsuitable for soil conditioning.

Make sure that there are air channels of some kind right through your heap. If a container is used, have it made of slatted or perforated material – not with solid sides – and mix in plenty of straw and similar plant fragments with any wastes that tend to be sticky or close textured such as fine lawn cuttings, for instance. Cow manure, if it comes from the modern type of intensive farm, often contains very little straw, and tends to go sour and malodorous if composted in this form. Mixing it with straw will soon give a fine, highly nutritious compost

BAN THE BONFIRE

One of the surest signs of uneconomic and inefficient gardening is the smoke signal rising from a bonfire. The nuisance is bad enough – clouds of acrid smoke blackening washing, turning leaves brown before their time – but even more serious is the wastage. Every pile of leaves, grass or weeds means a corresponding reduction in the fertility of the soil. In quite a small suburban garden, the nutrients contained in the annual crop of grass, leaves, weeds and vegetable waste could amount to a considerable amount of bought fertiliser. There are, admittedly, a few plant diseases so serious that affected produce must be burned, but these are so rare in normal gardening that they would scarcely justify one bonfire per year.

WHAT SHOULD STAY OUT

• Evergreen leaves, like privet, yew, pine needles or ivy. They poison the bacteria and slow down the composting action.

• Fresh perennial weeds – particularly buttercups, couch grass, convolvulus and bindweed. Dry them thoroughly in the sun to kill their roots or runners; then you can add them to the heap.

• Any plants that have been dressed with selective weed-killers or other herbicides. This can arise if you collect weeds or grass cuttings from neighbours who are not compost-minded. Some of the selective weed-killers used for grass are very persistent and could kill plants treated with the compost.

• Meat, fish and dairy are best avoided.

• Cat litter and non-vegetarian animal faeces should also be left.

• Plastic, glass, aluminium – anything which doesn't biodegrade at domestic compost temperatures.

The food that can't go in a compost – fish, cooked meat and bones – can go in a food digester which breaks it down, into water, carbon dioxide and a small amount of residue, using natural bacteria and the sun's heat. Digesters need to be rodent proof and must have their base below ground level since over 90 per cent of the waste will be absorbed by the soil as water. Once the digester is full – roughly every two years – the residue can be removed and dug into the ground. They should be placed in a sunny part of your garden.

with good texture and hardly any smell. If you cannot get straw easily, other 'hollow' plants will do almost as well. Long grass from road verges is often left to lie after cutting, and is less likely to have been treated with herbicides than grass from, say, the municipal park. Chopped-up cow parsley can be laid as 'pipes' to the middle of the heap. Even corrugated cardboard torn up into small pieces is better than nothing.

A layer of twigs, hedge cuttings, or similar stiff material at the bottom of each heap will let the air in, but do not make the layer too thick or spiky, otherwise earthworms will be discouraged from creeping up into the heap. Worms form the best aeration system of all; they carry on mixing and churning up the compost, leaving air channels behind them, until the natural rise in temperature gets too much for them. If you have a number of heaps at various stages, the worms may even be persuaded to migrate from one heap to the next as the process goes on.

Aeration is obviously assisted by turning the heaps over from time to time; this not only lets the air in, but makes sure that all parts of the heap have a turn in the warm interior.

• Weeds of all kinds – apart from one or two exceptions (see opposite) – should go in as you pull them up or hoe them.

• Leaves of most kinds rot down so fast that it is probably better to keep them in a separate heap (see 'Leafmould' box, page 36), but the tougher varieties, such as horse chestnut, can go into the general compost heap.

• The bedding of pets, such as guinea pigs or rabbits, can be used and will increase the nitrogen in the mix.

• Uncooked vegetable and fruit scraps from the kitchen can be composted.

• Tougher materials – such as hedge cuttings, cabbage and brussels sprouts stalks, the roots of docks and thistles, and cow parsley – will compost in time, but will disappear more quickly if they are sliced or chopped beforehand. In fact, bruising or shredding helps along all types of compost. The finer you shred the produce, the quicker the composting, so long as you do not make the mass too soggy and thus exclude air.

• Fine lawn cuttings may need to be mixed with something coarser, like straw or long grass, as they tend to rot down to an impervious mat; this does not allow air to penetrate and its centre begins to smell and turn black – evidence that anaerobic bacteria are at work.

• Old newspapers and magazines, well shredded, can be added to the heap – they do not add anything to the nutrient value, just increase the bulk of humus. (There must be a lesson for editors somewhere in this.)

• The contents of the vacuum cleaner can go the same way, and any rags, as long as they are animal or vegetable fibres – wool, cotton or linen.

In general, think of the compost heap as the natural resting place for all your wastes. Keep a large covered bin outside the kitchen door in which vegetable trimmings, tea leaves, coffee grounds, apple cores and leftovers can be collected before being taken to the heap. If you have a workshop, put all the sawdust, shavings and similar wood or paper scraps in a bin, and distribute these on the compost heap once in a while – shavings are very good for aeration. When you gather produce, carry a knife with you to trim away outside leaves and inedible roots or tops and put them straight on to the heap. Such simple time-and-motion study will make your kitchen and plot tidier, and your compost heap grow, without apparent effort.

3. WARMTH

Bacteria work about twice as fast at 30°C (86°F) as at 20°C (68°F). As the process of composting goes on, the temperature will begin to rise spontaneously, as fermentations get going, and it is this increasing warmth that is necessary to kill weed seeds and insects. The temperature of a successful heap should reach somewhere between 50°C and 70°C (122°F and 158°F), which is hot enough to kill nearly all seeds and insect eggs or larvae.

Some insects are remarkably hardy; flies' eggs can withstand temperatures of 45°C (113°F). A really well-made heap can get a lot hotter than this – we had one that caught fire, and we had to run water over it all night to keep it under control. So look out for overheating, and pour a few buckets of water over any heap that is getting too enthusiastic. Farmers used to poke an iron rod into the middle of a haystack and feel the temperature when it was withdrawn, as a check on overheating – this is quite a good way to test your compost heap.

• Worms can do the composting for you – 1lb (500g) of composting worms will eat over 2lb (1kg) of waste a week. You can buy wormeries or make your own (but don't use garden worms) – either way they will need constant warmth, moisture, and darkness. The good thing though is that a womery doesn't need much outdoor space – it will fit on a balcony or even sit indoors.

• The liquid that comes out of a wormery can be diluted (one part to ten parts water) to feed your plants. The rich, crumbly compost can be removed every six months or so but make sure you pick out the worms and put them back in with layers of cardboard, a bit of soil and some food.

• To make your own you will ideally have three containers that sit on top of one another – fairly large polystyrene boxes (the type used for packing vegetables or fish) with lids would be ideal.

• Make a 1in (2.5cm) hole in the centre of the bottom box and stand the box on some wood, bricks or concrete blocks. This way, liquid from the wormery can be collected by placing a container under the hole.

• Make eight or so holes in the second box for the worms to climb up and down between the boxes and place it on top of the first. Take the last box, make the same number of holes and place on top of the second then put the lid on top.

• To start, place kitchen scraps and small amounts of scrunched-up (not flat) cardboard in the base of the bottom box for bedding, along with 100 compost worms (source from an existing compost heap or buy online). Keep on filling with kitchen scraps and a little bit of cardboard and paper. When the box is full, place the next box on top of it (one with several holes) and start filling it. When that is full, do the same with the top box. The worms will move through the holes between layers in search of food. By the time the top box is full of food waste, the bottom box should be full of worm casts. Take it out and empty the contents (being careful to lift any worms you dislodge back into the wormery). You can put it straight onto the soil or use it as part of a mix for potting compost.

• Worms will eat almost anything that will decompose including weeds and garden waste, but they should be mostly fed on a variety of kitchen scraps. Foods to be avoided in large quantities include: citrus peel, seeds and diseased material, meat and fish. Overfeeding can also be a problem so do not add more until the last lot has gone.

• Don't allow the bin to get too hot or dry out. If not much happens it could be that the bin is too dry so you will need to pull everything out, water it and mix in some green material such as grass cuttings. Equally, it will start to smell if too wet and you will also have to pull everything out, and mix it well with brown material before returning to the bin.

Planning your plot

6. Where to grow

The first thing you need to do is decide where you will be growing.

A COMPLETELY NEW GARDEN

If you are taking up residence in a new housing development, you may be faced by a moonscape full of builders' rubble. Before making a first-time garden, you will need to shift all this, but don't get rid of anything until you've pondered on it. Stones, broken bricks and blocks, mortar and even broken glass will come in handy for making the base of paths. Lengths of scrap wood will be useful for frames and plant supports. Even small pieces come in handy as fuel and rotten wood will compost.

Having cleaned up the site, you are then probably possessed of an expanse of subsoil. It will hasten productivity if you can get a load of topsoil for it. On a new estate, the chances are that down the road the builders are still stripping topsoil from some other plot – find out where this is going and whether you can get your hands on some of it. If not, you could advertise in the local paper – this might get you a load of soil on your front path at 8.00am, but it will be worth the effort of shifting it. Or look in the Yellow Pages or online under 'Topsoil' or 'Soil' to locate bulk suppliers, which can be far cheaper than buying from garden centres or nurseries given the amount you are likely to need.

If you are buying topsoil then check the quality and origin. Avoid soil from weedy or contaminated areas. Look for rich, dark soil with plenty of organic matter and little debris, that is ideally similar in texture to your existing soil or to that commonly found in your area. You will need 3 cu yds (2 cu m) of soil to cover 1,000 sq ft (92 sq m) to a depth of 1in (2.5cm) – you should be aiming for 3–6in (7.5–15cm) deep for planting. Remember too, to ask your supplier to roughly spread the soil when they deliver.

A NEW, BUT EXISTING GARDEN

It could be that you have inherited a garden when moving into a new property. Hopefully it is in good condition (and not a sea of block paving) but it might be that your predecessors in the house neglected the garden, in which case there could also be some junk clearing to do. Again look out for things you can use, such as rusty water tanks that are quite useful as compost containers or rubble holders.

Some of the weeds can be put on the compost heap (see 'What can go in' box, page 39). Twigs and branches won't compost without treatment, but will be useful for protecting and supporting peas and beans. If it's a large plot then it could be that livestock would help with the ground clearance.

If you inherit a garden where the existing flowers and small shrubs are in the wrong place for your new plans then consider moving them (see 'Moving plants', page 70). You will also need to assess the soil condition (see 'Soil', page 55) and note the movement of the sun over the garden, the prevailing winds, etc.

YOUR CURRENT GARDEN

It might be that you are considering a change in your current garden – losing the lawn, reducing the terrace, creating beds in your front garden, increasing its productive potential in general. Remember what has worked for a lawn may not for vegetables – such as shade from larger trees or a high hedge – and again you may need to move some cherished shrubs and other plants to make way for your new raised beds.

AN ALLOTMENT

You will need to find out if there are any allotments in your district, whether one is available (or, more likely, how long the waiting list is) and how much it costs to rent. Local authorities have a legal duty to provide a sufficient number of allotments to meet local demand. Ask your local council and if they claim there is no space for allotments, remind them of their obligation in law (Section 23 of the Small Holdings and Allotments Act 1908) and guidance from Government (Planning Policy Guidance 17 which requires that local authorities make provision for all types of open space that may be of public value).

The Government has also produced good practice guidance (see Useful websites guide, page 246) to help local councils reduce the length of time someone has to wait before getting an allotment plot. It gives advice on making the most of existing allotment sites by reducing plot sizes and managing waiting lists. It also includes advice on providing new allotments sites and what temporary options are available for people who are waiting for a plot to become available.

Local authorities have a legal duty to provide a sufficient number of allotments to meet local demand

If you don't receive a satisfactory answer then the next step is to organise a pressure group, create a petition and lobby local councillors.

With a boom in their popularity, it is more than likely that you will be faced with a long wait. If this is the case it may be worth contacting the site manager to let them know how keen you are, just in case a plot that requires lots of work needs taking on. You may also find that one of the existing plot holders could do with some help and will consider sharing their plot with you – especially if they are not as young as they used to be.

The average allotment plot is 300 sq yds or 250 sq m (the traditional measurement is in 'rods' – ten rods is equivalent to 302 sq yds or 253 sq m), with a path around it. The rent varies, but it can be as cheap as £8 per annum, a truly remarkable bargain, although probably the average is £20 to £40 a year.

Allotments take time and effort to develop but the rewards are many and varied

Check that you have security of tenure for 18 months at least, or it will be no use to plant over-wintering crops like brassicas and beans. Also check if the allotment is 'permanent' – in which case it cannot be sold or used for other purposes without the consent of the Secretary of State; 'temporary' and therefore not protected from disposal; or on privately-owned land which can be let for use as allotments but is also not protected from disposal by your local council.

Find out whether water is laid on to the site, and if there are any odd regulations governing whether you can erect a greenhouse, for example. Some allotments forbid machinery; while others frown on children and animals. For the latest information on allotment legislation visit the National Society of Allotment and Leisure Gardeners' website (see Useful websites guide, page 246).

If you are planning to sell some of your surplus produce then you need to be aware of the legislation – there is a general prohibition in law on any 'trade or business' being conducted on an allotment garden and an allotment garden must, by definition, 'be wholly or mainly cultivated for the production of vegetable or fruit crops for consumption by the occupier or their family'. So allotment gardens can't operate as market gardens, or nurseries. But there is no restriction on the distribution, by sale or otherwise, of a certain proportion of the plotholder's crop, but the definition of 'surplus' is a grey area. The Government has said recently, however, that it will clarify that there are no legal restrictions on gardeners selling genuine surplus produce to local markets and shops.

If the allotments are far from your home, think about the time involved and cost out the journey. If you have to drive five miles each way, are you going to be able to pop out at night and cover this or stop that? If there is no water laid on, can you carry enough with you to satisfy hungry plants in a hot summer? In a one-car family, will the person with access to the allotment by day have the use of a car full-time? You can't go by bus if your wellies stink of dung or if you are carrying a bag of manure. But using a car will have a detrimental effect on the carbon footprint of your food so this may not be desirable anyway.

> If the allotments are far from your home, think about the time involved and cost out the journey. If you have to drive five miles each way, are you going to be able to pop out at night and cover this or stop that?

Take a look at the site of the allotments on offer. Are they fenced off? Is there any form of supervision in your absence? An unguarded site overlooked by other gardeners will probably be fairly safe, but more remote sites, where no one works an allotment, could be a target for vandals. You don't want to work for months and have your crop smashed or stolen.

Is there a shed for tools, to save a lot of carrying to and fro? Is it lockable? Are there any borrowable watering cans and wheelbarrows?

On the whole, the key to the matter is how close the allotment is to your home. The nearer it is, the less it will cost you to get there, in money, time and carbon footprint, and you will be more likely to keep up with the work. The more you are there at unpredictable times, the less likely you are to suffer losses from vandals. If there is a choice, go for five rods this side of town, not ten rods four miles away.

BORROWED LAND

Some elderly folk own large gardens where they would dearly like to be producing vegetables, but are just not capable of the work any more. They might be willing to let you work their land in return for a share of the fresh produce, which takes a lot out of a pension. Write to the local paper, use online community pages and so on – you might even start a local movement.

There would, naturally, be some control by the garden's owners over how much of it was dug and what structures were erected there. Against this, they would be on site to keep an eye on things from the security angle and for early warning of pest attack. Light work – like covering plants against frosts and limited watering – could be shared, to mutual advantage, while the arrangement lasted.

The reverse situation can arise, where a couple who are out at work for long hours and really can't cope with their garden during the week might be glad to let an able-bodied pensioner plant up part of it and share the produce. Obviously, there must be an agreement from the first about the area to be cultivated.

Schools, colleges and firms quartered in country houses often have spare land of which they make no use. In fact, there is a growing national movement to match those with land to those with the time and inclination to grow food on it. Even the National Trust is doing its bit to help – it has made food-growing spaces available at about 40 of its sites varying in size from smaller plots, suited to new growers, to larger areas suitable for community growing schemes. While in London the 'Capital Growth' project is trying to access more land for community groups to grow on by working with some major landowners such as British Waterways, Transport for London, various housing associations and Borough Councils.

It is even possible to make use of land that is currently unused or waiting development including stalled building sites or areas waiting for planning permission. The Development Trusts Association (a network of community enterprise practitioners) is to prepare standardised 'leases' so that organisations or communities can access land while it's waiting to be used. An example in London has seen local charity Global Generation create portable allotments in construction skips on a 67 acre (27ha) development site in King's Cross.

The lesson is, if you see some land with potential try asking if you can grow on it – they might say 'yes'.

7. What to grow

Once you have decided where you are going to grow, you need to decide what is going to be grown based on answers to these key questions:

WHAT DO YOU WANT TO GROW?

First comes the planning, which can be done largely in the cold days of winter – not the drawing of the diagram of where things will go, but deciding what you are going to grow.

The important thing is to decide what you or your family's preferences are. On the whole, if no one likes parsnips, it is probably a waste of time to plant them. However, if the dislike is based on a bad experience with some woody ones from a shop, then it's worth planting just a few to see whether the lovely fresh taste of them straight from the garden changes your mind.

If you have teenage potato addicts, then you may devote a lot of space to growing them, or at least plant enough earlies under cloches to cover the gap when the old ones run out and new ones cost the earth.

Allow for some crop losses from slugs or aphids, but equally beware of over-production. Seeds look so tiny in a packet that it is very easy to plant too many at a time and land yourself with a lettuce mountain. There isn't an awful lot you can do to preserve lettuce and even the nicest salads pall after the 15th appearance in one week. When your lettuces and other vegetables have exhausted deserving friends and even the guinea pigs go on strike, you will resolve to sow in very small pinches next time. Ordinary surpluses can be mopped up by freezing or preserving, provided you catch them in time, before the produce is past its prime. Freeze the best, not the left-overs. (See 'Harvesting', page 174 for more on storing surpluses.)

It is perfectly easy, though, to grow lettuce all year round, with slight glass protection, and a number of vegetables can be forced under cloches or in a greenhouse, though not in large quantities unless you have a whole lot of glass cover.

Now is the time to find out if other people in your street are thinking of growing vegetables this year. There are certain things you will all need – pots, plants, seeds – and it is often possible to get a useful discount when buying in quantity. Leave time to check prices online and do your research. You might also want to plan who plants what to ensure the whole community benefits – slightly different crops could be planned for each garden, so that a market and exchange for surpluses can be more easily found. But decide at the outset whether the exchange should be by simple quantity or not. A pound of carrots for a pound of parsnips, yes. But for a pound of asparagus? Beware of over-involvement, or you will find yourself giving away the tomatoes you wanted for your own lunch, or end up with nothing put by for the winter. (See 'Making it pay', page 214).

If you can restrain yourself, avoid growing for show. Maybe it would be fun to join the local horticultural society and carry off all the prizes in your first year, but it can't be reconciled with growing vegetables to improve your own standard of living or save money. Show vegetables are big, fat wallopers with little or no flavour left. To get them that way, you will have to feed and cosset the beasts all the time and this costs a packet in fertiliser, sprays and man-hours. You can't thin out any for eating because the very one cut off in its prime might have been the champion. By the time you harvest the reject monsters, they taste of old face flannels and have cost more per pound than anything in the shops.

If you are hell-bent on growing something for show, make it a marrow or pumpkin. Given averagely good soil – which you want for all plants – and plenty of water, they romp away without much effort and in such profusion that there are enough to eat young and still leave plenty to choose an exhibit from.

THE HUNGRY GAP

It can be difficult to plan for the 'hungry gap' – between the end of winter produce and the beginning of the new season's crop in May or June. Some root crops will stay in the ground through the winter, but there comes a time when they are frosted in or getting woody. It is then, about March, that you feel the need for something fresh, if only for the vitamin C content. Most of the possible vegetables belong to the brassica tribe – cabbage, cauliflower, sprouts, etc – some of which are cut-and-come-again plants. They take ages to grow, so they need garden space for a large proportion of the year. They are planted as seeds in early summer, transferred to a waiting bed as they grow and to their final wide spacing in autumn. The difficulty is finding space for parking in midsummer, when everything else is bursting out all over. If you want a lot of spring vegetables, allow for them in the overall plan.

Marrows of any advanced age are pretty dull vegetables cooked plain anyway, so being forced to turn your giants into curries or jam won't matter. Pumpkins also grow large without effort and are best mature. However, they have a distinctive flavour, which you either love or hate. It is a daunting prospect to find that you are the only member of the family prepared to eat a newly cut-open 42-pounder.

WHAT DOES IT PAY TO GROW?

It is worth costing up the profits on a crop by checking the price at a local greengrocers/box scheme or supermarket on or about the day you gather your own produce – weighing and pricing yours. Decide if you are going to cost what you freeze at fresh or frozen food prices and similarly with any other forms of preservation, like jams, sauces, bottling and pickling.

The profits will look impressive, but to get a true picture, you will have to set against them all the costs involved in running the garden (see page 242). To follow this plan, you will have to get into the habit of noting down all the expenditure – which is no bad thing anyway. At least you will know why you have got too much month at the end of your money and not vice versa.

When you come to planning the second year of planting, take into account what paid off and what didn't, what no one would eat or everyone wanted more of. You might also need to consider what sold, if this is part of your annual activities (see 'Growing for sale' box page 218).

WHAT CAN YOU GROW?

Whether a new or existing garden or an allotment, you will need to be sure you have the space, soil and climate for your choice of produce.

SPACE

Some housing developments (both old and unfortunately new) tend to devote the minimum possible space to private gardens. In some cases there is an unfenced 'landscaped' area in front of the house and only a tiny yard at the back. The same may apply to houses built on part of a plot belonging to an older property. Town houses may have hardly any garden space at all, and often this is paved or cemented over. Flat-dwellers may have only a balcony and people in bedsitters not even that. So what are the vegetable-growing options if space is at a premium?

Back-to-front layout
Anyone with a front garden available can plant vegetables – just go ahead and lay it out precisely as you would a back garden. This may cause comment, since Britons are a conservative lot.

A front vegetable garden can be laid out in an attractive way by using the more decorative plants and setting them out in patterns. Runner beans make a handsome fence, with red-orange flowers and light-green fruit. The rich wine-purple of red cabbage and beetroot; the contrasting greens of lettuce, parsley and the cushion-forming herbs like marjoram and thyme; the feathery foliage of carrots, narrow mid-green spears of onions; luxurious ropes of ripening tomatoes and elegant bushes of rosemary can be arranged to look like a very expensive piece of landscape design.

Avoid the messy plants, like potatoes, parsnips, swedes and savoys, and whip off any dying leaves from your chosen plants as they mature. The cucurbits – marrows, cucumbers, pumpkins – sprawl, but there is a certain panache about a single pumpkin, confined in a circular bed half-hedged with rosemary bushes or red cabbage. Cucumbers look fine planted in a raised bed with the fruit trained down the side. Judicious inter-planting with showy, bright blue or yellow flowers relieves the greenness of the vegetables when young.

An unfenced front garden may be a problem, because it can be attacked by marauding dogs and perhaps even the odd opportunist who might make off with your prize produce. Make sure the deeds allow fencing off before you pay for your house. Prickly mahonia bushes, roses or a series of tubs of plants do something to discourage invasion.

Patios and yards
The patio-only householder can make good use of pots, boxes, old sinks, tubs and wire baskets. It may even be possible to lift paving stones or break up a cracked bit of concrete in order to make a planting area. The bed can be filled with compost and good soil, after the sub-soil has been broken up and extracted. Top soil can be bought, or sometimes obtained from building sites or where driveways are being laid.

For any planting bed or container which is relatively shallow, choose dwarf carrots and round beet, onions, lettuce, radishes, herbs, tomatoes and cucurbits. Plant close together; feed and water them plentifully.

Even if you have little space or soil you can make use of growbags. These plastic bags hold good potting mixture, and there is no need to buy pots or boxes.

> There is a certain panache about a single pumpkin, confined in a circular bed half-hedged with rosemary bushes

Bought ready-prepared they can take two tomato plants, for example, or a number of smaller crops. It will be good for only one growing season, but the used medium makes a base for starting off new compost, mixed with fresh soil. Don't grow the same plant in it, though, as this would be a sure invitation to disease.

Equally, potatoes can be grown in sacks or large dustbins on patios – and even courgettes can be grown in potato sacks (one to a sack). Strawberry barrels will sit nicely on a sunny patio and tumbling tomatoes can be grown well in hanging baskets

If you have a dark little courtyard, paint the walls white to bounce back every bit of available light. Things can be grown all the way up the wall – trained on wires, in boxes of earth on long legs, or in pots and baskets hung from strong fixed nails. Wet earth weighs a lot, so err on the massive side for these supports.

Balconies

Anyone with a balcony can grow vegetables and herbs in pots and boxes – but make sure the structure is sound or it could come crashing down, which won't make you popular with passers-by or the police. As for window-boxes, a full-sized one is only possible when you have a sash window behind it. With a casement window, you are stuck with a half-width box and some interesting gymnastics.

Window-sills and other areas

Any indoor window-sill, French door or glazed porch will provide the necessary light and space for you to grow something. Just add water and ventilation. If you have no such space, there are always bean sprouts, which can be grown fast in a warm dark place.

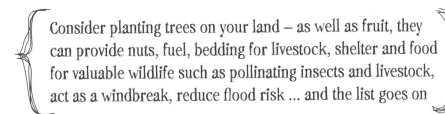

Consider planting trees on your land – as well as fruit, they can provide nuts, fuel, bedding for livestock, shelter and food for valuable wildlife such as pollinating insects and livestock, act as a windbreak, reduce flood risk ... and the list goes on

Larger spaces

Obviously the larger the plot the more you can do with it. Consider for example, the benefits of establishing an orchard – there has been over a 60 per cent decline in orchards over the past 30 years, so the benefits go beyond fruit – biodiversity will be helped by an increase in this valuable habitat (see page 144 for more on orchards). Certainly you could consider planting trees on your land – as well as fruit, they can provide nuts, fuel, bedding for livestock, shelter and food for valuable wildlife such as pollinating insects and livestock, act as a windbreak, reduce flood risk ... and the list goes on.

You may also have room for livestock (see page 222 for advice on how much room you will need) and certainly plenty of room for several compost heaps and perhaps a greenhouse or polytunnel.

SOIL

You will see a lot in books and magazines about acid and limy soils. Some plants hate one, some the other, and develop horrible ailments if planted in the wrong type. How do you find out what kind of soil yours is? As a general rule, most town gardens are liable to be acid and those on chalk hills are likely to be limy. But this is varied by the kind of past treatment each has received, so you can test your individual garden soil to be sure.

You can purchase soil testing kits at garden centres and online. These kits express the acidity of the soil in terms of its pH – a pH value of less than seven is acidic soil, seven is neutral and over seven is alkaline soil – most plants prefer a pH of 6.5 to 7 as it is the point where nutrients are easily available. Collect samples of your soil when it is wet, from three, four or more different parts of the garden. Put each sample in the container provided and add a few drops of testing solution, before shaking and leaving for the recommended period of time. By comparing the eventual colour of the sample with a colour chart you will be able to identify the pH value of the soil.

If your soil is noticeably acid, you can add garden lime to it (organic gardeners use natural sources of lime, such as limestone, dolomite, shell, and marl but avoid slaked lime or quicklime) and if it is noticeably limy, you will do no harm with compost, manure, grass clippings, and leafmould. However, don't be led into thinking there is a precise dose per square yard to be measured out with a fine scientific balance, even if you see this set out in a complicated table. Unless you tested every square foot of the garden separately, and then applied the prescribed dose to it from a dropper bottle, you could never cope with the local variations. One small area may have supported a greedy plant, and the next have been enriched by a natural fertiliser. In fact, you won't go far wrong if you follow Grandfather's British Standard Measures – 'a little bit, a middling bit and a tidy bit'.

If you are getting terrible results after a year of operation, with warped and stunted vegetables, then something may be deficient in the soil or you may have an infestation. Note down just what went wrong with each plant – yellowing leaves, coloured spots, wilting stems, etc. Check up in one of the hundreds of books on garden ailments; ask the expert down the road; or write to one of the excellent gardening magazines which offer free advice to readers.

If the answer seems to lie in the soil, you can get it analysed for mineral deficiencies. Some universities sometimes offer free soil tests so ask at your local ones. But, on the whole, if you treat the soil right and feed it compost, it will respond in a year or two.

Whether it is acid or alkaline, the actual structure can be improved organically. Assess what breed of soil you have by the 'fist test'. Half an hour after a moderate rainfall, pick up a handful of soil and squeeze it in your fist. If it powders away between your fingers, then it is thin sandy stuff which won't retain water. If it clags all over your fingers, it's clayey, which will flood in winter and cake into blocks in summer. Pale, starved-looking stuff with whitish bits and a gritty feel is chalk marl, no better than sub-soil. Good soil is deep coloured – black, dark brown, or red in sandstone country – and it holds the print of your palm for a minute or two, then unfolds in decent-sized crumbs with plenty of fibrous matter in them. It's rather like squeezing a good home-made fruit cake.

> The texture of good soil should feel rather like squeezing a good home-made fruit cake

If you haven't got good soil already, your object is to create it, by feeding in as much humus and nourishment as possible, ready for the demands the plants will make on it (see 'Feeding the soil', page 154 for more on this). It may take time to perfect, but every little helps, and you don't have to wait until perfection is reached. You may not get a brilliant harvest the first year, but there will be something to show for your labours and the promise of much more to come.

CLIMATE

Establish the patterns of sun and shade at different times of the day in your garden. With a compass or the map, find out where north is and, if possible, draw diagrams on a sunny day of where the maximum and minimum sun falls, in morning and afternoon. Any corner which never gets much light isn't going to ripen crops fast. The warmest spot is the place to be earmarked for the tomatoes. Note where the shadow of the house itself falls and whether there is an accessible bit of south-facing wall. Mark the direction of the prevailing wind and keep these diagrams by you when you are doing the detailed garden plan.

PLANNING YOUR GARDEN LAYOUT

No matter how big your potential growing area, you will need to decide how much space you are actually prepared to put down to vegetables. What area is needed for the children to play in and how boisterous are they? Toddlers must be under your eye while you are working, so a sandpit is something to make room for. Footballers can be a menace in the eyes of many a keen gardener, so bar them from the breakable crops with a line of gooseberry bushes, which give as good as they get, or well-staked broad beans. A fruit cage makes quite a good pen for games-players after the fruit is picked, which happens before the summer holidays.

Children enjoy lots of lurking places, and these are provided by any of the taller plants. Runner beans on a framework make a splendid den and double as a

HEDGES, WALLS AND FENCES

If any hedges or trees around the boundary of the garden are so tall they seem to shadow the whole planting area, you will have to think long and hard about the options. But definitely don't just wade in and grub the lot up – they would take years to grow again if you made a mistake and you could lose their value as places of food and shelter for helpful wildlife.

A tall privet hedge, so often found in town gardens of a certain age, takes most of the nourishment from the soil around it, in proportion to its height. A 10ft (3m) hedge robs the ground for 5ft (1.5m) on either side of it. But if this hedge acts as an important screen – such as from a public footpath – you might need to consider a replacement. You could replace the hedge with a fence or wall, bearing in mind that the maximum legal height allowed for rear and side walls is 6ft 6in (2m) and for front walls, or any adjoining a public highway, about 3ft 3in (1m) with local variations.

If you opt for a fence make sure the wood carries an Forest Stewardship Council (FSC) label which shows it comes from a sustainably managed forest (illegal logging is rife in many countries and you don't want to unknowingly support this business). Don't creosote the fence – this will make the ground nearby toxic. Instead choose woods that are better able to resist decay initially – oak and sweet chestnut will last 20 years in the soil and 40 years above it, while larch will last ten years when in soil and 20 years above. For fence panels above the soil, apply linseed oil that allows the wood to breathe.

A wall is a good choice for wildlife provided it has some nooks and crannies built in – bees often nest in these (the same applies to an old wall – so go easy on re-pointing or repairs in order to leave some bee nesting sites). Ideally try to source old stone for a wall – reclaimed stone found locally will have a much lower carbon footprint. You might also find a local craftsmen who is able to build traditional walls such as cob (local mud mixed with straw or heather); rammed earth walls; and wattle and daub (a hazel lattice covered in mud and straw).

But remember that even fences and walls cast a shadow, and the foundations of the wall make the 6–9in (15–22cm) beside it useless for deep-rooted plants. They are also less effective than hedges at providing protection from wind. Britain is a very windy country, and you may be glad of a windbreak to protect your small plants – especially from a northerly or easterly. Test the atmosphere near a gap in the hedge on a windy day, and imagine you are a tomato plant.

Oddly enough, walls and solid fences are less useful as windbreaks than apparently thin hedges. The wind hits any solid barrier, bounces up and comes down the other side with redoubled force. Hedges or open-weave fences filter the wind and take the sting away.

It is also possible to do quite a lot with low hedges to keep the wind off low-growing plants without blocking the sun. The Victorians used little box hedges around their vegetable plots, but mostly to conceal the utilitarian bits of the garden from the idle rich walking among the flowers. Dwarf lavender and rosemary make small neat hedges, if trimmed from time to time, and both give a bonus crop for household use.

So it would be better in terms of acting as a good windbreak, providing privacy, benefiting valuable wildlife and for its attractive appearance, to have hedges comprising native trees and shrubs. Consider using a mixture from these: native hawthorn, hazel, dog rose, dog wood, field maple, blackthorn, beech, hornbeam, holly and growing bramble or honeysuckle through the hedge will also provide more food and shelter for wildlife.

It is also better to have an 'informal' appearance since too much pruning will reduce the amount of flowers and berries produced, especially in the case of hawthorn, holly and privet. If you do need to prune then do so in late winter or early spring after winter fruits have been and gone but beware touching them from March to August as you may disturb nesting birds. Rotating your work on the hedge will always allow for one area to be left undisturbed.

If it's not yours:

Of course, you can only deal as you wish with a fence or hedge that is your own property. In towns, normally one side boundary is yours, the other your neighbour's. The deeds should have a mark showing who owns which side. If not, ask a local resident in the road or take a look at any nearby fenced garden.

The posts ought to be on the land of the person to whom the fence belongs. The same goes for any fence posts or wall piers you erect yourself. More often than not, it is the left-hand boundary, as you face the back of the garden, which is yours, but things get complicated at the corners of roads and with irregular street layouts. In case of doubt, try to come to an agreement with your neighbours before you start operations.

If it is not your hedge, you are permitted to cut back any branches which overhang your property but only to the point where they cross the boundary. And the prunings technically belong to the owner of the hedge. The same applies to any fruit-tree branches which violate your air space. You may cut them, but not damage the tree in so doing, and the fruit is not yours. You mustn't spray other people's weeds either until they invade your land.

a sheltered sitting out place for grandma. The clothes line needs to be sited where the vegetables won't get knocked over by the sheets or the sheets marked by the compost heap. A rotary line can be placed in the middle of a bed of low-growing plants, like herbs or roots. Washing hung out wet provides automatic watering in a dry summer.

If the garden is very small, remember that a lot of vegetables look really decorative as they grow and an edible herbaceous border laid out with just a few flowers here and there would look far handsomer than a conventional one.

Decide on the best place for a greenhouse or frames – these will prove a worthwhile investment if you have room for them. Any sort of glass protection or plastic propagator needs space for storing or setting out where they will not be damaged or a hazard.

Where there is a wide-spreading tree in the garden, draw a circle on the ground to cover the area reached by the tips of the branches. Nothing much is going to grow in that circle, because the tree is extracting all the nourishment from the soil. Normal roots go deeper the farther they get from the trunk or stems. Therefore, you can set plants with shallow roots above the outer tree roots, provided that, for a reasonable part of the day, the shade thrown by the branches is not too great. When trees have suffered from water shortage in their early years, the roots may have twisted up again in search of rain and can be seen or felt just below the surface. In this case, nothing will grow even under the outer perimeter of the branches, unless you pile earth on top of the soil surface.

Shade is a great problem in a garden. Plants need light, so any area permanently shaded by the house or any immovable object might as well be used for a path and storage of tools, pots and compost. If the shadow is caused by a hedge, you might be able to thin or shorten it a bit, to improve matters. If the culprit is a high wall, paint it brilliant white, to bounce back every scrap of light. If the back garden is a narrow strip completely overshadowed by the house, consider

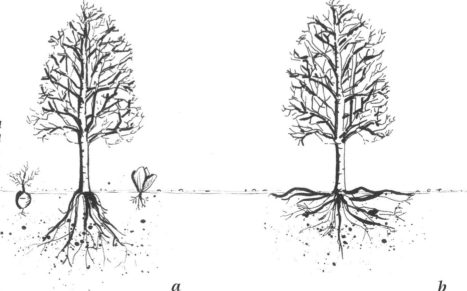

(a): Normal tree root pattern with plants around perimeter. (b): Tree starved of water in early years; no planting near it is possible

a

b

using the front garden for vegetables, although half shade, where the light strikes through leaves, is enough for some plants, especially in summer. The strong midday sun penetrates the canopy, so there is plenty of heat and enough light.

Light shade: Lettuces do quite well near trees, though not directly next to the trunk where the roots compete; they do in fact prefer this to being out in full sun, which makes them limp and exhausted.

You can grow very short carrots and baby round beet on the edge of a tree area, and winter-growing brassica, which are started in summer and spend a long period waiting for a home in the main plot, manage well in light shade, and thus save a lot of watering.

Full sun: Most other plants like a lot of sun and planning a garden is largely a matter of sorting out priorities. Tomatoes will not perform at all unless they have the best sun and good shelter. If you mean to grow them out of doors you must pander to their tastes. All the frost-tender plants, like melons, cucumbers, marrows, French and runner beans, and sweetcorn, must complete their growth cycle before the autumn bites, so they require a sunny place too. Onions need to finish with a coat of suntan if they are to keep well.

Partial sun: Most root crops will manage with only reasonable sun once they are past the seedling stage, so they have to take the secondary positions. Peas are tough and tolerant, once they get their heads off the ground, and broad beans cope with all but severe frosts when they are young, besides making good screens for weaker vessels.

Tall plants: Runner beans, and other tall plants, mustn't get between anything else and the sun, and should be located at the end or side of the garden, whichever most nearly faces south. Preferably all of them ought to face the sun, which means that, if you plant a double row, as is usual, the plants should be set out staggered, not directly facing each other.

Tomatoes do best with the whole row facing south and like a bit of shelter from behind, so set them out in front of the bean rows, far enough away for them not to cast their own lesser shadow over the growing beans. You need access to both sides of the rows

PLANNING FOR WILDLIFE

While considering the tricky issues of crop rotation, available light and so on, it is all too easy to forget that you need to be planning for wildlife in your plot as well. But by ensuring you create the ideal habitats for certain insects, birds, and animals you will be employing nature's help with pest control and pollination, while doing your bit to nurture species that in some cases are reliant on gardens, since commercial large-scale agriculture has left the countryside so depleted.

Consider these elements in your planting plans to maximise wildlife in your garden:

• shrubs and trees provide shelter and food for many creatures so are essential features in any garden, especially those that produce berries and provide nooks and crannies for nesting;

• ensure you have plenty of nectar-bearing plants for butterflies and bees;

• try to include a pond in your plans for toads, frogs, newts, dragonflies, birds, etc;

• a wood pile in a corner will provide a habitat for beetles, young frogs and newts, toads, centipedes – most of which will eat your slugs and in some case slug eggs;

• seriously consider creating a green roof on top of any garden buildings – a shed is ideal.

of tomatoes and beans, for tying up and regular picking, so there won't be much wasted space, and some of that can be used as a waiting bed for winter brassica, which don't mind light shade.

Phased planting: Beans and tomatoes are best started off in boxes or pots under protection and not set out until late May, so this desirable space can meanwhile be used for quick crops, like lettuces, or to start off other vegetables before transferring them to the main bed.

After the first year, you will probably have winter brassica on part of the rows. If the garden is ready for planting in early spring the first year, you could sow summer cauliflower or cabbage at the back of the plot where the beans will grow in February and March and transplant them to the main plot in May. Don't sow them where the winter brassica will stand, because of the danger of transmitting club-root.

Early peas could go in the tomato bed in February under cloches, to be picked in late May. Strawberries at the front of this bed would benefit from the sun and not interfere with the growing tomatoes later on. Rhubarb planted behind the bean site would have finished its cropping before the beans are tall enough to shade it. Once this sun spot is settled, any other very sunny areas can be allocated to cucumbers, sweetcorn, wall fruit or anything which needs glass protection for part of its life to ripen at all.

Companion planting: Carrots and onions discourage each other's pests, so do well together, and the feathery carrot foliage does not shade the onions too much if they are planted at right angles to the main sun path – running south (or south-east or west) to north. All the onion family are good policemen, so one or two spread around the plot, or next to wall fruit trees, will scare off pests, perhaps by confusing the scent. (For more see page 169)

> All the onion family are good policemen, so one or two spread around the plot, or next to wall fruit trees, will scare off pests

Crop rotation: Some plants have virtues. Peas and beans give back far more to the earth than they take from it, and can be planted anywhere which needs improvement for another crop. By contrast, the potato is the baddy of the vegetable plot: frost-tender, fussy about having rich soil, a greedy feeder, robbing the ground of nutrients, and leaving only its undesirable offspring and a host of infectious diseases. The potato is best kept right away from its more valuable cousin, the tomato, or it will encourage the unpleasant ailment, blight.

All the cabbage tribe tend to suffer from club-root, although they do not pass it on to others. It is best to take precautions against this disease when setting out and never to plant brassicas in the same place twice if it can possibly be avoided.

This is a good general rule: switch everything around next year, if you can, except the permanent beds, and feed those up to compensate. Even treasures like peas might as well spread their benevolence over as much of the garden as possible. This switching around is grandly called 'crop rotation', but in a small

ALLOTMENT LAYOUT

If you are growing on an allotment, the problem of layout is different. There will probably be no large buildings or fences casting shade, so you can rely on better sun distribution to all parts of the plot. There may be a wind problem, if the site is open to flat land all around, in which case, low windbreak hedges may be a priority, perhaps using edible bushes like rosemary.

If you are a newcomer, you will have no idea what was last planted on the plot. It may be possible to find out from a neighbouring allotment holder where the last person had their potatoes and cabbage, so you can avoid repeating these sites. All you can do otherwise is clear the site of weeds, lime it if necessary (except where the potatoes are to go), plant and hope for the best.

Allotment planting can be done on the rigid-straight-lines-all-going-the-same-way, compartmentalised style you see in many gardening books. This looks a lot tidier than varying lines to suit crop and shade requirements. Take a line which faces as near south as possible, and set all the rows parallel, varying the heights of the crops so that low always follows high; there should be enough light coming from all angles to develop the lot.

Onions, sweetcorn and the brassica seed-bed are best planted in blocks, most of the roots in double rows. Potatoes are generally planted all in one place, several rows wide, but in blocks within those rows – a square of earlies at one end, then second earlies, then maincrop, so that the ground can be cleared in sections and given a chance to recover. Rotate the whole plot the following year.

It is wise to set the more attractive crops, like strawberries, tomatoes and cucumbers, away from the edge so that passers by cannot easily reach them. We even lost pumpkins from our garden, which backs on to open farmland.

garden with limited space it is more like a juggling act.

PLANTING PLANS

Preparing some rough planting plans for a garden is a good idea. Two examples are illustrated on pages 66 and 67: one for a small garden and the other for a large garden.

When it comes to preparing these plans bear these points in mind:
  • If you are assuming morning shade from the house and/or a neighbour's high fence remember this will be worse in spring than summer when the overhead light is better, so concentrate all the early planting on the sunniest side. As the light improves, the successional sowings to mature a little later, can move across to the originally shaded side.

• With a larger amount of space available, you can lay down some more permanent planting, like fruit trees or bushes, asparagus or artichokes, according to taste.

• Because the layout of a larger garden is more flexible, it might be a good idea to get used to it before planting up all of it. Fruit trees, once ordered, must be planted right away, and if you change your mind a year later about the siting it will set them back to move them again, nor is it an easy matter with a mature tree. Always allow for its ultimate height and spread, even if it is a pathetic little twiglet when it arrives.

• Adapt your plans to your own family's requirements and cut out any planting or sowings which would produce a harvest while you are away on holiday. When you have decided how much space to allocate to any particular crop, check for the individual space requirement per plant of that type. This will tell you how many seeds to buy and sow. Most seeds will keep for another year, so store any half-used packets away in the dry.

• If you have room, remember to include green crops of nutritional value to the soil – comfrey, rye, Tagetes minuta, mustard – although the snag is that some need to grow in summer and would occupy a plot which could be growing vegetables. This is worthwhile in the long term, since these crops not only make valuable green manure to be dug into the ground but also bring up nutrients from deep down and have anti-pest attributes. (For more on 'Green manures' see page 155.)

• Draw out your planting plan in a notebook and write down each sowing, with date, type and variety. Make a note of any odd conditions of planting – warm, icy wind, thunderstorm next day, drought for a fortnight – which might affect the seeds. Add the date when the first seedlings show, and when most of them are through, with the rough proportion which germinated. Note the date of transplanting and keep a record of the crop-thinnings as well as ultimate harvest. Include any comments on pests or diseases which attacked the plant, and the family's reaction to the taste.

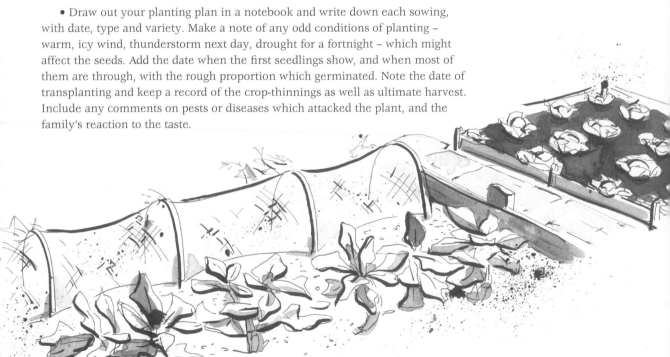

These are rough plans for planting ideas for a large and small garden.

If the garden is very small remember that a lot of vegetables look really decorative as they grow and an edible herbaceous border laid out with just a few flowers here and there would look far more handsome than a conventional one.

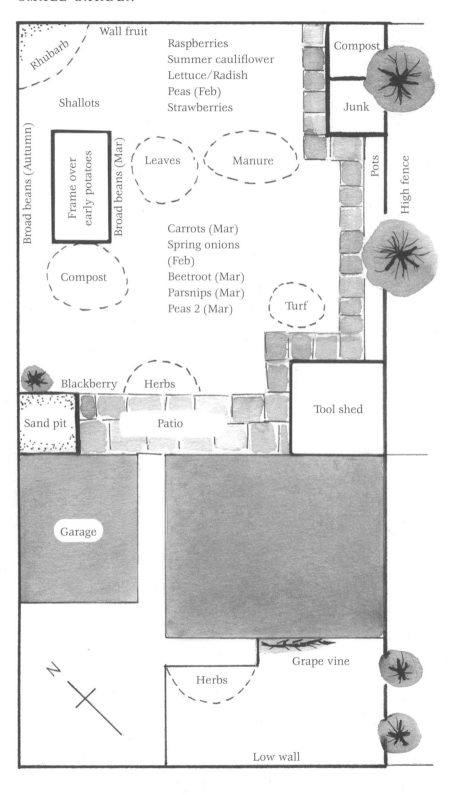

Wall fruit

Rhubarb

Raspberries
Summer cauliflower
Lettuce/Radish
Peas (Feb)
Strawberries

Compost

Junk

Shallots

Broad beans (Autumn)

Frame over early potatoes

Broad beans (Mar)

Leaves

Manure

Pots

High fence

Carrots (Mar)
Spring onions (Feb)
Beetroot (Mar)
Parsnips (Mar)
Peas 2 (Mar)

Compost

Turf

Blackberry

Herbs

Tool shed

Sand pit

Patio

Garage

N

Herbs

Grape vine

Low wall

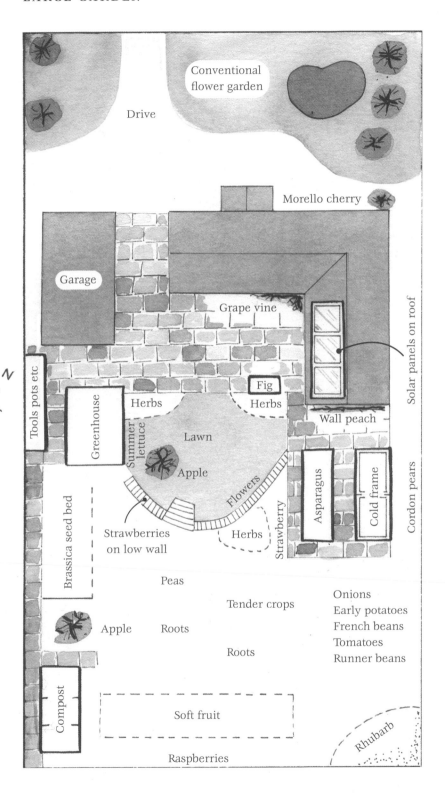

With a larger amount of space available you can lay down some more permanent planting, like fruit trees or bushes, asparagus or artichokes, according to taste

Conventional flower garden

Drive

Morello cherry

Garage

Grape vine

Solar panels on roof

Tools pots etc

Greenhouse

Fig

Herbs

Herbs

Wall peach

Summer lettuce

Lawn

Apple

Asparagus

Cold frame

Cordon pears

Brassica seed bed

Flowers

Strawberry

Strawberries on low wall

Herbs

Peas

Apple

Roots

Tender crops

Roots

Onions
Early potatoes
French beans
Tomatoes
Runner beans

Compost

Soft fruit

Rhubarb

Raspberries

Planning your plot 🌿 67

Growing

8. Essential preparation

There are some jobs that might need tackling before you start growing anything.

MOVING EXISTING PLANTS

If you inherit a garden where the existing flowers and small shrubs are in the wrong place for your new plans then consider moving them. They can normally be transplanted successfully, preferably out of their growing season. Autumn or spring, when the weather is dampish and the ground warmish, is best. Summer heat, winter cold or any sort of drought make things difficult. If necessary, soak the plant well before moving. The less time it spends out of the ground the better, to minimise the shock to the system.

First dig a large hole in the new place where you want your shrub to go, dumping the excavated soil on a plastic sheet or in buckets to save messing up the lawn and your feet. Then dig carefully around the transplant candidate, a good distance from the centre stem and outside the root run – poke around with a stick to find out where that ends. Then dig down below root level and lift the whole thing, with as much of the surrounding earth as possible. Edge the mass on to a plastic sheet or board and carry it to the new site. You will probably need a wheelbarrow or another pair of hands to accomplish this without dropping the lot halfway.

Enlarge your new hole if necessary and replant at the original depth. If you need extra earth, take it from the original planting site – try to kid the transplant that its environment has not changed. Water well in and take the displaced earth to the original hole.

> If you need extra earth, take it from the original planting site – try to kid the transplant that its environment has not changed

Larger shrubs and trees are a lot more chancy to shift, mainly because it is very hard to get them up with enough of their soil adhering. You may find in digging them out that one root appears to be going down to Australia. This is the tap root and in digging it out whole you may lose all the earth and break the fine root system higher up, which is more important. If you meet this problem, scrape back the earth round this tap root and saw the villain through as low as possible. Try to keep the earth around the upper roots in place, with a sacking nappy.

Make sure your new hole is deep enough, cutting slots and channels to fit any big roots that stick out in odd directions. Put potting compost in the bottom of the hole to retain moisture, sit your subject in place, very tenderly spreading the fine roots which will take up nutrition fastest. If the shrub is rather tall, plant a stake with it, between the roots, and tamp the earth down hard around it. Fill up the hole with earth from the original site, and make sure there are no air pockets which will allow the roots to flop about when the wind shakes the top of the shrub. When the roots are well cushioned, heap more earth on top, a few inches above the level of the surrounding soil, and then tread the whole lot down firmly and tie the trunk to the stake.

Water while you are filling in, and soak afterwards. Be prepared to water every day for a week, and at intervals thereafter, when more than a few days elapse without rain. If there is a hot spell, water over the leaves as well, since they will be giving out moisture faster than the unsettled roots will take it up.

PREPARING THE SOIL

If you are making a new garden, especially one on poor soil, try to get the preparation done in autumn if you can, so that it is ready to plant up in spring. Even if the whole garden plan isn't worked out in detail, you have probably decided where the main plot will be, or the total area you are aiming to use.

Mark off with pegs and strings the area you intend to prepare and slit along the edges with a spade. Pull up any large weeds and put them on the compost heap and strip off any grass. This is best done by cutting a slit, root deep, around three sides of a 10 sq ft (1 sq m) section, sliding a sharp spade under the flap and breaking back the piece. Pile the turf in a stack, face down, to rot quickly and re-use as humus.

When your plot is bare, you might want to dig it over to remove weeds and debris and to incorporate compost and possibly lime.

Although, before you embark on a back-breaking double-digging regime be aware that there is some evidence to show that it does not necessarily improve the structure of the soil. Some argue it can actually destroy the structure, that frequently dug over soil is more prone to compaction and reduced fertility, and that you might also inadvertently bury the fertile top soil.

The 'no dig' approach instead calls for adding a mulch of organic material such as any mature compost, strawy manure or well-rotted leaves (see page 155) to the top of the bed at the end of the season which will be gradually worked into the soil by earthworms and which will have the added benefit of suppressing weeds and preventing moisture loss. If you need lime (and make sure of this with a comprehensive soil test before assuming you do), then sprinkle it on top, or cover in lightly so it doesn't blow away. The average 'middling bit' of lime is 4oz (115g) or so per sq yd (1 sq m). Don't, whatever you do, put in lime and fresh manure. They react together and give off ammonia into the air, which smells horrible and wastes all the goodness of both.

However, digging may be worthwhile on compacted soils or on heavy clays where it is difficult for a mulch to be worked into the soil any other way. Especially in the case of clay soil, leave the dug ground rough and lumpy for the frost to break up. Try to keep the footballers off it, or the surface will form a hard pan and hold pools of water instead of letting it penetrate.

There is also some benefit in sowing a winter-growing crop like rye or tares, known as green manure (see page 155), just to dig in when spring comes to improve the texture of the soil.

Avoid using a rotavator or cultivator as you will end up spreading weeds by chopping up their roots and scattering them far and wide. You could spray the plot with a herbicide, wait for the weeds to die and then rotovate. But this costs money and your land will be saturated in chemicals – a no no for organic gardeners and a pain for others who will have to wait for some weeks before planting.

Although it is hard work, it is best to remove weeds by hand – working an area at a time (the area you haven't got to yet can be covered with plasic or carpet to at least slow down weed growth). Remove every scrap of couch grass. Its fat, white, unhealthy-looking roots spread everywhere, and any small bit left in the ground will multiply a hundred-fold and strangle your best plants. It is a nuisance to grub for it, but a lot easier than trying to get rid of it once the area is planted. The same applies to convolvulus, ground elder or any other perennial weeds.

PATHS AND WALKWAYS

It might seem logical to construct all the necessary paths and walkways before you get busy with the planting season. This makes sense in the case of boundary walls and paths which have only one possible position, next to a shadowing hedge. However, if you are new to the garden, and haven't seen where the sun falls in summer it might be as well to wait a while rather than running a path across what turns out to be the best tomato position. You can make a good temporary path from concrete paving blocks, laid on earth that has been tamped down level. Laying them on a bed of sand is better, but, if you change your mind about the placing, getting the sand up again may be a problem.

By the end of your first season, you will have a good idea of what your final plan will be, whether you are going to build a greenhouse or frames, and any other ideas which may affect the layout of your path.

Grass paths between or around plots are easier to alter if you feel inclined, but remember to make them wide enough for your mower to run on, unless you sincerely enjoy crawling around with a pair of shears. Paths in the actual vegetable plots are only trodden earth and of minimum size. In a very wet period it may be necessary to put down stepping stones or boards to stop yourself sinking in. You can get access to the back of a bed by mounting a board between two bricks or flower pots and doing a balancing act.

Ordinarily, if you prepare the ground in autumn, all you will have to do in spring is remove any weeds – including the couch grass of which you shifted every scrap – maybe fork the top lightly and rake the bed to a nice smooth surface, ready for planting. The earth should break to a nice open texture with plenty of air spaces between the soil crumbs, to allow warmth and moisture to penetrate to the roots of the plants.

If you are preparing the soil in spring, don't try to work the soil when the ground is too wet, because it will compact into lumps beneath the surface and cause trouble to the young plants. The digging should be easier this time, but on a heavy clay soil which has not been improved you will need to break up clods, and it is worth feeding in wood-ash to lighten the texture.

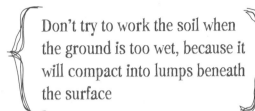

Don't try to work the soil when the ground is too wet, because it will compact into lumps beneath the surface

Also be much more careful about adding natural fertilisers, since there will be no time for them to break down and spread through the soil. Some plants react very badly to freshly manured or limed areas, so check exactly what you are going to plant on a particular spot before adding anything. This is especially the case with roots which get over-excited and coarse.

SOURCING SEEDS

Most vegetables can be raised from seed by most people, although in the north a gardener with no sheltered growing area may have to buy in tomato plants to get the full benefit of the limited growing season. Onion sets are often bought for the same reason and most of the common plants, especially of the cabbage family, can be obtained in market gardens, garden centres and online, for people starting late in the season, but the initial cost will cut your profit to quite an extent.

Seeds are selected from good strong plants in one season to be sold the following winter, and the packets will be dated with both years. All seed has to conform to a certain standard of viability, so there is no point in paying extra for the seed of common vegetables. The expensive brands aren't better, they just cost more, usually because the firms sell fewer in total than the big boys. Sometimes, there are fewer seeds in the packet too. This wouldn't matter if every seed you planted grew, since a few plants go a long way. But the ordinary grower isn't just dependent on fertile seed. What goes wrong may be their own fault, like lack of watering, or an act of God, like the cats having a fight in the garden and mowing down all the new seedlings.

What we need then is more seeds and this is what we get from the standard packets available in any chain store, garden centre or major seed suppliers. It may mean getting seed by post, so think about it early in the season.

SEED SWAPPING

Look out for local seed swapping events – often held by allotment or gardening groups – where you will find great advice as well as seeds. For example, 'Seedy Sunday' in Brighton & Hove which is described as the UK's biggest community seed swap - in return for a donation or in exchange for seeds they have saved, growers can choose seeds from traditional varieties of garden vegetables. These events also encourage the use of open-pollinated, 'heritage' varieties which are often no longer commercially available.

Look online as well for seed-swapping sites, (see Useful websites guide, page 246), which encourages people with surplus seeds to either swap them or pass them onto another gardener.

Most seeds will keep for several years but if you want to offset the cost in the first year, try sharing the seeds among a group

Most seeds will keep for several years, though the germination rate will drop as it gets older. If you want to offset the cost in the first year, try sharing the seeds among a group; there will be plenty for everyone.

You will also see pelleted seeds on sale. They are individual seeds coated with clay or a mixture of nutrient and clay binder until they are the size of little pills. They are easier to handle, especially for anyone with arthritic fingers, and so can be spaced out mathematically to reduce overcrowding. As they grow, the binder falls away and the nutrients are there, available for each plant personally. However, some of the binders are so hard that the seeds sit there in their little jackets doing nothing for months. You will have to water them much more than normal and sometimes even cut the coat open, which is a fiddly job and slows things up. They also cost more for less seed, but most of them will germinate if you are prepared to take the extra trouble.

Sometimes these seeds have been primed – given enough water to start off germination and then dried again. They are supposed to germinate more evenly and quickly, and often at lower temperatures, but may not last as long in storage as regular seeds.

Along the same lines as pelleted seeds, you can also buy seeds stuck on tape – convenience is the main reason for this, as well as reducing the need for thinning at a later date. But again you pay for it.

Look out too for treated seeds which have been coated in chemicals – usually a fungicide to prevent rot, or sometimes an insecticide. If you plan to garden organically you will want to avoid these. Instead buy seeds with an organic symbol from an approved organic certification body on the packet.

Some seeds are foil-wrapped, which is said to preserve their freshness and viability until the moment you open the pack. Since most seed lasts a fair time if kept dry, we remain unconvinced there is much advantage in this, except in damp areas where storage is more difficult even in shops.

Potato 'seed' consists of small potatoes grown and checked to ensure they are not affected by any of the ailments commonly afflicting local crops. An alternative is to use old potatoes bought for the kitchen and which have started sprouting. They may fall victim to disease more easily, but they may not, in which case you have ten or a dozen good potatoes from what you might have had to throw away. It all depends on your spirit of adventure which you choose.

Be wary of varieties labelled 'Best for freezing'. More or less any vegetable will freeze reasonably well (see page 202). These seeds are more suitable for commercial frozen food manufacturers, because they ripen all at once over a very short period and keep the production lines rolling. Unless you are in a position to drop everything and turn your kitchen into a factory for a week or more and freeze, freeze, freeze, you will be better off with ordinary varieties, which ripen over a longer period.

If you fancy growing unusual varieties – perhaps heritage types that have long since been dropped by the supermarkets for cosmetic or logistical reasons – then do some research online or look into seed swapping. Specialist suppliers exist and although they are likely to be more expensive than standard varieties you can feel good about your contribution to the genetic diversity of the planet.

It has been estimated that 75 per cent of the planet's plant diversity has been lost in the past 100 years and this is not helped by the dominance of major seed

VIABILITY OF SEEDS

If you don't use all the seeds in a packet in the first season, fold it over, keep it in a cool, dry place and use the seeds in following seasons. Date the packet clearly, with the first sowing year. Damp or mouldy seed should be thrown away.

Listed below are the average periods each seed will last, although some will deteriorate earlier, some later:

One year only – parsnips (butter and cream good for two), scorzonera, any F1 hybrids.

Two years – turnips, swedes, peas (some less), broad beans, French beans, runner beans, parsley, many herbs for preference, spinach.

Three years – leeks, carrots, mustard and cress.

Four years – lettuce, onion, radish, Chinese cabbage.

Five years – cabbage, cauliflower, broccoli, sprouts, kohl rabi, beetroot, spinach.

Six years – celery, celeriac.

Seven years – marrows, cucumbers, melons, edible gourds (but not if they dry out completely).

companies producing F1 seeds, and legislation that insists varieties can only be legally bought and sold if they appear on National Lists (the fee to be included in the List means that more specialised, lower-selling varieties often don't appear).

Saved seed, whether from your own crops or bought food, can be tried but you won't have much luck if your plants came from seeds marked 'F1 Hybrid' on the packet. These are crossbred plants carefully developed for some particular characteristic – like size, large yield or unusual colour. You should get excellent results the first year, but it is no use saving the seed as F1 seed doesn't 'come true' but reverts to the characteristics of one of the parents, always the least desirable one. Not a bad outcome for a seed supplier, but not great for a self-sufficient gardener – since for the first time in history it means growers have to buy new seed every year.

> Make sure seeds are thoroughly dry before storing them; store in breathable envelopes or packets, in a cool, dry room – never a greenhouse

If you want to save your own, then leave a plant to ripen fully, but make sure it does not drop its seeds around the garden. Start with the easier plants – bean, lettuce, pea, pepper, give the best chances of success since they produce seed the same season as planted and are mostly self-pollinating, minimising the need to be mindful of preventing cross-pollination. Make sure seeds are thoroughly dry before storing them; store in breathable envelopes or packets, in a cool, dry room – never a greenhouse. And don't forget to label them.

Potatoes tend to hide in the earth and set themselves next year anyway, but they are such robbers of the soil that it is best not to have potatoes on the same spot for two years running. This means that the 'volunteers', as farmers call self-set potatoes, are liable to come up awkwardly in the middle of other crops. Even old peelings thrown out on the compost heap can produce thriving plants.

Saving seed from bought vegetables is chancy. If you save exotics, like pepper seeds, or peach stones, they will probably turn out to be varieties which will only grow in tropical climates. However, people sometimes have remarkable results with orange pips, provided they have a sheltered south wall to grow them against. It is always worth trying anything like this which comes free, provided you don't spend more on bought fertiliser and heating than you would on the end product.

Growing

9. Planting

There is no 'right' date for planting any vegetable, because the weather is never the same two years running. Gardeners in the south can get going earlier than those in the north, but there are sheltered areas and windswept plains which affect planting. Town gardens, with the warmth spilling over them from the houses, are ready sooner than a country garden backing on to open fields. You can ask the old chap in the local pub, watch what the neighbours do or use your common-sense. The results will be about the same.

As a rough guide, in an average year when things begin to move in early March, parsnips and onion family from seed go in. Carrots are sown in late March to early April and beet a fortnight later. Even if you aren't sure, seed is so cheap that it is worth having a go with a small amount.

SOWING SEEDS IN SITU

Assuming your ground is dug and fed, rake it flat, removing all the big stones and weed roots. Then tread over the surface to compact the soil and eliminate air pockets. On heavy clay which is not improved, don't tread but smooth with the back of the rake. Then rake the top inch loose again. This sounds crazy, but the top inch is where you plant the small seeds, and if the soil is all loose underneath, they could fall straight through and never surface again. They need a soft mattress and a fluffy cover on top, until they are big enough to dig down through the mattress.

Having raked, trodden and raked again, set your garden line up where you intend to plant, twisting it tight with the stick. Cut a V-shaped indentation with the hoe along the length of the line. The recommended planting depth – given on the seed packet – is mostly a rough guide. It may vary from ⅛–¾in (3–19mm), but don't fuss with a tape measure, guess.

Take a pinch of seed from the packet and fold over the top before the rest spills. Sprinkle seed sparingly along the trench, aiming for one seed every 2in (5cm), which is practically impossible with small seeds.

Beetroot have bigger seeds and can be planted straight away at 4in (10cm) intervals for round (globe) beet and 6in (15cm) for long beet. Then draw the earth from the side of the trench over the seed to the required depth and pat down firmly with the head of the rake.

Take the line away and mark the ends of the row with small sticks. Write the name, variety and date of planting on a label or bit of paper, place it in a small polythene bag, and secure the bag, upside down, to one of the sticks. This will help you to check what does well and what doesn't in your particular garden.

Once you have started sowing in spring, repeat the operation at intervals of at least a fortnight or three weeks. The first sowings will produce some young vegetables ready for eating in roughly two or two-and-a-half months. If you leave half or a third of this sowing to mature, it will produce the largest size of that vegetable to ripen in summer or early autumn for storing in clamps (see page 174).

The mid-season sowing will give you a succession of young vegetables during summer and the main crop for storage. The last sowings may or may not mature, according to the mildness of the autumn, but it is worth trying to extend the harvest season.

The number of sowings will depend on the amount of space at your disposal and your personal fondness for a particular vegetable. Almost certainly, when you are starting, the sight of empty space doing nothing will lead you to plant too much, and there will come a crisis when the brassica start demanding space which is chock full of roots. If this happens, any deep container can be pressed into service to house the waiting plants, or you can pull more young vegetables and swap or freeze them small.

All small-seeded plants have to be thinned out as they grow into seedlings. They can be transplanted, but this gets less easy as the season progresses to summer, especially when there is little rain. You may prefer to increase the original planting distances to the spacings given after first thinning, to save wastage and the labour of thinning. Old gardeners will regard this as heresy, but modern seeds generally germinate pretty well, given reasonable warmth and moisture, so there is no necessity to provide for the failure of half the seeds to grow.

If you have doubts, plant a little clump of extra seeds at the end of your row ready to fill in the gaps – if they occur. This technique pays off, particularly in the case of exotic and soft-stemmed vegetables. With exotics, you get very few for your money and, if you plant two seeds and discard one seedling, you are doing the manufacturer a favour rather than yourself.

Soft-stemmed plants, like the cucumber family and runner beans, bruise if handled much, as they must be able to disentangle the roots of those which have been planted in bunches. Plant them as if you had faith that every one would grow, and you will mostly be repaid.

> Almost certainly, when you are starting, the sight of empty space doing nothing will lead you to plant too much

SOWING SEEDS IN BOXES, POTS OR FRAMES

If you are growing seeds in boxes, pots or frames, it pays to take a little extra trouble and start them off in good soil. Ordinary garden soil has weed seeds, plus roots and spores of plant diseases lurking in it, which might kill your plants before they mature.

The traditional medium for planting in boxes is seed compost. This isn't compost as in 'compost heap', made from decomposed weeds and kitchen gunge, but compost meaning 'mixture' – usually of peat, or a peat substitute, sand and sterilised loam – and it contains fewer nutrients than other composts since seeds contain all they need to germinate. Given the environmental issues surrounding the sourcing of peat (see box opposite), it would be good to use peat-free composts which often contain coir or leafmould.

> Seed compost contains fewer nutrients than other composts since seeds contain all they need to germinate

If you are short of money but have time and patience, you can make your own John Innes-type mixture. Look online for peat-free 'recipes'.

The seeds can be grown in plastic trays, yoghurt pots, old wooden boxes, egg boxes, or home-made newspaper pots (see 'Planting kit' page 22). Drainage holes must be made in the bottom at regular intervals. If the box has wide slats at the base, which would allow your valuable compost to trickle through, line it with newspaper. This will rot away by the time the soil has compacted with the roots sufficiently to stay put.

Fill your box or pot to within an inch of the top, water the earth well with a fine-rosed can and firm it down with the flat of your hand. Then plant your seeds, at regular intervals of 1–2in (2.5–5cm) according to size. Very tiny seeds, like those of some herbs, are difficult to separate; these can be mixed up with a little sand to spread them out a bit. Cover with compost to the required depth and pat the surface down again. Put a light-proof cover of black plastic or newspaper over the box or pot until germination starts, then remove it at once.

Small quantities of earth in a box or pot dry out a lot faster than in the garden, and there will be no natural rainfall to compensate, so you will have to keep watering. To reduce the need to water when the seeds are still loose and liable to be shifted, water the compost very well before sowing and retain the moisture with black polythene until germination.

Young seedlings can be watered from the top, with care, using a fine-rosed can held well away, or a little pot-plant watering-can with its thin spout pointed precisely between the rows of plants. A detergent squeeze bottle can be adapted for directional watering, or an old tin with tiny holes punched in the bottom can be held high over the box to simulate fine rain. The other important thing, apart from not flooding the plants out, is not to let blobs of water stand on the leaves when the sun shines brightly, or they will scorch and die.

Cold frames can either be used to house a collection of seed-boxes and pots, or filled with earth and treated like a gigantic seed-tray (see Protection page 26). When filling with earth, first put a few broken pots or stones in the bottom of the frame for drainage, add coarse compost – the garden sort,

THE PROBLEM WITH PEAT

Peat is actually partially decomposed plant debris, which can include trees, shrubs, herbs, sedges, grasses and mosses. In the UK, over 94 per cent of peatbogs have been damaged or destroyed partly in order to keep gardeners supplied with peat which is commonly used in seed and potting composts, and sometimes used as a soil improver. These bogs are hugely important sites for wildlife and also help absorb carbon dioxide from the atmosphere – it is estimated that globally peat stores twice as much carbon as forests. But this carbon dioxide is released back into the atmosphere when peatbogs are drained or disturbed. It can take from 7,000 to 10,000 years to produce a layer of peat 23–33ft (7–10m) thick, so replacing what's used is no quick and easy matter.

There are now a good many 'peat-free' potting composts available to buy, which are often coir-based mixtures. Coir comes from the fibrous layer surrounding the hard shell of coconuts. It adds bulk to composts so increasing moisture retention and porosity. Other possible ingredients are bark, wood chip, and garden waste. Alternatively, make your own.

> Young seedlings can be watered from the top, with care, using a fine-rosed can held well away, or a little pot-plant watering-can with its thin spout pointed precisely between the rows of plants

A sowing calendar

All dates are approximate and should be varied according to the weather in any particular year – and remember that climate change will in theory make for some warmer winters and the possibility of starting a few crops off earlier than you would have done some years ago.

sow = sow seed in the ground (in situ)

plant = set out seedlings, offsets or bought-in plants

glass = any form of unheated protected sowing

heat = protected and/or given additional heat

south = southern or mild areas of the country

north = northern or chilly areas

(tomatoes) = unusual, early or late sowing for a special date or purpose

late = towards the end of the month if mild enough

January	
sow	Jerusalem artichokes (late)
plant	shallots
glass	spring onions
heat	potatoes in indoor boxes, (tomatoes for early greenhouse crop)

February	
sow	Jerusalem artichokes, broad beans (south), lettuce (south), (onions), spring onions, parsnips (late), peas, salsify (south), scorzonera (south), summer spinach, (rhubarb seed)
plant	globe artichokes (late), shallots
glass	lettuce, potatoes in boxes. Also chit early potatoes
heat	onions, peppers (late), tomatoes for greenhouse

March	
sow	broad beans, beet, (brussels sprouts for autumn), summer cabbage, carrots, summer cauliflower, land cress, kale, kohl rabi, leeks, lettuce, onions, spring onions for early summer, welsh onions, parsnips, peas, radish, and most herbs (except marjoram, balm, basil)
plant	globe artichokes, asparagus crowns, early potatoes (south), pickling onions for June, rhubarb crowns, (tree onion)
glass	cardoons (late), celeriac (late), celery (late), mustard and cress, peppers (late), early potatoes under cloche or in greenhouse, tomatoes. Also chit maincrop potatoes
heat	celery, celeriac, indoor cucumbers (late)

April	
sow	asparagus, balm, broad beans for July, beet, brussels sprouts for Christmas, autumn cabbage, summer calabrese, carrots, autumn cauliflower, land cress, kale, kohl rabi, leeks, lettuce, marjoram, mustard and cress, onions, (spring onions for late summer), parsnips, peas, sugar peas, radish, spinach beet, (swedes), turnips
plant	onion sets, pickling onion for late summer, early potatoes (north), maincrop potatoes (south), bush fruits (early)
glass	French beans, soya beans, runner beans, cardoons (early), celeriac (early), celery (early), courgettes, Japanese cucumbers, ridge cucumbers, marrows, melons, peppers, pumpkins, New Zealand spinach, sweet corn
heat	aubergines; any of above in cold year

May		
sow	basil, French beans (late), haricot beans (late), soya beans, runner beans (late), beet, heading broccoli, winter cauliflower, sprouting broccoli for winter, brussels sprouts for Jan–Feb; carrots, cauliflower for Nov, winter cabbage, land cress, ridge cucumbers (late), kohl rabi, lettuce, marrows (late), Chinese mustard, mustard and cress, parsnips, peas, radish, Japanese radish, sweet corn (mid-late), spinach, swedes, turnips (both late, for August)	
plant	French beans (late), runner beans (late), soya beans (mid), cardoons, celeriac, celery (and bought plants), courgettes (late), leek plants, marrows (mid), potatoes, maincrop (north), pumpkins (late), sweet corn (late), tomato plants (late)	
glass	set out melons, indoor cucumbers, tomatoes in greenhouse bed, aubergines	
June		
sow	French beans, runner beans, haricot beans, beet, winter cabbage, carrots, chicory, Chinese cabbage (cauliflower), ridge cucumber, endive, kohl rabi, lettuce, mustard and cress, Chinese mustard, radish, Japanese radish, winter savory, swedes for August	
plant	winter celery plants, tender beans, marrow, cucumber, melon in exceptional summer, sweet corn	
glass	aubergines, etc, to final growing position	
July		
sow	French beans, runner beans, haricot beans, beet, cabbage for late winter, Chinese cabbage, corn salad, endive, lettuce, peas, spring onions (north), Chinese mustard, mustard and cress, radish, Japanese radish, Spanish and China radish, winter spinach, swedes and turnips for winter	
plant	winter celery plants	
August		
sow	French beans (south), beet (south), corn salad, land cress, endive, lettuce, mustard and cress, spring onions (south), radish, Spanish and China radish, winter spinach, swedes and turnips for winter	
plant	strawberry plants, globe artichoke offsets	
September		
sow	corn salad, land cress, lettuce, mustard and cress, onions (south), radish, winter spinach	
plant	plant bush fruits, strawberry plants, tree onions, Welsh onions	
glass	onions (late, south), lettuce (late, north); all tender plants may need covering late	
October		
sow	(glass later) broad beans for May (south), cauliflower for May–June (south), lettuce	
plant	tree onions, Welsh onions, tree fruits, autumn strawberries and raspberries	
glass	lettuce (north), radish (north), spring onions (south)	
November		
sow	(glass later) broad beans (south)	
plant	bush fruit in mild year	
glass	lettuce (south)	
December	sowings in heat or indoors only	

not seed/potting compost – or leaves, to about half-way up, then good soil. This should preferably be sterilised – which is possible if you have a solar dryer (see Harvesting page 184) – but at least well raked and sieved to remove weed seeds and stones. The surface of this soil should be three-quarters of the way up the box. Top it with seed compost, 3in (7.5cm) deep, and firm.

Plant your seeds, in rows 5in (12.5cm) apart, or in square blocks, marked off with labels. Sprinkle sand over the surface, close the frame and darken off the lid with black polythene or sacking until germination starts.

If the soil in the frame was well watered before planting, it should stay damp until the seeds are up and flourishing, after which fine sprays of water may be necessary. The lid will need to be opened during the day once the plants are growing, and eventually taken off, although by that time the plants may be ready for setting out in the open garden, after hardening off.

> Single seedlings – as of marrows and cucumbers – can be covered by an up-ended flower pot or jam jar, but remember to take it off in the daytime

If the seedlings in trays or pots have grown well but the outside atmosphere is still unsuitable they will have to be transplanted to larger, deeper boxes, and set farther apart, to prevent their growing weak and spindly or wilting altogether. Prepare the new box with the same sort of soil mix and water well. Place it in the greenhouse in advance, so that the seedlings move into a soil temperature they are used to. Water the seedlings well just before moving, to ensure that as much of the original soil as possible clings to the roots.

Ease the seedlings out of their box, a few at a time, working from underneath with a plastic label, lolly stick or old table fork. Never chop them apart from above with a trowel or half the roots will be damaged. Very gently edge one root system apart from the next seedling's and lay the separated plant on your hand or trowel. Don't pick it up between your fingers, as this would bruise the stem. Make a good-sized hole and slide the seedling in; let the roots spread and cover them in, firming the surface gently when the operation is complete. Shade the box for a day or two and water between, not on, the plants.

To reduce the need for transplanting – which is a shock to the system – it is a good idea to plant direct into large boxes or individual pots any seeds you know will produce large seedlings. Marrows, cucumbers, sweet corn, runner beans, melons, all prefer this treatment. Use the same mixture and they will be happy in their pots until the roots begin to show through the base holes. If you stand the pots in a saucer, watering from below is simplified too.

Biodegradeable pots are sold everywhere for germination. The idea is that plant roots grow out through the sides as well as the base and the whole thing can be planted without any check. This works if the pots are kept really wet. If they dry out, it is very hard to get them damp again. The roots cannot then penetrate the sides; instead, they start twisting around the root ball inside the pot. The only solution is to turn out the whole plant and repot or set outside, hoping the roots will unwind again before they choke each other.

When the time approaches to set your plants out of doors, they must first be hardened off. Gradually reduce the amount of heat and protection they have been used to, so that the open air does not come as a shock. Wean them slowly, first removing any heat, then daytime covers, then night-time covers, moving them steadily from the greenhouse or warm place to a cool situation, then outside in shelter, and finally into the open garden. Only when this hardening-off process is complete should they be shifted from box or pot to the ground.

To remove a plant from a clay pot, damp the soil and tap the sides with a trowel; from a plastic pot, damp the soil and wiggle the bendy plastic. Spread your fingers wide across the top of the pot on either side of the plant stem but not touching it. Up-end the pot, and the whole plant should come out into your hand. If it sticks, poke a skewer or plant label into the base hole and push.

Set plants from a pot a little lower than the ground surface. This is especially important in the case of plants in biodegradeable pots, which must be buried in soil or the sides will dry out and stop water getting to the roots and prevent their rotting down. All transplants need watering well until they are established.

If it suddenly turns cold, protect your set-out plants with plastic, newspaper or another cover. Single seedlings – as of marrows and cucumbers – can be covered by an up-ended flower pot or jam jar, but remember to take it off in the daytime.

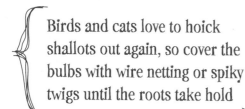

10. Spring

For most people, the garden year begins in spring – when the evenings are getting lighter and the air a bit softer and the trees are beginning to shoot.

You will hopefully have kept your soil covered with growing plants, green manure cover crops, or an organic mulch (see pages 154–156). If you planted a green manure crop, dig it up, let it die off and then bury it a few days later.

February is about the earliest time for normal outdoor planting and even then the soil is too wet and cold for small seeds. Two things which can always go in as they are large enough to take care of themselves are shallots and Jerusalem artichokes. Both are expensive compared with packets of seed but once you have one, you have them for ever by leaving offsets in the ground to grow next year.

Birds and cats love to hoick shallots out again, so cover the bulbs with wire netting or spiky twigs until the roots take hold

SHALLOTS
Shallots are first bought as offsets about the size of a young onion and reproduce themselves many times. Plant them 4in (10cm) apart with 9in (23cm) between rows, just sitting the bottom half in the soil. The top half projects and birds and cats love to hoick them out again, so cover the bulbs with wire netting or spiky twigs until the roots take hold.

The crop prefers soil which has previously been manured, but if you missed out in autumn let it take its chance. Firm the earth around them so there are no pockets to hold freezing water against the bulb.

JERUSALEM ARTICHOKES
These can be bought at the greengrocers. Plant any that are beginning to sprout. They do everything a potato does and have a much more interesting taste. The plants are a lot less fussy than potatoes and don't suffer from nasty infectious ailments. Give them a bit of compost, plant 6in (15cm) down and 18in (45cm) apart and they will do the rest. They can grow 6ft (1.8m) tall, so plant them where they are a useful screen, not a nuisance.

PEAS AND BROAD BEANS

The other major planting in spring is of the hardier pulses – early peas and broad beans. In some mild areas, broad beans can even be planted in November to stand the winter, but this has never worked for us, in a rather exposed garden. They don't like frost, but sometimes survive it if tucked up in leaves or earth.

Both have quite large seeds, which need to be planted more deeply, at 2in (5cm) or almost 3in (7.5cm). As they are easy to handle, they are planted in their final growing spacing. It isn't easy to guess distances down small dark holes, so it helps to have a dibber or cane marked at the required height.

A quick planting method, when time presses, gives moderate results. Just rake and firm the earth, then make holes on either side of the stretched line, in a zigzag pattern, with each seed opposite a gap at 2in (5cm) deep, 3in (7.5cm) apart for peas and 6in (15cm) for beans. Cover in, firm the soil and mark the rows.

Much better, but needing more time, is to make a trench where the peas or beans are to grow. Mark out a space between lines 6in (15cm) apart for peas and 12in (30cm) for beans. Dig out a trench one spade deep, and fill the bottom half of the hole with compost, lawn mowings, rotted leaves or even kitchen waste destined for the compost heap. Cover it with 2–3in (5–7.5cm) of the excavated earth. Tread down the mass firmly and water the trench.

Soak the peas or beans overnight before planting.

Set peas out in the bottom of the trench in a zigzag pattern about 3–4in (7.5–10cm) apart in a double row. Cover with 2in (5cm) of earth and tread firmly. This should leave the surface of the planted area about 1in (2.5cm) below the surface of the rest of the plot. This is useful if the weather turns dry, since they are thirsty creatures when growing pods.

Set beans out in the same way, but 9in (22.5cm) apart; cover them with 2in (5cm) of soil, and firm. Keep the spare soil beside the bean trench and, if there

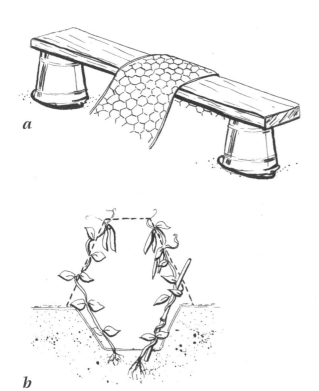

is a sudden cold snap when the young leaves are showing, earth them up to just below the growing tip as frost protection.

Peas, although they look frail, are tougher than beans, but they do need protection from birds. You can keep them off with fences of short twigs, stuck in the ground beside the planting holes. A better method is to make pea guards out of wire netting, 3ft (90cm) wide and long enough to cover the row with a bit of tuck-in at each end.

Commercial guards are sold, or you can make these yourself. Balance a plank on a couple of buckets and place the centre of the wire netting on the plank. Bend the two sides down to make a flattened tent. Mount the tent over the rows of peas as soon as they are planted and anchor sides and ends with canes at intervals (see illustrations left).

Close the wire together at the ends of the rows. This netting also acts as a support for the plants as they grow up. The size of the mesh should be a compromise between what will keep out the birds and what will allow your fingers through to pick – about 1½in (4cm).

Peas need very little attention when growing, provided you train the tips of the stems through the netting from the outset. Unless they are given encouragement to twine in the right direction, they will strangle the next plant instead. Peas need a lot of water to grow, which is easier to apply if you have set them in a trench. In a drought, soak the trench thoroughly, then cover it completely with a mulch of grass mowings, leaves, or compost, to stop evaporation.

Ordinary short peas need 3ft (90cm) canes and soft fillis to secure them at first. Tall peas are more trouble, needing 6ft (1.8m) canes and either wires or garden netting between each one. They are rather a nuisance in a small garden, and don't bear noticeably better than a good dwarf pea.

When they start to pod, be ready to pick every day. Pick whole pods of the French 'sugar peas' for eating. Ordinary peas are ready when you can feel peas in the pod. Keep picking a few and others will develop to replace them; if you leave the first peas to grow on, the plant will devote itself to the task and produce no more. Twist the pods off, don't tug the whole plant up.

When the crop is over the plant turns yellow and dry, don't pull it all up, but chop off the roots and bottom inch of the stem and leave them in the ground, as a valuable source of nitrogen.

Broad beans are sturdy plants, but they grow moderately high – 3¼–4ft (1–1.2m) – and carry a lot of leaf and weight of pods, so they can be damaged by the wind. They are helped by individual canes or a framework of posts and wires. A single line of canes and wires is fair, but a double line of wires with a pair of stakes at each end will stand anything the winds care to do.

When the beans are finished, the same framework can be left in position to hold up the brussels sprout plants over the winter.

If you planted in a trench, earth up each plant as it grows from the piles at the side. This shields the young plants from frost and helps the mature plant to take the weight of pods later.

Water well and mulch in dry weather (as described for peas).

Pick the individual pods as they ripen. When growth has finished, cut off the roots and leave them in the ground to contribute nitrogen to the next crop.

Blackfly is the great enemy of broad beans. It likes young growth, so 'stop' the plants by pinching out the top of the stem as soon as four clusters of flowers show.

SOYA BEANS

If you want to try these, soak before planting in mid-April. Set out 9in (22.5cm) apart in a double row. You can gather the pods to cook, although they taste rather nasty. Otherwise, let them ripen on the plant and use as dried beans for storage. Soya beans are an excellent source of protein. They are also surprisingly hardy, withstanding late frosts, and appear to have no ailments.

We tried sowing expensive seeds specially bred for northern climates and, for comparison, seeds taken from a much cheaper packet bought for cooking from a health food shop. The cheap seeds germinated better and grew larger and sturdier plants. Neither, however, produced enough of a yield to justify the space they occupied in the garden over several months. We don't consider soya beans to be an economic plant for English gardens, which is a pity.

CATCH CROPPING

Both radishes and lettuce are used as catch crops, to make use of the gaps between slower-growing plants which will eventually need more space. They do not need a designated part of the plot and one or two can fit into any tiny gap. This doesn't look so tidy, but it makes economic sense.

- Radishes you can plant at any time from early March to fill a space but not hog it for long. A tiny pinch of seed between rows of slow-growing plants will be ready for eating in about a fortnight as long as the plants get plenty of water. If radishes sit around in the ground, they will get old and woody and encourage the dreaded club-root since they are a member of the brassica tribe. Therefore, if you can't use them or give them away, pull them up and throw them on the compost heap before they cause trouble.

- Lettuce grows almost as fast but the seeds need warmer soil to germinate in. Cloche them or grow them in boxes under cover during March and let them out during April, according to the weather. Mature lettuce are tough and some kinds will stand the winter in most areas, so the planting season can go right on until October.

WEEDING AROUND SEEDLINGS

As the young seedlings begin to appear so do the weeds, generally looking much more vigorous. They must be removed for they are competing for every scrap of nourishment in the soil. Hoe them down ruthlessly and put them on the compost heap (provided it is going to be hot enough to destroy them) where they can rot down and do some good in the future.

If your lines are straight, pushing the Dutch hoe along beside the rows is easy. For weeds within the rows themselves, hand treatment is necessary. If you aren't too sure what the young seedlings should look like, study an illustration, and when in doubt await developments. Some seeds produce two totally uncharacteristic leaves before the familiar foliage appears. When you are sure which are the baddies, pull them out and use your fingers to firm back the soil round the seedlings.

Try to catch the weeds young and never let them run to seed on the plot, for each seed will produce another weed. On the compost heap they dry and die and the heat kills off future trouble. Deep-rooted weeds, like plantain, should be tackled when small or they will need digging out with a trowel, which disturbs the surrounding soil.

Chemical weed-killers are an easy though expensive remedy and will ruin your organic credentials. But be careful. Some just kill the foliage they are applied to, and all will be well if you keep them off the plants next door to them. Other weed-killers sink into the ground and destroy the whole weed, but they stay in the soil making it impossible to grow weeds or plants there for months. Make sure you know what you are doing before ruining the garden for a season and avoid their use if possible.

ONIONS

Onions can be grown from seeds planted in situ. It is useful to place rows of onions between other plants to discourage various pests. The maincrop can be planted in a rich bed of their own, with spring onions, or rarer varieties like tree and Welsh onions, dispersed among other crops. You can keep the latter going year after year from your own stock, just like shallots.

Because onions from seed are sometimes very slow to get going, it is common practice to buy onion sets and plant these as an insurance in late March to April. The richer the bed which can be provided for all onions – except those for pickling – the better the yield will be. Plant the little sets like shallots, with their tops showing and, until they are settled in, protect them from tweaking birds with sticks laid on top or wire netting. If these are your only onions, plant them 4in (10cm) apart for thinning. If you have others to pull and use, and wish to grow these for store, plant them 6in (15cm) apart, and leave 12in (30cm) between the rows – here you can catch crop lettuce or grow beetroot, if the soil is good enough to support both.

Pickling onions don't mind poor soil, since they don't need to plump up. Plant them in April, fairly thickly, in short rows and they'll be mature by August.

GARLIC

Another onion tribe plant, best bought at the greengrocers and set out. You won't need many cloves to provide a plentiful supply for yourself and possibly for sale, since the crop is marketable.

LEEKS

Another onion relative is the leek, planted as seed in March, 1in (2.5cm) deep, or bought in as plants later on. It develops slowly from seed and needs gentle handling while it is young so that the soft roots are not broken in transplanting.

POTATOES

The last of the spring crops is the potato. It is very sensitive to frost, so – except in the really mild south – it should not be planted until latish in April, unless the sowing is protected under glass or plastic. In any other circumstances, it is best to delay outdoor planting and start the seed potatoes off in a frost-free light shed or room.

Sit them in a box (egg boxes are great for this) with the rose end upwards. This is the part of the potato with the eyes which eventually sprout. For generations, good gardeners have divided up their seed potato into two or more parts, each with a growing eye, to increase the potential plants.

Potatoes which have run to seed in the rack make poor eating, but they will grow if planted out. If they have been in a bag, the shoots will be white and

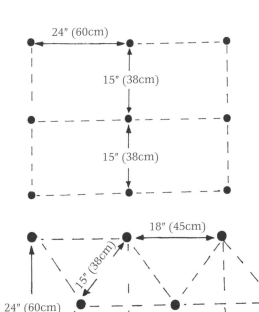

Planting pattern for maincrop potatoes; 15in (38cm) apart with 2ft (60cm) between the rows

Quincunx potato planting pattern gives more plants on a smaller area but this may reduce the total crop

scraggy, not purplish like the proper seed potatoes, and they won't do as well but you will get some return for nothing.

If you want early potatoes and the weather is still bad, you can grow them under glass or one or two at a time in a box of good earth, or a bucket, anywhere light and frost-free.

When they can be planted out, they will want a rich bed, with compost, manure or anything nourishing – except lime, which upsets their delicate skins. With a dibber, plant them 6–7in (15–17.5cm) deep, trying not to break off the shoots. The earlies are planted about 12in (30cm) apart with 18in (45cm) between the rows and maincrop 15in (38cm) apart with 2ft (60cm) between the rows.

> If the weather turns frosty after the crop is planted, cover the shoots with sacking, newspaper or anything available

You can reduce by 6in (15cm) the distances between rows by planting quincunx fashion, and this gives you more plants on a smaller area (see page 91). But don't do this unless you are pushed. The closer you get, the more the greedy beasts fight each other for the available nourishment, and this may reduce the total crop.

If the weather turns frosty after the crop is planted, cover the shoots with sacking, newspaper or anything available, otherwise they will blacken and die.

If you are caught out, leave the potatoes in. They will produce more shoots, but the crop will be lighter and later.

As the plants grow, earth them up by drawing soil against them with a hoe and patting it firm. This is done in straight lines for conventional planting or diagonals for quincunx planting. The earthing will smother small weeds among the plants, but large ones should be removed by hand and the gangways between the ridges kept hoed clean.

There are two reasons for earthing up. The first and most important is that the young potatoes grow close to the surface and, if they emerge above the soil, the sun turns the skin green. This isn't just unsightly – it shows the presence of the active poison, solanine, which can make people ill or even kill them. This is why you should never eat greened potatoes.

The second reason for earthing is that the potatoes on each plant develop at different rates, so some are ready while others are tiny. If you have to dig the whole plant to get the big ones, growth of the others is stopped. With a ridge, you can scrape away earth from the sides, take the big tubers and cover up again without shifting the plant root at all. The haulm, or foliage, will die off while the plant is still developing. When it is dry, lift the potatoes and destroy the old haulm by burning it or burying it in the middle of the compost heap, where the heat will destroy the many infections potatoes can spread.

Other spring plants: carrots, parsnips, scorzonera, beet, salsify, etc (roots proper) and swedes and turnips can be grown in spring. Roots like a deep-dug plot in order to grow straight. Lettuces and radishes can also go in now (see 'Catch cropping' box, page 89).

PROTECTED OUTDOOR PLANTING

If the winter hangs on well into spring, it is not much use to attempt outdoor planting. The ground is frozen or soggy, so that if you walk on it the top wads together into a hard pan. The soil is cold, which retards germination, or in extreme cases, kills the seed. Even if the seed lives, it doesn't start moving until conditions are right and will come up at the same time as a sowing made weeks later.

There are two basic problems: first, where the plant is hardy but the ground is not ready for it; second, where the plant is tender and the air temperature is too low. If you have a greenhouse or

A HOT BED

There is a natural form of under-soil heating – the hot bed — for which a supply of fresh manure, from horses, cows, pigs, or sheep (ideally from non-intensive or organic farms) is the main requisite.

Build a box with the cheapest sort of building block or from old bricks. Make it 3ft (90cm) deep and cover with an old window-frame. Fill the box with layers of decomposing leaves, manure, grass cuttings, old compost, more manure. Press the lot well down – tread it, if you dare, wearing long wellies. Top it with at least 6in (15cm) of good quality earth and cover the whole lot with your frame, tightly closed.

The whole thing will heat up to a very high temperature and will smell indescribable for a day or two. Let it heat as much as it will, testing the temperature now and then – you may have to cool it with water. Wait until the reading starts to fall before planting; when it registers 27°C (80°F) or less, the bed is ready for use. The soil on top will have been automatically sterilised by the heat. Plant your seeds and ventilate the bed a little from time to time. A bed made in winter will stay warm right through until spring or early summer, by which time cold-frame protection will be adequate.

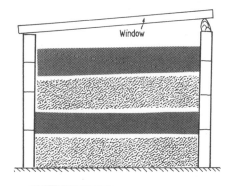

Window

frames, the matter is easily solved. If you haven't any structural glass, things are less simple but not desperate.

Cold ground can be improved from below by incorporating horse manure (or other fresh manure) just under the planting layer. This heats up as it decomposes and warms the soil around it. If you live in a neighbourhood where children go around on ponies instead of bikes, you should be able to find deposits of manure – although, not all plants appreciate fresh dung and you won't know the provenance of the manure, and therefore, whether it is from an organic farm. Or you can create a hot bed (see page 93).

Remember also that small seedlings often suffer damage from chill winds, even when they can take the ordinary air temperatures

A strip of black polythene spread along the ground and held down with bricks, will warm the soil a little, since black absorbs heat and radiates it locally. The amount of heat is increased if you weight the plastic with odd sheets of glass or an old window frame. This may raise the temperature just enough for planting, but you have to keep it that way if the cold weather continues.

There are a variety of cloches and covers available both to buy and make (see page 27) which will protect new plantings in early spring. Remember also that small seedlings often suffer damage from chill winds, even when they can take the ordinary air temperatures. A board or two propped up to act as a windbreak; a fence of flower pots, sticks or old bricks along the row, even cardboard or newspaper draped across the plants when there is a frost warning may all help to prevent a total loss.

If you can afford a greenhouse or can construct a frame (see Protection, page 29), half your problems are over. There are refinements, some of which can be employed outside a greenhouse or frame. Electrically-heated propagators are mini heated greenhouses; propagating trays with their own plastic covers are little cold greenhouses; and a box with a bit of glass on top is an embryo cold frame.

Seed trays can be lined up on a warm windowsill or along a sunny south-facing house wall, sheltered by a few panes of glass leaning at 45° against the wall. Cats love this arrangement and tend to use the boxes as sofas, unless you block the access.

TRANSPLANTING AND THINNING

Unless you have a really steady hand, too many plants will have emerged from the sowing. Thinning out is necessary to reduce them to numbers which will grow to maturity. To do this, select a sturdy seedling at regular intervals and ease the others away from it, using a trowel to loosen the earth and taking care not to cut the plant or break the roots. Firm back the disturbed earth and water over.

Traditionally, the reject seedlings are thrown away, but those which look healthy and have unbroken roots and leaves can be saved for transplanting. Do this as soon as possible after lifting, on a damp, overcast day for best results, handling the seedlings as little as possible. Make a hole longer than the longest root – using a short cane for small plants and a dibber for the big ones. Slip the plant into the hole, making sure the roots are well disposed and shake down earth to fill the hole. Firm round the plant on the surface and water in if there is no rain to do it for you.

If the weather suddenly turns sunny, shade the transplants for a couple of days with plastic, cardboard, newspaper or a strategically placed flower-pot. Water well at night until they are settled in. Some will droop and die, but most should mature about a week or fortnight after the seedlings that were left undisturbed.

Carrots

Where you have planted a double row of carrots, say, with 12in (30cm) between rows, thin them to 2in (5cm) apart. Set the surplus seedlings in a row down the middle of the two rows, where you have been taking a catch crop of radish. As the carrots grow larger, take every alternate one in the outer rows for eating young or freezing, then every alternate in the centre row. This leaves 4in (10cm) between each carrot and 6in (15cm) between rows. This is fairly tight packing, but it should smother weeds. Keep the shoulders of the carrots covered or they tend to discolour and split at the top.

Parsnips

The same principle applies to other roots. Parsnips, with more spreading foliage, are planted in wider spacing, in rows 9in (23cm) apart. Thin the seedlings from 2in to 4in (5cm to 10cm), and move the spares to a separate row. Use alternate roots and leave the final spacing at 8in (20cm) apart in the rows.

If you want to grow really huge parsnips, make a hole 12in (30cm) deep and almost fill it with a mixture of sand and sifted soil. Set the parsnip seedling in this, firm down and water well. Very large parsnips can go woody in the middle, but some varieties will become huge and edible, if there is enough to drink while growing.

Beetroot

Beetroot needs slightly different treatment according to the variety and ultimate use. Each seed, like a cork granule, produces a clump of seedlings clinging very closely together. It is very difficult to get them apart without damaging the roots and sometimes even the stem, so these will have to be discarded right away as compost. Some of the others will transplant successfully, providing they are kept damp at all times.

Having planted widely apart, as recommended, you will only have to select the best seedling in each bunch and remove the rest, carefully firming back the disturbed earth. But if you planted closer, whole bunches of seedlings must come out, so you will need to stagger the work over more than one day.

The long beet are generally grown on towards maturity like other root crops, with some half-grown ones pulled at intervals during the season. Your original rows should have been 8in (20cm) apart with 6in (15cm) between the plants. You can transplant suitable spares; they do rather well between well-spaced rows of onion sets. By the time the beet foliage is spreading out, the onions are harvested and can be replaced with lettuce, which like a little shade in summer.

Round beet can be grown on to maturity in the same way, in which case they need an ultimate 6–8in (15–20cm) to bulge into. Most people like to eat or pickle them young, at about 2in (5cm) diameter. If you intend to use all your globe beet this way, keep them planted at the original 4in (10cm) apart in rows 8in (20cm) apart and transplant into the centre of the row opposite gaps in the outer rows.

Use the outer rows first, by which time the inner will be ready. If you want to compromise – using some small, some large – plant at 4in (10cm) overall spacing, and use every other one in the outer rows and every one in the centre row as babies, and let the rest, now 8in (20cm) apart, grow to full size. They can get huge without going woody.

Onions

They are harder to transplant because their soft stems tend to bruise. Spring onions are usually left unthinned, jostling each other until they are a sufficient size to pull for salads. Firm back the earth around the roots of those which remain.

Ordinary maincrop onions are transplanted as soon as they are big enough to handle. Apart from soft stems, they have fat roots which snap easily, so they should be carefully eased out with a trowel from well below and handled as little as possible. Plant them 4in (10cm) apart, if you mean to use alternate ones young, and 6in (15cm) apart when growing on for store.

Once onions are growing, most of the bulb sits on top of the earth but it is difficult to make it do so if you transplant it so high. Set each bulb sufficiently into the ground to make it firm and press the earth well down beside it. As the transplants grow, they will raise themselves up to the right position.

They need plenty of water in the first six weeks or so, to help them increase in size. After that, they spend a while consolidating their gains and then the tops droop, at which stage they are ready for the harvesting process.

Although onions will grow perfectly well in three ranks, like other vegetables they are very handy as a policeman for other plants, warning off certain pests. For this reason, it is useful to plant your onions in single lines between other crops, like carrots and beet, but never where they can be overshadowed. They will not grow out of the sun.

Leeks

Leeks need slightly different treatment, since they sit low down in the soil. When they are ready to transplant, cut a narrow trench about 3in (7.5cm) deep, piling the spare earth on each side. Make holes 3in (7.5cm) deep in the bottom of the trench with a dibber and slip in the leek seedlings.

Sprinkle loose earth into the holes and between the well-spread roots and water in, but don't firm around the top more than enough to steady the plants. As they grow, draw the spare earth into the trench and bank it up against the stems. This is to blanch the stems, and stop them getting coarse in flavour.

Leeks for show are put into huge holes drilled with a crowbar and packed with manure down below and fine potting compost at the top. The earthing is reinforced by anchoring slates along the sides of the heaps against the stems. These leeks can grow enormous but they are strictly for astounding others, not for eating, since they taste of old dishcloths.

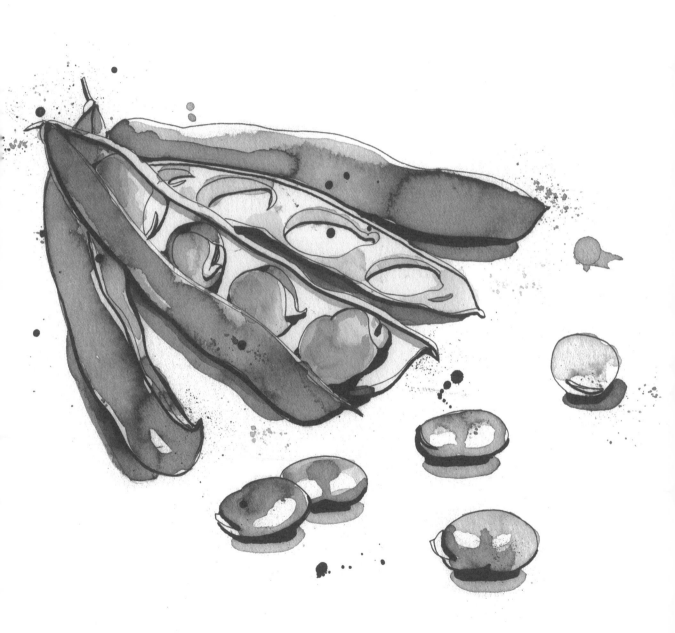

11. Summer

Between late May and August, a wide range of crops can be grown out of doors without protection.

First, there are various beans: dwarf French, climbing French, runner and haricot, and less common sorts which have much the same habits.

Dwarf French beans are the simplest to handle, and they are quite often planted in situ. Rake the soil over very thoroughly to a 3in (7.5cm) depth and turn it over, so that the warmth penetrates – beans sulk in chilly earth. They like land which has been well fed, but not recently, so incorporate compost low down or let it take its chance. Do not firm down after raking – the stem is soft and can't push hard against compacted soil.

Plant 2in (5cm) deep, 6in (15cm) apart with 12in (30cm) between rows; or in zigzag fashion with 9in (23cm) between individual plants. If you set them in a trench, 1in (2.5cm) deep, they can be watered more easily and mulched with a top dressing of lawn mowings or compost in time of drought. If there is a sudden chill after planting, cover the rows with a strip of black polythene for a few days but remove it the moment there is any sign of activity.

Place spiky twigs or a netting over the rows to stop birds fishing for the seeds. Not all of them may germinate, so plant a few spares at the end of the rows and transplant when you are sure there is a gap. As soon as the seedlings are 3–4in (7.5–10cm) high, draw the earth up around the bottom of the stems and firm in to help the plants stay upright when bearing.

These dwarfs do not normally need staking but in a windy area support them with short pea sticks or twigs. Pick the pods regularly, as soon as they are big enough, to maintain the succession of cropping. When they finish, leave the roots in the soil to provide nitrogen for the next crop.

Haricot beans are selected varieties of French beans planted 6in (15cm) apart in a staggered row. Set up your line and plant beans on either side of it, clearing it by 1in (2.5cm). They are not gathered young but allowed to mature on the plant. When the plant has finished, pull it up, apart from the roots, and hang it on a nail or rack to dry out before picking out the dried beans for storage.

Tall beans are slightly different because they need support. It is easier to set this in position first since there is a lot of treading around involved. The simplest framework is a wigwam of three or four 6–8ft (1.8–2.4m) canes, tied at the top, with the base of the canes about 12in (30cm) apart (see right). Set a bean at the foot of each cane, with some horizontal strings to help them. The snag about this arrangement is that heavy cropping plants jostle together at the top, tangling and reducing the yield.

A more common means of support is to set pairs of canes about 12in (30cm) apart, crossed near the tops, with other canes laid across the 'V' to steady them. The two ends need staying with uprights. You can buy a commercial metal framework with a triangular frame and netting to hold the beans. In our windy garden, we have made a stronger frame of 2in (5cm) roofing batten, braced at 10ft (3m) intervals with uprights and covered with netting stiffened with canes every 2½ft (75cm). This defies the gales which collapsed the ordinary framework of canes.

When the supports are safely in position and the soil trodden down hard against them, plant the seeds or young plants in a staggered double row, 10–12in (25–30cm) apart, by the canes or along the nets. Normally, beans train themselves but some may need guidance at first.

Water well, since the high bank of foliage loses a lot by transpiration. Spray a fine mist of water over the flowers to aid 'setting' of pods. Once the growth of the pods starts, you will need to pick daily. The produce from one packet of beans can be enormous. Freeze some as you go, not waiting for the tougher ones at the end of the season.

Climbing beans also grow well against a wall, on a single-sided net or wires anchored with metal 'vine eyes'. Being tall, both types of bean need to be at the end or side of the garden. The growth is very attractive, with bright orange or red flowers, and can be used as a living screen or sitting-out area in summer. They look good in the front garden too – the framework is very rapidly covered with leaves and beans. In both cases, when the plants are finished, leave the roots in the soil to release nitrogen and compost the rest.

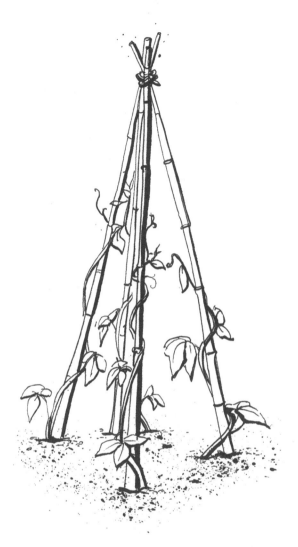

A wigwam support for tall beans

SWEETCORN

Maize is a tender plant and must not be put outside until the middle or end of May when it can then be planted in open ground. It needs rich land – although not freshly manured or it will produce foliage instead of cobs.

Set the young plants out in a square with 18in (45cm) between individuals. They will then give each other some shelter from the wind, and pollinate more easily than in a long row. Firm the ground well around the plants and repeat at intervals as they grow. Keep a flower pot or box ready to cover the plant if the weather turns cold even in late May.

The plant produces tassels of seeds at the top which should fall on the sheaths of coiled leaves below to pollinate. If necessary, encourage the process by inserting seeds in the sheath. The plants are greedy for water when the cobs are ripening and, unless you can satisfy this need, they are not worth growing.

CUCURBITS

These include marrows, courgettes, cucumbers of all types, melons and pumpkins, as well as such fancy varieties as vegetable spaghetti and edible gourds. All of them react badly to the cold when they are young and shrivel at the first touch of frost. They are usually started in sheltered pots or boxes and not planted out until the danger of frost appears to be over.

Marrows can manage reasonably well on any but the poorest soils. Eaten small, in the form of courgettes – or as young marrows about 12in (30cm) long – they are more palatable. The great monsters reared for display at harvest festivals and shows are for impressing people, not eating – you would need an axe just to get through the skin.

Plant seeds about mid-May, under jam jars or cloches, once the frosts are past. Otherwise raise under cover and plant out your seedlings in late May. In either case, set them in a circular depression, about 9in (23cm) in diameter, which will make watering easier. Plant bush marrows about 18in (45cm) apart – the ordinary trailing kinds need even more space. In fact, it is as well to keep marrows right out of the vegetable plot, since they will rampage across it, twining around any plant they meet. They do well in a separate bed of reasonable soil, and will trail up over a coal bunker or old tree stump, and will even climb a tree, given the chance.

Marrows need little aftercare, except weeding until they are big enough to smother opposition, and plenty of watering. Always remember to water around the stem, not over the leaves and fruit, as this could cause blemishes. Just occasionally, they may need help with the first pollination (see Melons, page 102) but in the ordinary way they manage perfectly well. The only problem is to stop them proliferating. If you have more than you could possibly want, pinch out the growing tip to stop them.

When the first frost is forecast, gather all the remaining marrows, big or small. Frost will blacken the plant and turn any fruit left on it mushy.

Pumpkins are just as easy to grow, but they become so big that they need even more space between plants. You can use them when they reach the size of footballs, but they are just as good as mature 40-pounders. They need a lot of water to flesh up and prefer fairly rich soil. The fruits have rather soft skins when young; to prevent scratches it is best to cushion them on straw or a smooth tile while they are growing.

Cucumbers are rather more work. First, you must select an outdoor variety, particularly if you intend to grow tomatoes in your greenhouse, as the two don't mix. The outdoor cucumber looks coarser, but tastes just as good.

Secondly, if you start them in pots, as is usual, it is important not to let them get pot-bound – with the roots starting to twist around the soil ball. Cucumbers grow fast under cover and, once the roots show through the base holes of the pot, they must go out or into a larger pot right away.

> Once cucumbers get going, they do very well in a good summer, and fruits will keep appearing all over, however fast you eat them

They do benefit from rich soil. If you can, obtain some horse manure. Dump it on a vacant bit of garden, or on top of the compost heap for a few days to let the ammonia go off, then dig a hole 12in (30cm) deep and wide at the planting station. Put in a good ration of manure, add a bit of compost or rotted leaves, then top off with 2–3in (5–7.5cm) of earth.

Obviously, pick the sunniest place available, and use the spare earth to form a rampart around the pit, into which you plant your seedlings. Each plant should be 18in (45cm) apart. If the weather turns chilly, shield it with a jam jar or a pane of glass balanced across the earth rampart.

Cucumbers normally have male and female flowers, but if the males fertilise the females the fruit is bitter and twisted. Therefore, whenever you see a male flower, pinch it off before it makes trouble – they are the ones without the little fruitlet starting behind the flower. F1 varieties of seed have been bred to produce only female flowers. This is stated on the packet.

Growing cucumbers need a lot of water; run it into the pit but don't allow it to stand in a pool around the stem. They like a dampish atmosphere, so in dry weather give them a fine spray of tepid water at night. The leaves will scorch if they get large drops of water on them in hot sun.

Once cucumbers get going, they do very well in a good summer, and fruits will keep appearing all over, however fast you eat them. Support them on straw or old tiles to keep the slugs at bay. Frost will cut the plant down, so when the first one is forecast, go out and gather all the remaining fruit, otherwise they will go soggy and useless. A good cloche and a lot of straw packing may, however, save them for a week or so.

Japanese cucumbers look like indoor cucumbers but are darker and smoother-skinned than ridge types. They will grow out of doors in the most favourable circumstances only. Don't let them trail on the ground, but train them up fences. Alternatively, bend a length of stiff plastic trellis into a tunnel shape and train the plant over the top. The cucumbers will hang down inside and can be easily given extra protection if needed (see page 102).

Indoor cucumbers are longer, darker and smoother than the ridge varieties. They must grow under glass. Minimum shelter is a cold frame, in which they can be started, or planted out as seedlings, on a well-manured and composted bed. They will need covering at night, and at the beginning and end of their careers, but during the day and for the best part of the summer, the top can be removed or opened. One plant will fill a small frame easily. Spray the frame with tepid water from time to time and keep the soil as damp as possible but not soggy.

Japanese cucumber supported on a plastic trellis

If you are growing tomatoes in a greenhouse and want to grow cucumbers there as well, things get difficult. Tomatoes like it warm and dry, cucumbers hot and wet. If you wall off a section of the house with plastic — perhaps an old shower curtain – you can keep just that area steamy. One cucumber, planted in a well-manured bed, or two in pots, will fill the whole space, trained up wires to the ceiling. More plants than that will produce too much fruit for any family, however keen.

Those in pots will need feeding with fertiliser, and all of them will require mist spraying over the leaves on hot days and the removal of male flowers. Stop the tip of the plant when it hits the roof, and pinch out inconvenient shoots. Some heat will be needed if the growing season is to be extended past the end of October.

You can grow cucumbers on hotbeds (page 93). They will grow fast and the soil will stay warm until the air temperature catches up. Proceed as for cold-frame cultivation.

Melons

The Canteloupe melon grows well in a cold frame or greenhouse and fairly well out of doors in the south or in a good summer. The other main types of melon are likely to grow only in a heated greenhouse, although look out for new varieties which are being trialled to grow in the British climate.

Don't give melons fresh manure, or they will run to lots of leaf and no fruit. They like a bit of compost, and good soil on top sieved to remove stones and weeds. Start the seeds off in pots while you prepare and warm up the bed – with black polythene if the sun does not cooperate. Two melons can go in a 6 x 4ft (1.8 x 1.2m) frame. In the greenhouse, if you have a bed at ground level, you can set one plant every 18in (45cm) square and give them a framework of canes and wires to climb.

Left to themselves, melons may not bother to reproduce; you encourage productive sideshoots by pinching out the plant's growing tip as soon as three hairy leaves appear on side shoots. It will respond by doubling up on the side shoots. When each new side shoot has three leaves, pinch out again (see below). The plant will begin to feel threatened and therefore grow female flowers, with little lumps like baby melons behind them.

As soon as there are enough – say, four per plant for large melons, six or eight for little ones – you will have to help again. The male flowers have pollen on their stamens, so either tap them towards the females, or pick off the male and dust the female flower with it. You will soon know if a 'set' has occurred, because the baby melons start to swell.

> Low-hanging melons can be supported on up-turned flower pots which is the usual method for those grown in frames

Once the plant is pregnant, feed it with plenty of water and general fertiliser or liquid manure. This should be poured on to the earth near the main stem, not touching it, and not on the leaves, which will blister if left wet under sunshine.

As the melons get bigger, they will need support. Tie the stems to the canes and wires regularly, and fix small nets under each fruit attached to the framework. Low-down melons can be supported on up-turned flower pots, which is the usual method for those grown in frames. In the greenhouse an alternative is to sling a whole fruit-net to the roof and loop it up at intervals around the growing melons, like a hammock. Make sure that no net is fastened tight, or the melons will warp to odd shapes. Slugs are very fond of melons, so to prevent grievous losses keep the plants surrounded with slug traps.

first stop

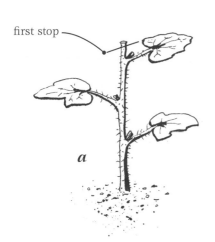

a

second stops

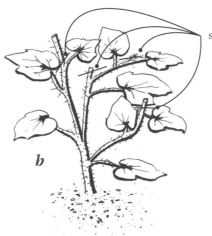

b

Melon stopping: two stages

The melons are ready when they begin to smell sweet. The stem end forms a slight callus around the neck and the other end feels slightly soft when you test it with your thumb. Don't leave them unpicked – they rob the plant and suddenly get overripe and rotten.

Before all the melons are ripe, the air temperature will drop, at least at night, below what they can stand. Close the greenhouse each day while the air is still warm, and keep it closed on chilly wet days. The frame light, which has been open daily through the summer and even at night for some of the time, must now be closed early. If necessary, in the event of a chill autumn, cover the frame with black polythene at night – it will pick up some warmth from the morning sun. Reduce watering as the weather gets cooler, but never let the earth dry out completely.

Tomatoes

Tomato seeds can be started in heat as early as January, but the plants are best grown on in a greenhouse. Plants intended for outdoor planting can be started in a cool greenhouse or in the home in late February to March and, after hardening off progressively, planted out in late May or even June, when the frosts are past.

Outdoor growing

The growing season out of doors is very limited – three or four months in which to grow into a mature plant, produce fruit and ripen it – so the tomato needs all the help it can get. First, it must be placed in a really sunny and sheltered place. Second, it must have good soil, but not fresh nitrogen, which makes it put on leaves instead of fruit. Third, it needs support, since the fruit gets very heavy. Fourth, it needs adequate water.

The best site is one backed by a south-facing wall or fence. Failing this, runner beans, Jerusalem artichokes or, to an extent, gooseberry bushes serve very well as a windbreak or shelter.

> Runner beans, Jerusalem artichokes or, to an extent, gooseberry bushes serve very well as a windbreak for tomatoes

Make a hole 12in (30cm) deep and about the same across and put in a good layer of compost and some wood-ash, if you have been shifting tree stumps, or useless prunings, as tomatoes need potash. Part fill the hole with good earth and set the root ball of your plant well down into it, so that about 3in (7.5cm) of the lower stem is also buried. Strip off any leaves which grow this low. Mound the earth immediately around the stem and make a circular trough 2–3in (5–7.5cm) deep about 5–6in (12.5–15cm) away from the stem. This is for easy watering later in the season without upsetting the plant.

Set the stakes or canes firmly in before planting, 18in (45cm) apart in a straight line, or at slightly closer intervals in staggered rows where space is limited. Set every other plant 3in (7.5cm) forward of the planting line, but keep the individual distance between plants at 18in (45cm) or they will shade and rob each other.

As the tomato grows, it will need to be tied to the stake at intervals. Don't tie it tightly, since this will break the stem right away or bite into it as it thickens. A 2in (5cm) ring of space is best, with the string crossed between stem and stake to ensure security but freedom of movement. Elastic plant ties are available commercially, which can be copied by cutting strips from old bicycle tubes. Bits of rag, plastic, soft fillis or twine can be used. Avoid thin, hard string, which chews through the stem when the fruits add pressure. Secure the stem 'under the arms' at leaf junctions, where it is less likely to slip.

Left to itself, the tomato will try to branch out, by producing a side shoot in the junction between leaf and stem. Pinch these out ruthlessly as soon as they appear. Frustrated, the plant will then turn to producing fruit trusses – little sprays of flowers which fall off and leave tiny fruit in their place. The number of these will vary according to the state of the weather. However far the plant has reached by the middle of July, pinch out the growing tip of the main stem. There are only six or seven weeks of good weather to go and the plant will need all its energy to mature the fruits already started.

If a plant gets very heavy, help it with another short stake on the other side, and prop up any low-growing trusses of tomatoes on a bit of tile, straw or any old packaging material, to keep them off the ground and away from the slugs.

Apart from slugs, which should be regarded as enemy Number One and destroyed on sight, tomatoes are liable to blight. This strikes late in the season, when they are full of fruit and promise. If the weather is warm and muggy in mid-July to August, you may expect trouble.

You should be able to gather tomatoes from July, depending on the weather. If the trusses are very heavy, pick any fruit which is starting to blush – it will redden off the plant. Some people become addicted to fresh green tomatoes and have to be fought off in the interests of getting some red ones. It is worth braving a storm to drape plastic over the plants, as the fruit skins can be split by hail or heavy rain.

Tomato plants are on sale in May or June ready for planting. If they look healthy, treat them as you would your own stock and water them well in.

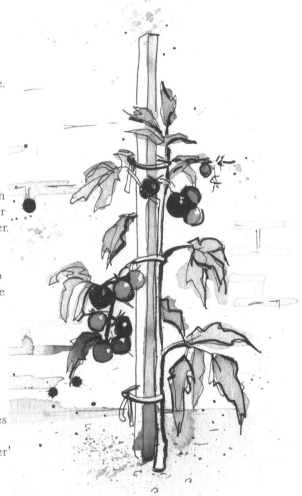

It is worth braving a storm to drape plastic over the plants, as the fruit skins can be split by hail or heavy rain

Growing in containers
If you have no suitable ground, but a nice sheltered corner of the yard, tomatoes can be grown in pots. The larger the pot, the less trouble you will have with watering at the height of the season, but the more spare potting earth you will need to begin with. A 12in (30cm) diameter pot is about the minimum practical size for full growth.

Put broken pots or stones at the bottom of the container, then a layer of coarse compost, leaves or peat, which will retain moisture. Fill up with good soil, preferably sterilised, or a mixture of half compost and half soil. Set a bamboo cane firmly at one edge of the pot and then put in the young plant.

In any sort of container, it will need feeding with liquid manure, or any fertiliser recommended as soon as it produces a truss – at first once a week and, when it is heavy with fruit, twice a week. Never let the soil dry out, and pick off any broken or sick-looking leaves as soon as seen. Note the colour of those leaves and check what deficiency needs correcting.

In a smallish pot, moisture will evaporate very fast. You may need to water the plant three times a day in high summer. If this is difficult, try standing the pot in a bowl of water during the day, but take it out if the soil gets soggy or dank. You might move the plants – being careful not to shake the trusses – to a spot less in the full sun for a while. As long as the air is warm, they will continue to grow.

Growbags – plastic sacks of prepared compost and sometimes with added nutrients – are popular. The bag lies on its side and the plants are grown through holes in the plastic. Two or, at a pinch, three plants can be grown per bag; they are treated in every way like pot-grown plants. They must be kept watered, and dosed with the liquid fertiliser (sometimes supplied as part of the kit – but check what it is first). This saves all the trouble of making up your own soil mixtures, but they are going to cost much more than doing it yourself and, so therefore, are the resulting tomotoes.

After one using, the compost must be discarded; the mixture is good for the soil and can be put on the garden.

No tomato plant with a restricted root run, in a pot or any other container, will cope with more than four trusses of fruit out of doors. In pots smaller than 12in (30cm) across, two or three trusses will be enough. When this number has set, pinch out the growing point.

Towards the end of summer, they will need some protection, from a plastic cover at night or newspaper loosely tied around. As soon as frost threatens, either move the plants inside to finish, or pick all the tomatoes, red or green, before they are damaged.

> No tomato plant with a restricted root run will cope with more than four trusses of fruit out of doors

Under cover
Tomatoes grown in a cold frame can be protected more easily, provided they are not too tall for the lights to close. A plant can be finished under cover if the cane is removed and it is tipped on its side. It may be as well to grow a bush tomato – designed to grow low from the outset. Fruit trusses will need padding with straw or packaging to keep them off the ground.

A tomato plant can be made to bush by taking out the growing point when three leaves are on the stem and letting lateral shoots develop. This is chancy, but worth trying if you particularly like the flavour of one of the climbing varieties. Don't stop a shoot when the weather is muggy – it encourages blight to take hold.

Tomatoes grown in a greenhouse, even without extra heat, have a longer growing period – by two or three months. We have picked fresh tomatoes at Christmas grown this way. The lean-to mini greenhouses will do quite well for this purpose.

Greenhouse plants can be grown in pots on staging, in which case they must be watered and fed regularly, but can normally cope with six trusses of fruit before stopping. Wires from the roof will be needed to support them.

The ring culture method is popular with enthusiasts. It encourages the development of two root systems; short roots within the ring, which take up the food for the plant, and a second, longer root system which reaches out to a gravel base to take up water. The plants are placed in bottomless straight-sided pots, about 10in (25cm) in diameter, filled with potting compost. Sit the pots on a tray full of clinker and gravel. All the fertiliser goes into the rings and the plain water in the gravel. If you are keen on the idea, research it, since the prescribed quantities of this and that are complicated and the whole operation can be time-consuming. It keeps some gardeners happy for hours.

In a Dutch light greenhouse with glass to the ground, it is much simpler to grow the plants directly into a bed of soil. You can make this up on a solid floor by marking off a box with building blocks or bricks. Put in a drainage layer – of crocks, large stones, etc – then coarse compost or leaves, and finally sieved soil mixed with a peat substitute and a bit of sand. Sterilise if you can, but weeding is easier on this scale.

Plant the tomato seedlings diagonally 15in (38cm) apart. Fix canes, or run wires from the roof to short stakes in the ground. Cross wires at various heights fixed to the side of the greenhouse are useful too.

Treat the plants much the same as outdoor ones, removing side shoots as they appear and tying the stems loosely to the canes or wires as they grow. Don't stop the plants until they have filled all the space available – right up to the roof ridge, provided all the weight can be supported safely at maximum growth.

Under cover, tomato plants are less easily pollinated and may have trouble setting trusses of fruit. One way of helping them is to go in early in the morning, after a night-time closing of the greenhouse, and tap the canes or wires smartly, which should release a cloud of pollen and do the trick. Another method is mist-spraying the plants – ideally, squirt a fine jet of water from a hose at the roof, and let the mist fall on the tomatoes. Once the first trusses have set, they usually get the idea.

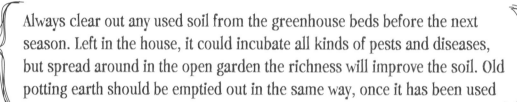

Always clear out any used soil from the greenhouse beds before the next season. Left in the house, it could incubate all kinds of pests and diseases, but spread around in the open garden the richness will improve the soil. Old potting earth should be emptied out in the same way, once it has been used

Tomatoes grown under cover need a lot of water, though the soil mustn't stay soggy around them. Always water around the roots. If the leaves ever droop, they may need the mist-spray treatment – done late in the day so no drops of water will catch the sun and burn the leaves. The fruit does not relish being splashed with water, so it is risky to set top trusses by mist-spraying.

Tomatoes like the air warm and dryish, but wilt if the heat is too fierce, so greenhouse roofs are traditionally washed over with thin emulsion paint, whitewash, muddy water or 'special greenhouse shading compound' (whitewash) once the tomatoes have got going. Greenhouse blinds on rollers can be pulled up and down much more easily than the whitewash can be scraped off, but they are expensive. A fine net curtain can be lashed across the roof or a semi-opaque plastic lining fitted. The greenhouse could, of course, be sited in the first place beside a tree with summer foliage, which filters the amount of light when needed and obligingly drops its leaves as the heat of the sun lessens (see Protection, 'The best spot for your greenhouse', page 32).

As the cold weather advances, all the shading must be removed and replaced with clear polythene as a barrier against heat loss. Soft polythene film is cheaper, but a semi-rigid sheet is a lot easier to fix, especially to a metal-framed greenhouse.

Always clear out any used soil from the greenhouse beds before the next season. Left in the house, it would incubate all kinds of pests and diseases, but spread around in the open garden the richness will improve the soil. Old potting earth should be emptied out in the same way, once it has been used.

ENDIVE

Endive is another blanching plant, but easier in cultivation. It is sown directly into the ground in late June, and should germinate extraordinarily fast. It likes reasonable soil, but not fresh manure or any pampering. It should not be sown in a trench, or it rots. A light cloche helps the seed to start well and can then be removed. When the seedlings are big enough to handle, set them out in a staggered double row, with about 10in (25cm) between plants.

Keep weeds and slugs away and never let the plant dry out, though don't stand it in a puddle. From September, reduce watering, and in October cover plants with cloches to keep off the rain, as they must be dry before blanching. Set slug traps, or all the plants will be eaten. Tie the top leaves around with fillis.

Blanch just as many as you want at one time, by covering the required plants with peat and an up-ended large flower-pot or plastic bucket. At first the blanching will take about a week, but as the weather gets colder it will take two or three. Keep checking, because there is only a short period when they are blanched and perfect, then they rot.

> Endive is sown directly in the ground in late June, and should germinate extraordinarily fast

The plants will stay out of doors in a certain amount of frost but die in hard winter, so either use all the crop by Christmas or lift part of it in autumn and replant in a cold frame. You can blanch several heads at once in a frame by putting matting on top to exclude light from a selected number, or make a thick paper cone and up-end it over one. The plants must not get wet or dirty at any stage, so be careful when cutting off the blanched heads in bad weather.

> Chinese cabbage is another strictly summer crop. It is far more like a lettuce than a cabbage

CHINESE CABBAGE

Chinese cabbage is another strictly summer crop. It is far more like a lettuce than a cabbage. It needs warmth but can't take direct sun, so find a sheltered but not too shady corner. Sow directly into the ground in June or July – possibly August in the far south. Thin to 6in (15cm) apart as soon as possible. Keep well watered – over the soil, not the leaves. Take half-grown specimens for kitchen use.

In the north, pick it all before the frosts come or cloche it over in October. In the south it will grow on to full maturity in November, or even December if left in the garden; but it must be watched closely, for there are only a few days between maturity and bolting.

It will not keep fresh for more than a matter of days after cutting – like a lettuce – so keep on thinning all the time. The last plants, standing in isolation, may need fillis tied around the leaves to stop them dragging in the mud.

CHINESE MUSTARD

A similar summer plant, to be grown in partial shade between about May and early August, Chinese mustard likes good soil, and is a safer substitute for spinach. Sow in situ and thin as soon as possible to 6in (15cm) apart. Water well and use as soon as it reaches half-maturity. It is fully mature in about six weeks from sowing and after that it bolts – runs a stem up to flower – which makes it grow tough and rather unpleasant to eat. It will not stand frost at all.

DANDELIONS

The humble dandelion, which grows as a weed, can be turned into an appetising salad vegetable. Pick the young leaves green, and up-end a flower pot over the stump to blanch the second growth; this tastes nutty and tangy.

BRASSICAS

The major class of vegetables involved in summer planting are the brassicas – including cabbages, cauliflowers, brussels sprouts, broccoli, turnips and swedes. They will stand worse weather than most other vegetables and will come through the winter relatively unscathed. For this reason, most people do the sensible thing and grow them for winter use, when others are scarce.

They could, by carefully planned sowing, be available all the year round in one form or another but, unless you have a lot of space, you will probably not aim for this. The big snag about brassicas in general is their long maturing period and the amount of room they take up. They need 2ft (60cm) or more between them, and their large leafy heads cast shadows over other plants during the major part of the good growing period.

Some varieties, especially summer cabbage and cauliflower, can be sown in spring like the root vegetables. We always grow a few swedes and cauliflower in spring because we like to have some ready in the summer. Pick your varieties with care – some need to be started in January to give them a long enough growing period. Most of the brassicas needed for summer use should be planted under shelter in January or February, or in the open in March. Brussels sprouts required for the autumn should go in during early April and the winter plants in May. Stagger the sowings by a month or so if you want to gather regularly from growing plants, or sow in larger groups if you intend to pick them all at once and store for later use.

Early summer sowing
Because of their long growing season, the seeds have to be started off in early summer, when space is short. Brassicas are therefore grown in seed beds, and kept there for as long as possible while young, to leave the main plot free for summer-ripening vegetables.

> The major class of vegetables involved in summer planting are the brassicas – including cabbages, cauliflowers, brussels sprouts, broccoli, turnips and swedes

Much the same method is used for making a seed bed as for preparing the rest of the plot for sowing. Dig out all the weeds; you may also need to rake in lime thoroughly to discourage club-root (the major disease of cabbage-family plants) – but test the soil first to see if its pH is too low (lower than six). Then firm the soil by treading, and loosen the surface again. Because the plants are going to remain in place, close packed, for a long time, it is really important to shift every scrap of weed root and seed you possibly can, by vigorous raking initially.

You don't want to encourage fast leggy growth, or to have to water every day in a hot summer, so try to place the seed bed out of the sun – anywhere unsuitable for your summer growers. To economise on space, plant the seeds in a block rather than in rows – although the more they can be set out at 2in (5cm) apart in any direction the better they will grow. This is a job which a patient child can do – it takes ages and needs small fingers. If you haven't the patience, sprinkle the seeds over the block and hope that not too many come down in clumps or gaps. Cover ½in (12.5mm) deep and firm the soil well.

Don't let the ground dry out, particularly at germination and small-seedling stage. As the plants grow taller, a mulch of lawn mowings or compost tucked around them after the ground has been well watered will keep in the moisture.

Let them grow undisturbed – unless they clump – for as long as possible. When they start to jostle each other, they will have to be thinned out. Those which ripen in late summer to autumn can move into the main plot as soon as the early peas are done, but the rest, including all the winter stocks, must move to a waiting bed at greater distances apart – 9in (23cm) if you can manage it. At any stage, brassica plants should be set very firmly in the ground, because they have a lot of top weight and catch the wind easily.

Planting out in autumn

As the summer crops are cleared, rake lightly over the top of the earth to remove dead leaves and decaying mulch which isn't quite ready to sink into the ground; but don't dig, since most brassicas like a firm soil. If their roots are not held tight, they flop about and produce blowsy plants.

Plant with a dibber or thick stick and make a hole deep enough to take the roots without doubling, plus half or more of the stem, plus 2in (5cm). In that 2in (5cm) space, put a chunk of rhubarb leaf and leaf stem, as a precaution against club-root – rhubarb leaves are full of oxalic acid, which poisons the club-root virus. Spinach past its prime is also full of oxalic acid although we have no evidence as to its effectiveness if similarly used. In the absence of any of these, dust the soil around the roots of the plant with lime.

Lift the young plant with as much earth attached as possible – wet the soil well first – and sink it into the hole. Keep individual plantings about 2ft (60cm) apart. The tall plants – sprouting broccoli, heading broccoli (winter cauliflower) and brussels sprouts – may need provision for staking in windy gardens since they carry a lot of top weight. Broad bean wires can be left in place for one of these crops.

Brussels sprouts

These can be planted out in mid-summer to crop from about October; in September to crop by Christmas; or in October to crop at intervals during January to March.

Broccoli

Sprouting broccoli produces a stalk with a loose tassel of cauliflower-like florets. Planted in October, it crops in late January to March, with a few late starters running on into April. The purple variety looks very decorative as it grows, but disappointingly it cooks dark green. Heading broccoli (winter cauliflower) produces small cauliflower heads in February to April. Both these can be frozen if they come in a rush, to extend the season to cover the 'hungry gap'.

Cabbages

The various cabbages are slightly shorter, but need watching in case the plants tip sideways. The firm-ball sorts – red and white – are mostly planted out in late August to September and produce in early winter, although some will stagger production until spring. After that come the savoys, which are very hardy, stand the winter and crop in March and April. The leaves are floppy and crinkled and tend to cook soft.

Kale

Kale – the cabbage's poor relation – grows in any sort of hard winter, not even needing good soil, and is highly resistant to club-root. It crops from January and goes on until April or May, since leaves are pulled off a few at a time, not the whole plant. Though not to everyone's taste, it is a splendid standby when no other fresh food is available.

Radishes

Radishes, the baby of the brassica family, used as a catch crop are ready for eating within a fortnight of planting, but the Japanese, Spanish or China Rose types, planted in summer, can be grown for winter use. They need plenty of water all the time, since they grow large and would otherwise taste woody. They will reach maturity in the autumn. One goes a long way, so either restrict planting or pickle some of the crop. They will keep for a time in damp sand, like any other root crop, then wither away to nothing.

Summer watering

In a hot summer – or a drought – even the strongest plant will die or fail to produce a crop. With the growing likelihood of hotter, dryer summers due to climate change, coupled with huge pressure on our water supplies, this is likely to become an increasing problem for growers. The good news is that there's a lot we can do to save water and keep our plants alive.

First, you should hang on to every scrap of rainwater and use other sources of water (see 'Watering equipment' page 25). But also remember that the more humus there is in the soil, the better it will cope with the extremes of rainfall. Thin soil lets rain run straight through to the sub-soil. Heavy clay gums up and holds pools of water on the surface. Good, rich soil is evenly wetted and holds moisture for a long time a few inches down, where the plant roots can get at it. The more compost and similar humus-producing material we can get into the soil, the less of a problem it will be.

When a long drought comes, the soil dries from the top, so small seedlings and shallow-rooting plants die first. Any plant with a lot of leaves will give off moisture to the air fast and, if it can't replace this, it will be in trouble. This loss of water can normally be replaced by long sessions with the hose, drenching the earth and spraying over the leaves. But, in time of prolonged drought, this is not allowed (and is also best to do all you can to avoid using a hose in order to save water).

It is easier to water effectively around the roots of a plant if it has been set in a shallow trench or pit; this is the best method for most of the summer-growing plants. Those which have a soft stem may

SETTING UP A SOLAR STILL

Except in desert areas, there is usually some water in the soil, even during a drought. The trouble is that it is rarely where you want it; established trees get plenty, but thirsty new seedlings find none. You can get over this to some extent by setting up simple solar stills on any unplanted piece of ground – even between rows – to catch every drop of the moisture that is constantly being sucked up by the sun.

A plastic cloche is set up to condense the moisture rising from the ground, with its edges arranged so that the water collected will not run back on to the soil but drips into lengths of plastic guttering. These are slightly sloped so that the water eventually runs into a storage tank set into the ground – this could be something as simple as a large plastic bottle with a funnel in the top (see illustration below). You can lift this out when full, or pump the water out of it in situ by fixing a piece of plastic tube through the bottom of the bottle before you sink it into the ground.

You can also use a simple still of this kind to get (fairly) clean water from brackish or even salt supplies. Simply place another piece of gutter down the middle of the polythene cloche and allow a slow stream of your contaminated water to flow down it. As the sun evaporates it, clean water will collect in the still reservoir.

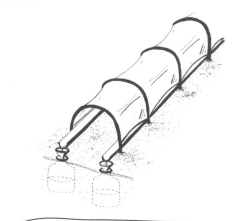

need a little rampart close to it, with a circular trench outside that, to ward off rot. If drought threatens while you are planting, start the plants off with a handful of wet compost in the planting hole. It will retain this moisture and future waterings just where the roots need them. Newspaper or tea-leaves in the bottom of the planting trench will serve the same purpose, rotting down slowly as the amount of moisture in the soil increases. Old sacks will do – or even old socks provided they are woollen, for nylon and other synthetics won't rot and may interfere with plant growth.

Water late in the day, after the sun has gone down, especially if you are spraying leaves. In the daytime, drops of water left on leaves act as burning glasses for the sun and the leaves would be scorched to death.

Your trenches could be lined with plastic to keep in all the water you supply. However, unless you buried the plastic very deeply – which would mean a lot of watering to get the area damp – the roots would soon hit the plastic and be unable to proceed to the deeper layers of soil where the nourishment lies. Also, if it rained, the plastic trench would flood and wash out or rot the plants.

You can line a wooden box with plastic, but be sure to make a lot of drainage holes in the base. An inch of compost in the bottom of the box does the same job less riskily.

Always water plentifully at one time. It is heavy work carting cans of water around, and the temptation is to spread it over as large an area as possible per can. Too little water only wets the surface of the soil above the plant roots though. Either it evaporates in the heat of the sun before they get to know about it, or they start struggling upwards towards it. The nearer the roots are to the surface, the more likely they are to be dried up by the sun or attacked by surface pests looking for something juicy to eat.

Once the soil is really wet, you can mulch by covering it with compost, grass mowings, newspaper – anything which will rot reasonably quickly. Don't let it wad together and block the air from the plants. Even a dust mulch is better than nothing. Hoe the top surface of the soil loose to keep the sun off the lower layers.

> It is easier to water effectively around the roots of a plant if it has been set in a shallow trench or pit; this is the best method for most of the summer-growing plants

Shade plants, particularly young seedlings, from the fiercest sun, with pots of shrubs, wooden screens, paper, doubled-up netting – even strategically placed washing, which can drip over the garden too.

And, if you have faith, pray for rain.

HOLIDAY PLANS

A really dedicated, not to say manic, gardener would take a holiday only in dead of winter, but not many people are going to be that self-sacrificing. But going away at more or less any time in the summer poses problems, mostly concerned with watering and gathering of ripe crops

In the normal British summer, outdoor crops will probably get enough rainfall to manage on. But a sudden drought may well occur, and even the semi-dedicated gardener will want to do what they can to preserve the crops they've worked for.

Just before you leave, soak the planted area very thoroughly – 2 gallons (9 litres) of water for each sq yd (1 sq m) is about right. To prevent the moisture being evaporated by the sun, cover the wet earth with a mulch of any absorbent material – lawn mowings, tea leaves – or top it with stones or straw.

Tall plants, like runner beans and tomatoes, lose a lot of moisture through their leaves, so apart from watering and mulching see that they are shaded by a nylon net with bits of foliage stuck in it, a white net curtain, an old sheet hung on wires a couple of feet away – anything which will impede the sun's direct rays. Less light will slow down the growth a little, but this is no bad thing while you are away.

Stake everything firmly and check that tomatoes are tied as high as they can be. Stop rampant growers like marrow and grapes so that their long tendrils do not roam all over the garden. Net fruit against birds, and set slug traps.

Plants in pots can be thoroughly watered and then sunk to their rims in the ground. Cover with lawn mowings or ashes to keep in the moisture. Raise them very carefully when you return, as they may have rooted into the earth.

Pots and boxes from the greenhouse can be stood outside in a sheltered place or in a frame. Plants in pots which must stay in the greenhouse can be placed inside a second pot or bucket of compost or sand, which will hold in the moisture. To sink them in a bucket of water would be too much, causing their soil to go soggy or float away, and the roots to rot.

> Plants in pots can be thoroughly watered and then sunk to their rims in the ground. Cover with lawn mowings or ashes to keep in the moisture

You can place several plant pots around a large bucket or tank of water. Trail a strip of rag or, better, candle-wick, from the water to each pot and tuck its end well down in the soil. The wick should transfer water to the plants as they need it by capillary action. An equally effective method is to sit pots on a tray of gravel filled with water to half its depth. If you can trail a bit of wick from the base holes of the pot to the water reservoir, so much the better.

Plants in beds in the greenhouse can be watered and mulched, but they are subject to much higher temperatures than outdoor plants and thus lose their moisture much faster. Shade the greenhouse roof with whitewash or blinds and arrange a capillary watering system if possible.

Leave all doors and ventilators open – also frame lights.

A fairly simple automatic spray-watering system can be set up for the greenhouse. Outside, you need a reservoir of water large enough to last for the holiday. Inside, you need a waterproof pump, controlled by a time switch set to go off twice a day, in the morning and afternoon. Attach a hose to an oscillating lawn sprinkler – the type which waters in an arc rather than a horizontal circle.

It is as well to try out any of these devices in advance to make sure they work. Ensure that the automatic sprinkler system is thoroughly safe in operation, with all the electrical connections and the pump shielded from water penetration by secure plastic barriers. Even so, it is wise to put a fail-safe cut-out between the time switch and the electricity source in the house.

However, it would be much better – in terms of reduced power bills and water wastage – to make use of a reliable and cooperative neighbour instead. Although some of these measures will ensure you are leaving as little to be done as possible, so that goodwill doesn't wear thin. You can offer an incentive by encouraging the waterer to help themself to ripe crops. This will be an act of mercy in the case of beans and peas, which must be regularly picked or they stop producing new pods. If the neighbour isn't much of a gardener, take them on a tour first and indicate which plants are which – especially if there are any particular instructions concerning them.

If your neighbours are incapable or unwilling, and you can't make a reciprocal arrangement with a gardening friend, you may have to consider paid help. Payment in kind is best if it can be arranged – someone expecting to benefit from the produce is likely to be more careful with it.

If at all possible, install a tap on the outer wall of your house to make life simpler and easier for you and the waterer (especially if you would rather they don't have keys to your home).

If you know well in advance when you will be away, plan your crop sowing accordingly. Leave out the successional sowing which would ripen then. Plant – in trenches or circular dips lined with compost – a main crop earlier or later, so that it is not too small or too far advanced to manage by itself for a week or three. Early to middle July isn't a bad time, if you have the choice. The further you get into August, the more things are bursting out all over and will need dealing with daily.

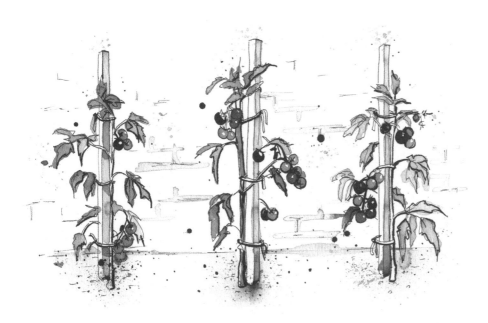

12. Autumn

Apart from setting out the brassicas in the main plot (page 112), your major job of autumn planting will be to install any trees or fruit bushes you have ordered. Prepare the soil well by removing perennial weeds, add as much muck and compost as you can spare, and set the plant in firmly. The soil in autumn is still warm and the roots have a chance to take hold before winter stops growth. Stake any such trees or bushes firmly, and check occasionally that winds haven't rocked the stake and plant loose, leaving a hole down which icy water can go.

BROAD BEANS

These can be sown in sheltered gardens in November; they stand the winter as young plants which get going again in early spring. Don't plant them in the same place twice, since their valuable work of producing nitrogen should be spread around the plot. Don't set winter beans in a trench, since they might get water-logged, but earth them up almost to the tips to protect them from frost. If they survive, they will be so tough that the blackfly are scared off. In colder areas, plant in October and cover with a cloche, but don't forget to water from time to time.

PEAS

In sheltered gardens a November sowing of peas will get off to a flying start in spring, but icy winds are their enemies. Sow an early variety like 'Feltham First'.

LETTUCES

Lettuces sown in September stand a good chance of maturing in mildish winters. Sown in October or November, lettuce will produce crops all through the winter in a cold greenhouse or frame, and possibly under a cloche. The variety 'All the Year Round' lives up to its name, with very slight protection.

TREE ONION

This useful perennial isn't readily available, but snap it up if you see it (you can find suppliers online). Plant it in the autumn if you have any choice, although it will have to be put in at whatever time of year it arrives, otherwise it will dry away to dust. You may get it as a handful of cocktail-size onions – which are planted

12in (30cm) apart, or by themselves. Or you may buy an older bulb, probably sold singly; this should go in at 2½–3in (6–7.5cm) deep.

In the first year, it will just grow bigger, looking like an ordinary onion, but mark it so that someone does not dig it up and eat it. Leave it in and the following year it will throw up a stem, on which little bunches of tiny onions hang at intervals. The stem grows quite tall, and will need propping up, or the weight of the onions will snap it. Pick these tiny onions in autumn for use.

At the same time, the base bulb produces offsets, which will send up their own stems the next year, and so on. Left in, the clump becomes very congested in the third and subsequent years, so either eat some of the offsets, or lift and divide the clump in autumn. The original bulb gives up after five years, but by that time you will have younger plants to succeed it.

WELSH ONION

Another rareish plant, the Welsh onion is occasionally found as seeds. Sow in spring in a box, plant out into a nursery bed during the summer and transfer to the final position, 9in (23cm) apart, either in autumn or the next spring. Set the young seedlings well into the ground, about 2–3in (5–7.5cm) deep, according to size. The most forward ones planted in autumn will produce a number of little offsets, like chives or spring onions, early in the year. Use some of these and save the others to start the process over again for next year. If possible, leave the continuation clump in the ground until autumn before dividing the plant up, but do this at any time if they get too congested.

> In the first year the tree onion will grow bigger, looking like an ordinary onion, but mark it so that someone does not dig it up and eat it

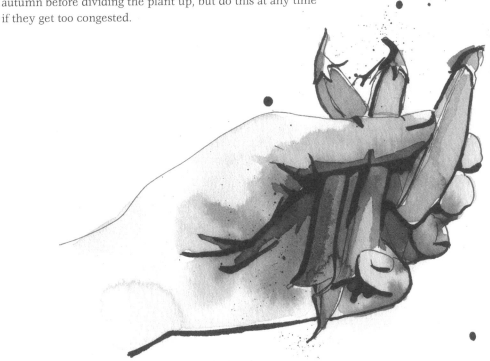

13. Long-term producers

If you are reasonably sure of staying in the same house for some years, it is worth considering growing certain vegetables which show no return in the first year but then bear increasingly for the next two, three or even twenty years.

These long-term producers will be living in the same soil for some years, therefore, the better quarters you give them, the better results you will get. All of them do best if you prepare the site by digging out a whacking great hole and filling it with horse or cow manure, compost, rotted leaves, etc, and topping off with soil carefully sifted to exclude large stones, weed bits and insect pests. You can't overdo the food for perennial plants; if you haven't the means to do the job properly, either wait until next year or settle for inferior results. It isn't nearly as easy to add the food afterwards.

GLOBE ARTICHOKES

Globe artichokes are planted on a rich bed one spring for first use the next summer. March is early enough, unless the winter is very mild. They can be grown from seeds, under protection, but are normally bought as offsets and set in the ground with just the tip showing. If the weather turns chilly, protect the tips with a bit of compost until the plants are established.

Globe artichokes are an acquired taste, so one plant may be enough for your family. Indeed, one plant may be enough for your garden, because it will eventually need 1 sq yd (1 sq m) of space. This will not be filled for the first two seasons, so initially you can plant other crops nearby.

The plant grows about 4ft (1.2m) high when mature. In an exceptional year, it may produce a head or two that same summer. Strictly, you shouldn't touch them for fear of weakening the plant but, if they look very vigorous, sample not more than one-third of the total output, and leave the rest. The bit which is eaten is the fleshy flower head when young – if left it goes as tough as boot leather. Don't let them run to seed, but cut them off ruthlessly. In the second summer a whole mass of little heads will be produced. If you take the main head first, this will encourage the side shoots to produce more.

The plants are pretty hardy, but it is as well to protect them for the winter by packing earth, compost or old leaves around the stems, and removing it again when the milder weather comes. Chop off the foliage in November for compost and don't let the plants get waterlogged in winter, or they will rot.

A plant will go on producing for about four years, with luck, so in the third year take an offset from the bottom and start it growing again, as you have done with the first one, so that when mother dies, junior is ready and to continue production.

When the old plant is on its last legs, you can take a different crop from it – chards. After gathering the heads, cut back the leaves to 6in (15cm) to produce new growths, or chards. When about 18in (45cm) high, wrap the whole thing up in paper, leaves, compost – anything to exclude all the light. In six weeks' time, the growths will have blanched and be ready for cooking. These chards aren't to everyone's taste, but it is interesting to try.

At all growing stages, globe artichokes need plenty of water if the crop is not to be tough. In winter they shun it.

RHUBARB

Although rhubarb is a sort of fruit, it is usually planted in the vegetable plot and has more of the characteristics of a vegetable. Technically it could be raised from seed, but by far the simplest way is to plant a hunk of rhubarb root with a growing point, called a crown. Rhubarb owners are usually only too pleased to give a bit away to try to keep a vigorous plant within bounds.

Dig an ample hole (on well-fed land) and spread out the roots, shaking soil well down around them. If you are planting more than one crown, keep them 2ft (60cm) or more apart – they will expand to fill any given quantity of space.

> Never eat any of the leaf – it is poisonous to man and beast. It is also poisonous to club-root in brassicas

Don't take any of the sticks produced in the first year; in the second year be moderate, and after that you will be overwhelmed. Pull the sticks off the base with a twisting motion and take a few from each plant at a time. When you have pulled a stick, cut off the leaf and throw it straight on the compost heap. Never eat any of the leaf – it is poisonous to man and beast. It is also poisonous to club-root in brassicas so throw some rhubarb leaves in their planting holes in autumn.

After ten years or so, the oldest part of the plant stops producing. Either hack it out or take away crowns from it and plant elsewhere. Antique rhubarb is virtually indestructible. We have burnt fanged monsters on a fierce November 5th bonfire and they have reappeared, fresh and invigorated, from the ashes the following spring.

Rhubarb ripens naturally in early summer but it can be advanced by about a month by forcing. This is quite simple. At Christmas-time cover one plant with an old dustbin or bucket with a holey bottom. In severe weather, fill the container with leaves and a bit of compost and cover the top as well – this is easy with a dustbin lid. As soon as you spot any action, take out some of the packing so that the sticks will be a good colour. The forced plant will be no good for further rhubarb production that year, but will recover the year after. Always cut off the central stem if it tries to flower, and feed the plants now and then with a dressing of compost to keep them healthy.

ASPARAGUS

Asparagus is the king of long-term plants. It gives no returns until it is three years old, and then produces magnificently for up to about twenty years. The bed does need careful preparation, because of the very long residence the plant will have there. Every scrap of perennial weed must go, since it is very difficult to get it out once the asparagus roots have filled the bed. Bury a good helping of manure, compost, etc, and cover with 12in (30cm) of good earth.

The site must be reasonably sheltered, with a dwarf hedge – of rosemary, possibly – to filter the wind. The crop is produced from April, and the tender shoots are turned soggy by frost, so plant where it will be in the sun at that time and have a supply of protective material ready.

Traditionally, asparagus beds are built up high. There is no need to do this unless the area is badly drained, which the plant cannot stand. The bed will get a little higher each year anyway from additions made to it. If possible, separate the bed from the ordinary vegetable plot with a strip of path, then the plants can have the nourishment from the soil under that as well. At full maturity, the root system can spread to 4ft (1.2m) apiece. The individual plants can be set 18in (45cm) apart, with 9in (23m) at least on the path side, so you can get 16 plants on a bed 5 x 6ft (1.5 x 1.8m).

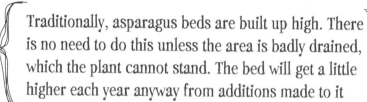

> Traditionally, asparagus beds are built up high. There is no need to do this unless the area is badly drained, which the plant cannot stand. The bed will get a little higher each year anyway from additions made to it

The plants can be raised from seed in a small bed and transferred into the asparagus bed two years later, or bought in as one- or two-year old crowns to save time. The one-year crowns settle in more easily, but the two-year ones flourish with just a little attention and produce the next year. 'Connover's Colossal' is an excellent variety commonly available. Prepare the bed before you buy and don't open the bag until you are ready to plant.

Cut a trench, about 9in (23cm) wide and 4–5in (10–12.5cm) deep, down the centre of the bed and along the two sides, and set the earth beside it. Then draw the point of a hoe down each side of each trench, to make a deep 'V'-shaped indentation, which leaves a ridge of earth in the centre of each trench.

Take out one plant at a time, closing the bag again – they are very sensitive to drying winds and if allowed to dry out at any stage they wither away to nothing. Sit the centre of the crown on the ridge and let the roots dangle down each side. Cover the crown with damp earth to about 3in (7.5cm) and firm down; this will leave a mound of earth and a slit depression beside it to channel the water down in summer.

Complete the planting and covering of one crown before lifting out the next. Plentiful watering down the channels should send the roots downwards instead of poking out sideways into the space between the trenches. Sprinkle seaweed meal, wood ash or other fertilisers over the bed at intervals during this first summer and cover each dressing with a little earth from the spare trench soil. Firm it well down each time.

If your plants are one year old, take another crop, like carrots or baby beet, between the rows. Let the asparagus produce its crop of fern in late summer, but resist any cutting of this by flower-arranging addicts. When it dies down in October–November, cut it off and compost it.

With two-year-old plants, which have longer roots, pull a shallow dip between the trenches with a hoe, to stop the roots going sideways; pile the earth in ridges on the plants and grow a shallow-rooted crop, like lettuce, between the rows, in the half shade of the fern. Give the same feeds early in the season. You may get a few genuine asparagus sticks, but try not to cut them, for fear of weakening the plant. If you can't resist, sample no more than two and let the rest run to fern. When the fern dies, cut and compost it.

Flatten the ridges out every November and cover the whole bed with a good layer of rich compost or strawy manure, and top that again with a 2in (5cm) layer of dead leaves as a frost precaution.

In spring of the third year, brush off all the loose leaves and any strawy bits which have not decomposed, but keep them handy. Ridge up the three rows again, making a really deep dent down the two middles and the sides. Sprinkle on a fertilizer (seaweed meal for example) and wait for action. Cover with leaves in frost.

Soon, the spears of asparagus will start poking up through the ground, a few at first, then lots. Cut them with a sharp kitchen knife at the height you like them. Brush the earth back from the side of the ridge and select your spear. Cut away from the plant to avoid damaging the next little spear. You can break off the spear by twisting and pulling at the same time, which makes sure the next spear is unhurt. In either case, replace the earth until next day, when more will be ready. The speed of growth is fantastic, so keep eating. Freeze some as you go, before it gets large and coarse, or give it to friends who only know the restaurant variety, where size is often preferred to flavour.

> The speed of growth is fantastic, so keep eating. Freeze some as you go or give it to friends who only know the restaurant variety

Don't take any more asparagus after early June the first year and mid-June later on. The production starts slacking off to warn you when to stop. Let the fern grow through the summer and cut it down when it dies in November, flattening the ridges and covering with 2in (5cm) of compost or manure plus leaves every year. In spring, clear the leaves, ridge up and stand by to gather asparagus. And so on for years and years, with increasing crops.

The only other attentions needed are removing annual weeds when seen; watering in spring with soot-water (old soot steeped in water for weeks), and scattering wood ash between the rows when any is available. The only pest seems to be asparagus beetle and you can control them by regularly inspecting plants and hand picking adults and larvae from the spears and fronds. Plus removing dead stems and clearing old plant debris around the base of plants prevents larvae pupating.

Female asparagus plants reproduce by throwing berries to the ground. If these take root between the rows, it is best to shift them to another bed or they will complicate the ridging up in spring. They are also good trading currency when one or two years old.

HOPS

At one time, hops were grown everywhere in England, except the north, and there is no reason why they should not be grown now by anyone with a lot of space or an overriding thirst. The main commercial growing is done in Kent.

The chief problem with hop growing is the sheer size of the mature plant, which is a vine (called a bine) about 15ft (4.5m) tall, needing light and air all the way up. The ideal support for the plant would be a windmill pylon, which it would clothe attractively. A post-and-wire framework, 15ft (4.5m) tall, would be very difficult to keep upright safely, so the best arrangement for a row of free-standing hop bines would be to erect a 6–8ft (1.8–2.4m) frame – as for runner beans – and train the remainder of the bines out over strong nets or wires to a second frame 6ft (1.8m) or so away. A redundant football goal would provide a basis for this set-up – it would make a cosy though strange-smelling arbour. Other possibilities include using an outdoor lamp-post and wires, a carport side and roof, or a trellis on a south-facing wall. The plant is quite elegant and unusual when growing, and would certainly make a talking point.

You can purchase a sett or rhizome online – this is the base of an old bine, which is grown on in a nursery bed for the first year. Then it is planted out in spring, not closer than 5–6ft (1.5–1.8m) to any other bine. The soil must be quite rich, with manure and compost in a good hole in deep-dug land. The crown is set just below ground level. Great care must be taken in preparing a soil bed near a wall, for this is liable to be a shallow planting area unless a deep hole is excavated and refilled with good stuff.

There is only a little growth in the first year, but in the second the full height is reached and a crop is produced. Once moving, the hop rampages away like a grape-vine and needs the same tying in to wires and stopping of unfruitful or over-vigorous shoots (see page 145). It may need spraying with Bordeaux mixture or soapy water (depending on your stance re: chemicals in the garden) against mildew or aphids in summer or autumn.

In late August or September, when the cones are dry and rustling and smell hoppy, the hops are ready to gather. Take them piecemeal or cut down a whole stem and lay it on the ground for ease of stripping. Don't drag up the root of the bine, which grows again next year.

DRYING HOPS

Hops must be dried artificially and as soon as possible after harvesting. This should really be done in a kiln, but it could be managed in an oven. Start at 37°C (99°F) slowly rising to 65°C (149°F) after four hours and then to 71°C (160°F), but no higher. Keep a draught going at intervals. (Take a look at some ready-dried hops, obtainable from wine-making suppliers, to help you check when the process is complete.) The hops will be brittle when they come out of the oven, and must be handled carefully. Leave them to cool down in an airy place, then pack in jars or tins for use (see beer recipe, page 211).

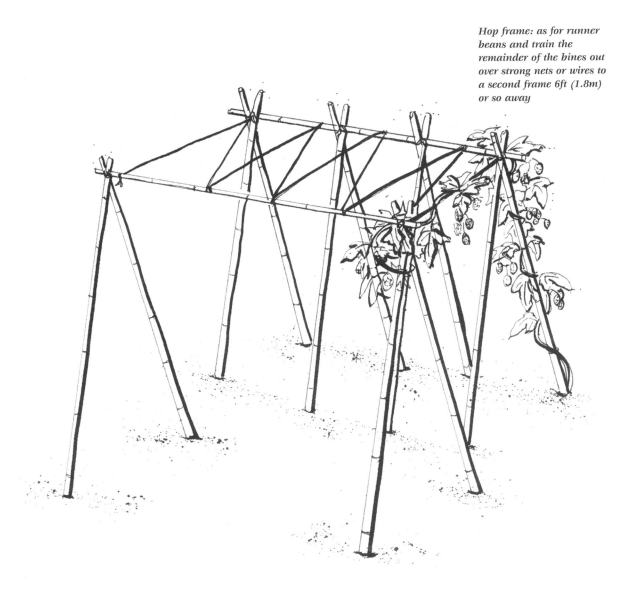

Hop frame: as for runner beans and train the remainder of the bines out over strong nets or wires to a second frame 6ft (1.8m) or so away

14. Undercover plants

A few plants really need a greenhouse or a warm frame before you can grow them at all. Even in an exceptionally good summer, when they can stand being outside for some time, they have to be started and finished under cover.

CAPSICUMS (RED AND GREEN PEPPERS)

These can be grown from seed. Start them early, in March at the latest, because they take ages to germinate. Place a plastic propagator or glass jar over your seed tray or pot. Transplant the seedling each time it outgrows its container until it is eventually in a 8–9in (20–23cm) diameter pot.

The plant must be kept damp but never soggy. Stand the pot in a saucer of water. The soil in the final pot must be rich – try a mixture of potting compost, garden compost or a little manure left to air for a day or two. Wait until late June before putting them outside and choose a very warm, sheltered corner. Bring them in again before the nights turn at all chill.

When the young peppers develop they may need a little support from small canes to stop one fruit squashing another. Pick when green or wait until they turn red. When frost threatens, shelter them with an individual cover inside the greenhouse or pick all the fruit, otherwise they will turn mouldy.

Their only pest seems to be green aphids, which retreat before a soapy water spray, although red spider mites and whitefly might also be a problem in a greenhouse.

CHILLI PEPPERS

These are grown in a similar way to peppers. They can be picked and used fresh or dried. Being very 'hot', not many will be needed.

AUBERGINES

Aubergines also need very similar treatment to peppers. They are not really keen on being out of doors except in really warm climates. Keep them well watered but never let the soil puddle. As they ripen, the fruits will certainly need support from nets attached to canes or an overhead hoop of wire. They too are upset by the first frost.

COFFEE TREES

These must be kept in a constant temperature of 18°C (65°F) plus, and in a humid atmosphere. They can grow to 23ft (7m) tall and 10ft (3m) across, but are also easy to keep to 6ft (1.8m) high and 4ft (1.2m) across. It would take an estimated five years for you to get back 3lb (1.3kg) of coffee, so it is not a productive proposition.

EASY GROWERS

Bean sprouts

Bean sprouts are very simple to grow and cheap to buy. A packet of mung beans can be obtained from a delicatessen or good grocer. Find a suitable covered container – a jam jar will do, or a plastic lunch-box or deep tray. The lid must be perforated or slightly raised – a cardboard-box lid works well for a tray. Line the base of the container with a piece of blotting paper and spread out the beans. More than one layer can be put into a jar, but don't fill more than one-tenth of it with beans.

Cover them with off-chill water and put in a warm, dark place. An airing-cupboard or a cupboard near the kitchen stove is ideal. Let them swell for 24 hours, then water them, twice a day, with tepid water, damping them thoroughly and running off the surplus each time. The beans will grow and grow, and are ready for eating in four or five days, depending on the temperature.

Pull off and eat at the white-shoot stage – when they begin to grow their first leaves, they are past it. They can be eaten raw, or very lightly cooked, in spring rolls, chop suey and as a delightfully fresh accompaniment to any meal.

Mustard and cress

These can be grown indoors, very simply, and by children, on a tray, plate or saucer covered with a piece of damp flannel or hessian. Sprinkle up to half the area with a thin layer of cress seed. Three days later, spread the remainder with mustard seed. In a week's time, the little seedlings will be ready to eat; strip them off and start again.

Mustard and cress can also be grown on a tray of soil or a window box. Cover up the seeds as you sow them, and keep the cover on until the stems are 1in (2.5cm) high. When the crop is ready, use it all very quickly – the next day, it flops or coarsens, having no nutrients to sustain it.

If you want your crop to last a few days, or need more than a plateful, grow the same mixture on soil, which should be fine and well firmed. This can be done in a seed tray, with another up-ended over it to exclude light until the seedlings are 1in (2.5cm) tall. Unless it is kept indoors, wrap the double tray in polythene, fleece or put it in a greenhouse for warmth. The ideal temperature is approximately 13°C (between 50 and 60°F) at all times. When the seedlings are ready, remove the covering tray and put back the polythene cover propped up on sticks. You will get about ten ¼lb (112g) punnets of mustard and cress off a standard seed tray. It will stand for about a week ripe.

The seeds can be grown out-of-doors in moderately mild weather, on a finely raked and firmed bed. Plant the seeds, with the cress always three days ahead of the mustard, on damp soil. Cover with a sheet of sacking or thick paper and top the whole thing with a black plastic cloche or a cardboard box painted black. This excludes light and absorbs the necessary heat. After the seedlings are 1in (2.5cm) high, take off the covers, but replace with a clear cloche if the weather is cool. This crop will be ready in about ten days, and will last about a week before it goes off. The quantity will vary with the box size.

Mustard and cress grown on soil must be kept wet, though not soggy. Water with a fine mist-spray, which can be improvised from a detergent bottle, or by using a hose with your thumb across the nozzle. Any wet soil tends to splat up into the crop and is very hard to shift. You can avoid this by planting the seed on a sheet of damp cloth on top of the soil. When the crop is ready, strip off the whole or part of the cloth plus mustard and cress, all clean.

> Plant the seeds with the cress always three days ahead of the mustard

Mushrooms

Mushroom spawn is easy to come by from garden centres and online but getting good results is not so easy. In their natural state, mushrooms grow wild in pasture fields with a short, close turf, grazed regularly for years, enriched by the droppings of cows, horses or sheep, or in woods with a lot of rotting vegetation lying about. Packets of spawn will enclose instructions which may imply you can copy this by lifting a square of lawn turf, stirring a bit of compost into the soil, planting the spawn and standing back to await results. If your lawn is an ex-pasture, with the right soil, this may work; if not the spawn will just die.

You will get quite good results from buying a kit, which provides a packet of spawn and another of compost, sometimes even ready-mixed, with a plastic growing container. You add water, stand it in a warm place in the dark and, hey presto, up come the mushrooms. They do too, and very good and fresh they taste, but the quantity will only just cover the cost of the kit plus heat – though you do get a free container out of it. This is the only way for a flat dweller to grow the crop.

Also available, are mushroom kits where wooden dowels are impregnated with mushroom spawn; these dowels need to be pushed into drilled holes in freshly cut logs, and the mushrooms can be harvested four to ten months later, continuing three to five times a year for up to five years.

But, if you have more space and want to grow mushrooms in a fairly big way, you must have access to a lot of fresh manure and straw – and somewhere to keep it while it is in the smelly stage. You also need a dark or half-dark growing place, and either a brick box or trays for the compost. More or less any very rich compost will do – it is a matter of trying out what is readily available to you personally and judging the results. If it doesn't work, vary it; if it does, stick to it.

Mushrooms must have organic fertiliser, which could be any animal manure – cow isn't much good, but better than nothing; straw or decomposing wood, to provide the natural sugars, and calcium; they also like a touch of phosphate (rock phosphate is the preferred option for organic gardening and lime (again choose your source carefully if you wish to grow organically) to protect them. They cannot use simple chemicals as such, so they need plenty of bacteria to break down all these ingredients into compost and this is encouraged by the fresh manure, which provides an ideal breeding ground.

Mushroom spawn is easy to come by from garden centres and online but getting good results is not so easy

You can make up all these ingredients into a simple hot-bed (see page 93) and sow the spawn in it when the temperature is falling. This will confine the operation to a single, manageable place, but it will not produce the maximum possible yield from the amount of valuable manure you have collected, and it will run out of steam in a matter of months instead of the greater part of a year.

If you are prepared to take more initial trouble for a much greater crop, first find out what you can collect together at the same time – odd bits acquired at intervals work at different rates and spoil the set-up. You will need a solid floor to work on, which can be cleaned down afterwards. A yard (just under 1 metre) is ideal, but don't work too close to your – or the neighbour's – kitchen windows.

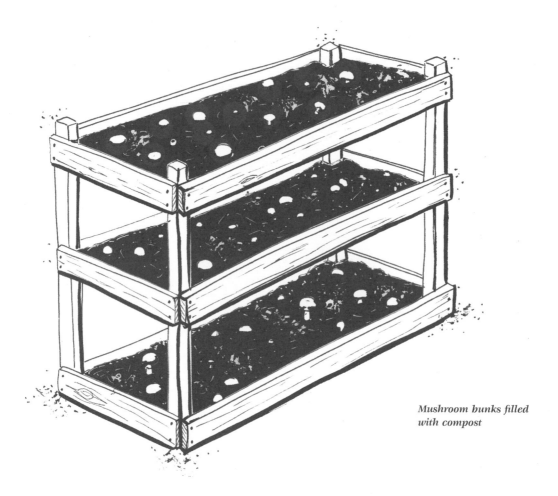

Mushroom bunks filled with compost

Make arrangements with a local farmer or stable to deliver a load of manure, and get in a couple of bales of straw at the same time. One expert claims that wheat straw is the only one to use, because it has xylan, which converts to xylose in the heap. All straws have xylan, and most have more than wheat straw. If you want to be scientific, choose rye straw. Wood refuse has the same effect, so clean sawdust could be added, especially to cow manure.

The process of making the compost begins by spreading straw on the floor, wetting it thoroughly, adding a layer of manure, a layer of wet straw, and so on, until the whole thing is about 4ft (1.2m) high. Top with straw and bang the sides to shape it into a tidy heap. Keep it damp, but don't hose it loose. It will heat up, quite fiercely, and smell powerfully rich and farmyardy – this isn't nasty, just strong.

After about five days, pull down the heap, turn it over and pile it up again, with the former sides in the middle, so there is even fermentation.

If you want to grow mushrooms in a fairly big way, you need access to a lot of fresh manure – and somewhere to keep it while it is in the smelly stage

If the heap overheats enough to smoke, damp it down at any time, but don't drown it. Keep it moist but not soggy and cover it from heavy rain. Turn once or twice more, packing it well together each time. It will gradually turn into a uniform, brownish, pleasant-smelling compost or mixture, moist if squeezed but not dripping. After several heatings, its temperature starts to drop from 60°C (140°F) to under 26°C (79°F) and then it is ready for use, as quickly as possible. Add the calcium – in the form of real gypsum (not gypsum plaster from the builder) and stir it in.

You can check if the compost is ready, first by smelling it. If a urine/ammonia smell lingers, air it by spreading and re-heaping. Test the pH (see page 55) which should be neutral, about seven. More important, take the temperature, which should be 26°C (79°F) or less, and falling. The whole process of preparing compost will take about a month.

Meanwhile, make the growing beds or trays. Ideally, the shed or room should be of solid material like rendered blocks or bricks, since the very humid atmosphere would soon rot wood. If the only available place is wooden, line it with polythene and paint with ship's varnish or several coats of gloss paint. At least back the growing trays with plastic deflector curtains to keep the wet off the walls. You can build beds 12in (30cm) deep and the length of your arm across, and set trays on staging or make triple bunk beds with about 9in (23cm) access space between each tier (see illustration page 132). Beds and bunks take less material to build, but trays are easier to fill and empty.

Fill each tray or bed with compost and firm it down well. Plant the spawn, 2in (5cm) deep and about 6–8in (15–20cm) apart. Keep the atmosphere moist by covering the trays with damp newspaper and lightly spraying it if it dries out. The temperature should stay at about 15°C (59°F) while the spawn is growing, so a small heater may be needed for a while. If this dries the air in the room, spray the walls, but never directly on to the compost at any time, or the spawn will rot.

Soon, in about a fortnight, the spawn will have spread little white mycelium threads all over the tray, under the compost. Little whitish patches show on the surface, which look like mould. This is reasonable – mushrooms are a sort of mould, which happens to be edible. At this point, remove the paper and case the beds by covering the top with 1in (2.5cm) of sifted garden soil. Pat it firm and dust with lime (if required). Preferably sterilise this soil; the crop is worth the effort. You can mix in a little peat-substitute (coir perhaps) and chalk too, which reduces the risk of the soil panning hard on the surface and retains moisture.

Now relax and collect the mushrooms. You should not need any extra heat at all once the beds are cased but, if the air is very cold, production will slow. Keep the casing moist but not soggy, preferably by watering where no mushrooms are visible. Ventilate well in summer and spray the walls to keep the air humid.

> You can check if the compost is ready by smelling it. If a urine/ammonia smell lingers, air it by spreading and re-heaping

15. Herbs

Make room for herbs – either in a dedicated bed, pots near to the kitchen – or dispersed throughout your vegetable plots. They can be used year round in the kitchen, adding huge amounts of flavour and aroma to dishes, and can also be used to deter pests in the house and garden and in bath and aromatherapy oils.

A lot of herbs or wild plants can be grown for medicinal use. They may need special treatment or harvesting according to which part of the plant is required. Some of the uses are incredible and rather terrifying, so on your own head be it.

There are no rules about using herbs for culinary purposes – anything goes with anything you personally like it with. Experiment a bit and get some interesting combinations – but be light-handed at first. Home-grown herbs are much stronger than shop-bought ones and a little tends to go a long way.

a   *b*

PLANNING YOUR PLANTING

From the gardener's point of view herbs can be grouped into four types according to their growing habits (see illustration below):

• those which make relatively neat cushions or mats of low-growing plants, eg. thyme
• bushy plants, which at least start small, eg. rosemary
• the invasive type which sprawl across half the garden, eg. mint
• tall, mostly umbelliferous plants, grown for seeds or stems, eg. coriander

The first three groups need to be stationed somewhere near the kitchen, so the cook can rush out and pick a handful before the pot boils over. This is especially important in winter, when the trek down a muddy garden isn't inviting. Many of the herbs also stay permanently on their sites, and would interfere with crop rotation if planted in the main vegetable plot. Therefore, it is best to keep them separate from other plantings, near the house and at the edge of the bed where you can pick from the path.

Most of the first two groups of herbs are decorative and can be grown in the front garden if you are short of space. They make good edging plants, will grow on rockeries, and in pots or old sinks, which makes them useful for windowsills or balconies. They are generally not very demanding about their soil. Some will even go without watering for ages, provided the container isn't too small. They stand all kinds of ill-treatment – like being walked on (some are used for lawns) or given a rough haircut with scissors or clippers – and live in peace with babies and cats.

The bushy plants, like rosemary, sage and lavender, make useful windbreaks for small seedlings, and mobile ones if they are in pots. The sprawlers, like the various types of mint, keep sending out shoots and putting down roots.

Herbs
(a) Cushion
(b) Bushy
(c) Sprawling
(d) Umbelliferous

Although herbs are mostly pretty easy to grow there are a few things to look out for:

Light – most herbs like the sun, if they are in pots you can try moving them to sunnier spots if they don't appear to be thriving.

Water – herbs dislike heavy, clay soils that are prone to water logging. Either add some mild organic material such as leafmould or compost (but not manure) to the soil or grow in raised beds or containers filled with soil-based compost

Running to seed – some annuals, such as coriander, tend to run to seed in hot weather. Shading the plants might help prevent this.

Tired perennials – as they get older some of the perennial herbs may start to wane unless propagated in late spring. There are various methods depending on the type of herb: clumps (eg. fennel) can be dug up and divided; tarragon produces offsets that can be dug and separated for planting on; take cuttings to propagate thyme and sage.

Pruning – for perennials give them a trim after flowering, for others, harvesting will be keeping growth in check

Most herbs will fail to flourish in acid soils, heavy soils with poor drainage and in deep shade

Unrestricted, they will spread everywhere and strangle other plants beneath them. Therefore they must be grown in a space confined by brick or stone walls or in an old sink or other container, but they must be deep, as they need more moisture than can be maintained in a shallow sink. You can also plant them in containers set into the soil (and you can buy bags designed for restraining pushy roots for this very purpose as well).

The tall ones look handsome at a distance but untidy at close quarters, so they should be planted well to the back of the garden. Mostly they are allowed to ripen before use, so you will not need daily access. If the seeds scatter, you could have an invasion of huge monsters – 4–5ft (1.2–1.5m) tall – and far more caraway, dill and coriander than you could use this century.

GROWING

Most herbs can be started from seed in spring, and the commoner ones are readily available. The less common herbs are advertised, but it is a lot cheaper to beg a cutting from someone with an established herb garden. There are always plenty of bits to spare. Some plants divide easily, giving a bit of rooted plant ready made. Others will be presented as a short length of stem. If you have the choice, take a piece that is about 4in (10cm) long, not too young, not old and woody or with flowers on. Strip back the lower leaves, and sink about half of it in wet, sandy soil. You can put rooting hormone on the cutting, but this is over-elaborate. Shove it in, keep it watered, and it will grow.

Any of the seeds can be started out of doors in spring, with protection for basil or sage. The seeds are mostly so tiny that it is easier to mix a small quantity with sand before sowing in small pans or pots of mixed sand and soil, so that you know just where they are. Label the pots, to show which is what. When they are big enough to handle, plant out – quite wide apart for the cushiony type – in a well-firmed bed Some of the plants have hard little seeds which are slow starters, so you tend to lose track of them in open ground.

Most herbs will fail to flourish in acid soils, heavy soils with poor drainage and in deep shade. But on the plus side, herbs rarely suffer from insect pests and diseases and nutrient deficiencies are also unlikely. Once you have a herb, you usually have it for life. There are three growth patterns. Annuals produce, flower and die off all in one season. You can collect the seed carefully and sow it next spring, or let the seed fall on the ground and set itself. Only the odd tender plant doesn't react well to this. Biennials produce young leaves for using one year and then run to seed the next. This means a gap of one year unless you sow from bought seed for two springs, after which you have your own seed to work from.

Perennials go on growing from year to year, although the plants tend to get tired and leggy after a time and should be divided, or restarted from cuttings or seed. They generally drop seedlings all around the mother plant which can be moved and grown on.

HARVESTING

Annuals are mostly used first by picking some of the young leaves; later hang the whole plant upside down on a nail to dry off, then powder the leaves between thumb and finger and put the bits in a small, closed pot.

Perennials, and biennials planted in spring and again in summer, will be usable fresh all the year round, or pick a piece off and dry it as before. You can hurry up the drying in a cooling oven.

The following is a guide to growing some common culinary herbs:

A = Annual
B = Biennial
P = Perennial

Angelica B
huge, striking umbellifer

PROPAGATE AND PLANT seeds sown in situ, very slow starters. Try keeping them in pot of sand through winter to break down hard coat and plant out in spring. 3ft (90cm) apart final position
HARVEST young leaves (dull) stalks in second summer for candying (see page 193)

Balm P
lemony, medium bush, invasive after first year
PROPAGATE seeds in late spring, cutted, rooted bits in summer
PLANT 12in (30cm) apart
HARVEST young leaves or dried

Basil A
lowish cushion or bush version
PROPAGATE seeds under shelter in late spring; frost-tender
PLANT in May, 8–10in (20–25cm) apart
HARVEST young leaves or whole plant dried for winter use; collect seeds for re-sowing and store until spring.

Bay P
evergreen bush or small tree like laurel
PROPAGATE cuttings of half-ripe wood
PLANT sheltered place or tub; rather frost-tender
HARVEST young leaves and dried whole leaves most of year

Borage A
medium low, attractive blue flowers
PROPAGATE seeds in early spring, reseeds itself easily after first year
PLANT 12in (30cm) apart at first, later fills 1 sq yd (1 sq m)
HARVEST young leaves, old leaves dried quickly

Caraway B
tall, untidy umbellifer
PROPAGATE seeds in situ in summer
PLANT well back, 2ft (60cm) apart
HARVEST seeds, next summer, before they drop

Chamomile A
small cushion, bright yellow flowers
PROPAGATE seeds in spring, reseeds itself
PLANT 8–9in (20–23cm) apart
HARVEST flower heads for chamomile tea, shampoo additive

Chervil B
floppy cushion
PROPAGATE seeds in spring, reseeds itself
PLANT 12in (30cm) apart
HARVEST leaves fresh most of year. Don't allow flowering except one for seed

Chives P
narrow spikes in small cushion; onion family

PROPAGATE seeds in late spring, division of clumps
PLANT 6in (15cm) apart
HARVEST stems by snipping off about 2in (5cm) at a time from top – 'haircut'. Small onion bulbs from old plants

Coriander A
medium height, messy appearance

PROPAGATE seeds in situ in spring or summer
PLANT 12in (30cm) apart, out of sight but in sun
HARVEST seed heads, well dried and extracted from husk

Dill A
tall, untidy umbellifer
PROPAGATE seeds in situ in spring or summer
PLANT 10–12in (25–30cm) apart in sunny corner
HARVEST seedheads, well dried, used whole in pickles

Fennel P
tall, feathery foliage
PROPAGATE seeds in April, divide plants in spring
PLANT 12in (30cm) apart
HARVEST leaves, whole young sprays of leaves, dried seed heads

Florence fennel (finocchio)
same, with turnip root
PROPAGATE AND PLANT as for fennell, earth up root in summer
HARVEST as above, plus turnip root as vegetable

Garlic P
medium spiced, onion family
PROPAGATE offsets (cloves) in spring, like shallots

PLANT 6in (15cm) apart, good in rich pocket of earth near fruit trees, especially peach
HARVEST whole bulbs when ripe, dry in sun and hang in net

Horseradish P
about 3ft (90cm) tall, broad floppy leaves, very invasive

PROPAGATE small thong (root section) about 4–6in (10–15cm) long
PLANT 18in (45cm) apart, good soil, in a corner
HARVEST roots when mature, cut off still-growing plant; re-generates at any time from small roots left

Marigold, pot A
ordinary garden plant, orange or yellow flowers and wide leaves

PROPAGATE seed in spring or summer, reseeds easily
PLANT 6–9in (15–23cm) apart, flower garden
HARVEST flower petals, young leaves

Marjoram, pot P
small cushion
PROPAGATE seed in spring or cuttings
PLANT 10in (25cm) apart
HARVEST leaves, fresh or dried

Marjoram, sweet A
low cushion; slightly tender
PROPAGATE seeds in late spring or in shelter earlier
PLANT 12in (30cm) apart
HARVEST leaves, fresh or dried, flower buds

Mint P
low, sprawling, very invasive
PROPAGATE root cuttings (stolons) in autumn in greenhouse, spring out of doors
PLANT in container or walled-off bed, one plant will expand to sq yd (1 sq m) if let; 3in (7.5cm) deep
HARVEST leaves fresh or dried, or as mint sauce

Nasturtium A
garden flower, orange, yellow, red trumpet flowers, sprawling
PROPAGATE seeds in spring in situ
PLANT about 12in (30cm) apart; will fill square or drape over walls, etc; space accordingly; sunny spot
HARVEST young leaves; seeds fresh or pickled

Oregano (wild marjoram) P
large cushion
PROPAGATE AND PLANT
as for pot marjoram, but twice distance apart

HARVEST as marjoram, but stronger
Parsley B
crinkled foliage; medium height
PROPAGATE seeds in spring (treat as annual); runs to seed second year; successional sowings in summer
PLANT 9in (23cm) apart in sunny place; good soil
HARVEST sprays of leaves

Pennyroyal P
very invasive and sprawling
PROPAGATE AND PLANT as mint
HARVEST young leaves only, old ones very bitter and toxic

Rosemary P
neat grey-green bushes, about 4ft (1.2m) high, feathery foliage, mauve flowers
PROPAGATE cuttings (or seeds, but slow)
PLANT solo bush or as hedge 20in (50cm) apart
HARVEST handfuls of leaves or sprays dried and powdered

Sage P
evergreen bush about 2ft (60cm) high
PROPAGATE cuttings (or seeds, very slow); tender when young
PLANT solo or 2ft (60cm) apart, sunny position
HARVEST not in first summer, then leaves at any time, fresh or dried

Savory, summer A

loose cushion, sprawling stems

PROPAGATE seeds in spring

PLANT 12in (30cm) apart, warm damp place

HARVEST summer, when flowering, gather and tie up to dry

Savory, winter P

short bush, about 12in (30cm) high

PROPAGATE seeds in summer, cuttings in spring; under cloche

PLANT 18in (45cm) apart, sunny place

HARVEST from second summer on, young leaves, coarse after flowering each year

Thyme P
low cushion, sprawling

PROPAGATE seeds in spring; layering in spring; (cuttings in summer reluctant); division of clump in autumn

PLANT 12–15in (30–38cm) apart, well-drained soil

HARVEST not in first year until well-grown, then whole side shoots at a time, fresh or dried, to keep it tidy

Tarragon P
low, sprawling cushion

PROPAGATE cuttings, rooted stems (seeds reluctant)

PLANT sunny place, early summer (tender when young); will fill 2 x 2ft (60 x 60cm) eventually

HARVEST leaves regularly fresh; collect before flowering for drying, or make vinegar

Thyme, lemon P

sprawling, invasive

PROPAGATE cuttings, division

PLANT grows anywhere like weed, set in cracks in paving or by door

HARVEST leaves any time, fresh or dried

16. Fruit and nuts

Summer is the time when fruit of all kinds is available in profusion – lovely taste, lovely smell ... and a lovely price too at times. Wouldn't it be lovely to grow your own and always have top quality fruit? Producing your own nuts is also entirely possible – almonds, chestnuts, hazel, and walnuts, will all grow happily in many parts of Britain. The choice of what can be grown is expanding too – due to climate change and developments in fruit breeding – kiwis, peaches, cranberries and more can all now be given a go.

FRUIT TREES

Fruits – such as apples, pears, plums, damsons – provide more than just a bountiful harvest that can be eaten fresh or dried or preserved in jams, chutneys, etc. They will also help feed and attract useful wildlife – pollinating insects, for example – and they can provide shade and shelter for other crops (even livestock, depending on the size of your plot).

GENERAL VARIETIES

In general, bearing trees need all the nourishment of the ground under their branches, which means that you can't grow anything on that whole area. A standard apple tree – which is the same size as any other standard fruit tree – will eventually cover a circle about 18ft (5.5m) across, so you must allow this final space for it. You can grow vegetables around it while it is very young, but never closer than 6ft (1.8m) to the trunk and only top vegetables, not roots. When the tree is fully grown, all you will be able to grow beneath it is grass, and not very good grass at that.

There are though a huge number of specially bred dwarf trees – fruit trees that are propagated onto different rootstocks which produce trees far smaller than a standard variety. Those labelled M27 or M9 will suit most gardens; the Royal Horticultural Society provides a helpful guide to rootstocks (see Useful websites guide, page 246).

A bush apple covers 10ft (3m) across and a dwarf pyramid 9ft (2.7m) or even less (it is best not to grass the area under a dwarf tree, because of the competition for food). They are not likely to go on for thirty, forty and fifty years, like the big ones, but they do grow much lower making it easier to pick the fruit (and the fruit is the same size as it would be on a traditional tree).

Most standard fruit trees don't bear until they are five, six or seven years old and are mostly sold as three-year-olds. Older than that, they are more difficult to get settled in and well rooted before they are ready to crop, and they may die in the effort. Bought younger, they are cheaper, but you have to wait an extra year or two. Dwarf trees get going sooner, but die off earlier. You won't get anything from them in a year or two, in any case.

Older alternatives in a limited space include espaliers, fans and cordons, grown on walls or fences. A fan-trained tree is systematically pruned, from its youth, to have a fairly limited number of side shoots. These are tied firmly to a wooden trellis or strong wire and cane framework

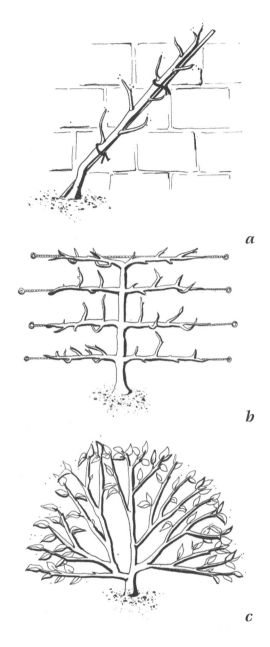

a

b

c

Different ways to prune or train fruit trees
(a) Cordon – a single main stem trained diagonally at 45°
(b) Espalier – a central stem with tiers of side branches at right angles
(c) Fan-trained – has a limited number of side shoots

CREATE AN ORCHARD

Traditional orchards, made up of varieties of fruit trees such as apples, pears, plums, damsons and cherries, have been disappearing at an alarming rate – over 60 per cent have been grubbed up since the 1950s as development spreads and small-scale fruit producers have lost out to bigger commercial growers. As a result, there are fewer varieties of traditional British fruits available to buy and many rare species, such as the lesser spotted woodpecker, are finding it even harder to survive.

If you have space on your land, then you could do worse than create a traditional orchard – defined as having at least five fruit trees, where the trees are widely spaced, and the site is often grazed by animals such as sheep, or cut for hay.

Even if you don't have your own land, you could join forces with others in your neighbourhood to create a community orchard – providing fruit to the community, a way to pass on horticultural skills and a centre for other local activities. The organisation Common Ground has spent years championing community orchards and has published the 'Community Orchards Handbook' giving advice on how to go about creating them. Hundreds have already been established, providing locally grown fruit to communities and providing a way to share knowledge and horticultural skills (see Useful websites guide, page 246).

attached to the wall in a fan shape. Anyone with a lot of patience can buy a very young tree and do this themself – they need regular summer pruning. It looks best if the fan is a decent size, and this needs a high, old-fashioned orchard wall or a house wall.

An espalier is pruned leaving only a central stem and side branches at tidy intervals, trained at right angles. They are most suitable for growing apples and pears and you can buy ready-trained trees with two tiers of branches that will quickly make three or four tiers.

A cordon is even more severely pruned to a single main stem, and trained diagonally up the wall at an angle of 45°. These can be bought from a nursery ready trained, but both have to be kept that way with annual attention to pruning. They bear well in their limited area. Because they have the shelter of walls and can be covered quickly, they often do well in a year when trees in the open have lost their blossom through frost or winds. Peaches and apricots, which bloom insanely early for such delicate trees, do very well as wall fruit. Soil near walls and fences is not very good, so the trees will need an extra ration of food at planting and regularly each year.

Look out too for dwarf 'step-over' trees which are horizontal cordons grown on very short trunks. They are grown as free-standing trees supported on wires and can be used as a decorative and productive edging to beds.

POLLINATION

If you have room for a single apple tree, the question is 'Is it self-fertile?' It may need another variety to pollinate it. There is no point in choosing as your pair of apples a dessert apple which produces an early crop and a cooking apple which produces a late crop. The two types must bloom at the same time so that bees can fly from one to the other doing their good work. Some apples need two pollinators before they will produce. Unless you have space for two or three trees in your own garden, you must either do without apples or persuade a neighbour to plant the pollinator, so that you both have a good crop.

Alternatively you can buy a 'family tree'. These trees are produced by grafting a number of compatible varieties on to one stock, so that the pollinator is there all the time. They cost more, naturally, but might be the answer for a small garden.

> Cordons have the shelter of walls and can be covered quickly, so they often do well in a year when trees in the open have lost their blossom through frost or winds

Specialist suppliers (check online) will have a wider choice of pollinating varieties available and possibly be cheaper than a nursery. If they offer a collection of six pollinators, these could be shared with neighbours to be sure of fertility. The local nursery, on the other hand, will have stock bred for your sort of soil and the plants might spend less time out of the ground and won't dry. This is important for success in establishing them. Container plants get over this difficulty, but can be damaged in transit because they are awkward to handle.

Much the same considerations apply to pears and plums. One or two pears are described as self-fertile but they are still likely to crop more heavily if they are cross-pollinated by another variety. Several plums are self-fertile, including the popular Victoria, and so are damsons, but again they will benefit from cross-pollination. Plums and damsons prefer clay soils which are slightly alkaline, in a sunny position sheltered from winds, but care for them as you would for apple trees.

Some fruit trees need careful placing. Cherries will grow perfectly well in the open, but they are a magnet to birds. Even covering the branches with black filament webbing does not protect the fruit for more than a day or two. Word goes out and clever Uncle Fred Bird comes to show the others how to get underneath.

Some apples need two pollinators before they will produce but you could persuade a neighbour to plant the pollinator

GRAPEVINES

Grapevines can be grown indoors or outdoors but will need some sort of support system no matter where you grow them. A greenhouse or conservatory is the place for growing dessert grapes (although some varieties can survive outdoors) and outdoors for wine varieties.

If you opt for indoor growing be sure you have the room – allow 3ft (90cm) between each vine if you are going for more than one – and ideally plant the roots outside the greenhouse, with the vine entering through gaps at ground level. If you have to plant inside the greenhouse border then you will need to stay on top of watering – at least every seven to ten days in the growing season.

Plant vines from late autumn until early spring when the plant is dormant. All varieties of grape need fertile, well-drained soil with a manure mulch in spring helping fruit production later (in the greenhouse an additional straw mulch in summer will help pollination by keeping the air dry).

Careful pruning is also essential in order to restrain rampant growth and ensure the plant puts its energy into producing fruit. This is mainly done in early winter when the temperature will ensure the vine doesn't bleed, they will also need regular thinning during the growing season. There are two main pruning systems: the Guyot system used for outdoor vines and the cordon system for indoor grapes and grapes against walls. (Look online for detailed instructions.)

Cherries do best on a wall, where you can cover them with thick nylon netting anchored top and bottom as protection (varieties grafted onto dwarfing rootstock will also be easier to net). They like similar conditions to plums. So also do peaches, apricots and nectarines, which in the open – except in the sunny south – are liable to damage by late frosts and winds. On a wall, they can be covered with curtains against the elements when necessary. This makes for competition for your sunny, south-facing wall. Morello cherries (cookers), however, will flourish on a north or east wall, preferably a tall or house wall.

Figs need special treatment. Brown Turkey, is well-suited to life in Britain (although 'Brunswick' and 'White Marseilles' are also worth trying in our climate) but it must be planted with a restricted root run, in a large container or brick-walled bed 3ft (90cm) square, or it will never fruit. In warmer parts of the world figs will fruit two to three times in one year, but in the UK they only produce fruit once a year.

The small fruits can first be seen in late spring – they should swell over the summer ready for picking in late summer or early autumn when they are soft to squeeze (you might also notice a drop of nectar at the bottom of each fruit). If you do get a second crop of small fruits developing later in the year leave this on the tree to hopefully survive the winter and ripen the following year.

The tree must be in a very sheltered spot to carry its fruit through the winter unharmed, so here is another candidate for that south wall. They can tolerate temperatures as low as -10°C (14°F) but you should cover the bare branches with layers of horticultural fleece, or by packing fan-trained branches with straw – both of which should be removed by the end of May.

> Don't be alarmed, by the way, if a tree full of little apples suddenly drops what seems like half of them in July. Despite the month, this is called the 'June drop' and is nature's way of disposing of what she can't ripen

Another familiar fruit from warmer climes are oranges and lemons, which can be grown in this country but which certainly can't cope with any frost. They can be started from pips and grow into neat little bushes which, in the very best circumstances, will produce small fruit.

Orange and lemon plants are able to survive temperatures as low as 4°C (39°F), and we know of one orange tree growing out of doors in Dorset, in a sheltered angle of a wall, but in general these trees are happiest when situated in a heated greenhouse or conservatory.

They need a large tub of good compost and soil; plenty of water in summer; freedom from frost; and warmth and light at all times. And it is worth remembering that they are mainly fun plants, not serious croppers.

NUT TREES

These can be overlooked but they form a useful role in a productive plot – especially if you have room to play with. Hazel, walnuts, chestnuts and almonds can produce lots of nuts in many parts of Britain.

Walnuts

Walnut trees can take eight or nine years to start bearing although 'Rita' will crop within four to five years. This variety, along with 'Hansen' and 'Lara', is also the most suitable for growing in smaller gardens, as it reaches only 20ft–25ft (6m–8m) in height; most walnuts reach around 39ft (12m). They like a heavy but free-draining loam soil and will not take kindly to areas in your garden that are prone to late frosts. You should also be sure to only prune walnuts in late summer/autumn to avoid sap bleeding and weakening the tree.

Once going, they will keep it up for the next hundred years or so, producing very discreet flowers early in the season and surprising you in autumn by dropping their fruit cases. If you inherit a walnut tree, let it do what it will – it is older than you are, for sure.

Hazel

Hazels are easy to grow on well-drained loamy soil and they don't mind our cold, wet winters. They are best in open areas as they are wind-pollinated (a group works well as they are only partially self-fertile) and they are also good as part of a native mixed hedgerow.

Sweet chestnuts

Best grown in warmer areas where it is rare to get a frost in late spring and for larger gardens. Some varieties produce nuts four to five years after planting.

Almonds

Growing your own fresh almonds can be tricky since the trees tend to flower when frosts are common and they rely on a good spring to attract pollinating bees out of their hives. If you are happy to live with a bit of uncertainty, however, they are worth a try. Grow 'Lauranne' and 'Mandaline' if you are short of space since they are self-fertile. Pick the fruit in autumn, opening the stone to remove the single nut.

Planting and after-care

Whichever tree you choose, plant in autumn or spring, when the soil is warmish and dampish. Follow the directions for careful transplanting of a tree given on page 70. Prepare the earth well, removing all weeds and filling the bottom of the

OLIVE TREES

More gardeners are having success growing olive trees and this is likely to continue if climate change has its way with warmer winters and hotter drier summers (they are extremely drought tolerant so should suit these summers perfectly, although are less likely to fruit if the soil dries out). They can be grown in the ground or containers – ideally in a sunny, protected spot against a south-facing wall – but will need some protection in cold winters (ideally, if in a container, you can bring them indoors in winter – either the greenhouse or the conservatory would do nicely). They are self-fertile but as with other fruiting trees cross-pollination is likely to improve yield.

Keep moist in the growing season and don't let the compost completely dry out in winter. For fruit, olive trees actually need around eight weeks of cold weather (ideally below 10°C (50°F)) but not too cold (below 7.5°C (45°F)). The fruit will appear on the tips of last year's growth so don't get too enthusiastic with your pruning, but they will benefit if thinned to three or four fruits per 12in (30cm) of branch.

large hole with manure or compost. Stake the tree well and make sure the tie will allow for growth. Water until it is established and whenever in the first year the weather is dry for long.

Most fruit trees need pruning to some extent. The general principles are to keep the middle open – which means removing crossing and centre pointing branches; take out any diseased or ancient non-fruiting wood, and trim short any branches going where you don't want them to.

You could guard against pests and diseases by spraying with some new chemical every few days, but the cost of this would make your crop very uneconomic and less than appetising. Better to stick to the simple things, such as banding the trunks with a grease bandage in autumn to catch insects looking for a home. If woolly aphids appear on the twigs, squirt them with detergent-water. If that doesn't shift them, is it so serious if you lose a few apples? They might have rotted in store anyway. Left to themselves, pests tend to cancel each other out.

Don't be alarmed, by the way, if a tree full of little apples suddenly drops what seems like half of them in July. Despite the month, this is called the 'June drop' and is nature's way of disposing of what she can't ripen.

SOFT FRUIT

Soft fruits, grown on bushes or plants, are much easier for the small-garden owner with limited space. Even so, bushes of gooseberries and red- or blackcurrants need a sq yd (1 sq m) – what the old gardener called 'a square yard and a bit for luck' – or even more for access.

Plant in spring or autumn, no deeper than the soil mark on the stem in a prepared hole with a tidy dollop of manure about 12in (30cm) deep, topped with compost and good weed-free soil. Spread the roots out well in the hole and make sure there are no gaps in the earth. Tread well in – it will be there for the next twenty or thirty years.

If the bushes arrive unpruned, cut back any long shoots to the third or fourth bud on each. Remove broken or twisted shoots and leave an open middle to the bush. There should be no fruit at all the first year; take off anything that shows or the plant will be weakened. The next year there will be a small crop and, after that, a lot for the foreseeable future. Don't prune unless you must, and then confine yourself to old, diseased or straggly branches. Blackcurrants can be semi-pruned every harvest time by cutting off a whole bunch of fruit plus a little stem when picking the berries.

You can increase stock at any time by layering. Anchor a long, low branch to the ground with wire and cover with soil where it touches. Gooseberries will throw down roots very quickly; blackcurrant stems may need cutting half through where they enter the ground to encourage them. Healthy cuttings of wood 9in (23cm) long may also be stuck in sandy soil and will probably root. The resulting bushes should be moved to their own planting station where they will fruit in their second year.

> Soft fruits, grown on bushes or plants, are much easier for the small-garden owner with limited space

RASPBERRIES

Raspberries can be grown as bushes, but being taller and floppier than gooseberries and currants, they are generally grown on frameworks. These are quite simple: just two posts, set firmly in the ground every 6ft (1.8m), projecting about 5ft (1.5m) above the surface. String four or five wires tightly between the posts at intervals.

Raspberry canes can be planted in October or April. To extend the season, you can buy autumn-fruiting raspberries, which are always labelled as such.

Plant the raspberry canes to the depth of the nursery's soil mark, 15–18in (38–45cm) apart, and tie them to the wires. They will probably have three stems cut to about 2ft (60cm), if not, trim them to this length. Sideshoots will develop, but no fruit in the first year. In November, cut off the old brown canes and trim the six best side shoots to different heights so there will be fruit at every level. Tie these to the wires, so that they are trained to grow straight instead of sticking out in all directions. The next year they will fruit, and for many years after. Each year just cut out the old canes and tie in the new.

Autumn-fruiting raspberries planted one October will produce a little fruit the following autumn and plenty afterwards. Normally, cut them down in spring to produce new growths during the summer which will fruit that year.

All raspberries send up dozens of suckers from the base. These can be detached, plus their own bit of root, and planted in a new line, but not within 5ft (1.5m) of the first row or they will shadow each other.

> You can increase stock at any time by layering. Anchor a long, low branch to the ground with wire and cover with soil where it touches

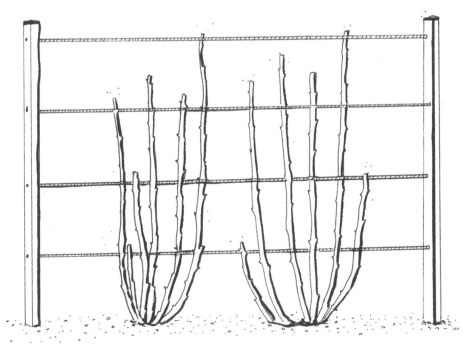

Raspberry canes: trim the six best side shoots to different heights and tie to wires

BLACKBERRIES

These sometimes arrive in the garden of their own accord as a result of berries dropped by birds. However, the cultivated forms like 'Himalayan Giant' are much better croppers. Plant them on a fence or a post-and-wire framework, but give each one 6ft (1.8m) of space – more if possible. For your own convenience, tie the shoots in a rough fan if you can – they are vicious beasts, which will savage their owners as well as marauding small children, so use an old walking stick, leather gloves and an iron determination. Trim off any dead wood and any stem which is wildly out of line, but don't touch healthy old wood, since there will be another crop from it. The prunings are excellent as guards for seedlings against the birds.

> Blackberries are vicious beasts which will savage their owners as well as marauding small children

LOGANBERRIES

Loganberries and some of the fancy crosses, like Boysenberries, related to blackberries and raspberries, need fence or wire support and 6ft (1.8m) of space. Cut out all the old wood of loganberries after fruiting and start again; follow the growers' instructions for the hybrids. The fruits are mostly sourer and less vigorous than raspberries or cultivated blackberries, so they can serve as thief deterrents.

STRAWBERRIES

These are the easiest fruit to place in a small garden, since each plant can manage on a sq ft (0.09 sq m) – or less if you never want to increase the stock. Some varieties fruit in June – 'Cambridge Rival', for instance – and others carry on until early August. The old 'Royal Sovereign' is what most people think of when they visualise a strawberry and interesting new varieties have been bred for size of berry. Once the summer crops are over, autumn fruiters like 'Hampshire Maid' carry on until the frost comes. There are also perpetual varieties that fruit from mid-summer to mid-autumn. All are widely sold and advertised, and some claim to be virus-free stocks which would be vital if you were thinking of growing them as a cash crop.

> The original strawberry lasts about three years, after which the crop decreases greatly

Clean the site of perennial weeds and put in a good dose of manure at one spade's depth. Cover with compost and good soil, then build up a shallow ridge or mound, on which the straggly roots of the plant are spread out. Firm down the soil over the roots and water well around them. Summer-fruiting strawberries should go in during August or early September; autumn fruiters can wait until October–November. These will all fruit the following year. If you wait until spring for planting, there will be no crop that year, except in very favourable climates.

The crop can be advanced by covering the plants with a cloche in February. Water the young plants, but reduce the amount sharply once the fruits have formed, or the plant will run to leaf. Tuck straw or dried grass under the stems to

Strawberry plants: setting out

fill in with soil
and good compost

protect the fruit while it is ripening. A polythene collar can be used instead but this encourages slugs and holds water around the stems which rots the fruit.

After fruiting, the plants send out little runners which produce tiny plants at the end. Anchor these stems down with a stone or wire and they will root, to produce new plants. These can be set in the space left between the rows, if you planted the strawberries 12in (30cm) apart. If you planted closer, pin the runners down into pots of earth on the path or adjacent soil, which must be kept watered. Restrict the number of runners to one or two per plant or it will be weakened.

The original strawberry lasts about three years, after which the crop decreases greatly. So, each year, take the rooted runners and set them out in a separate bed of their own. They will fruit the next year, which will double or treble your crop, and eventually take over from their parents. You will have a permanent succession of strawberries, as long as disease does not strike.

The worst offender – grey mould (botrytis) – can be sprayed with chemicals at the flowering stage, never later or the fruit would be poisoned. However, if trouble strikes when you have two or three different strawberry patches in the garden, or if you would rather avoid chemicals, it would be better and cheaper to quickly root out the affected few before the rest are hit. The other healthy plants will remain to crop then, with no risk of poisoning.

Strawberries will also grow happily in flower pots, barrels, frames, and greenhouses. They cope quite well in window-boxes, provided they are given good earth and plenty of water. Some will grow up trellises; although this looks pretty, the crop will be a bit miserable, since they are putting a lot of effort into clinging on.

Alpine strawberries
Available under various names, usually concealed as 'continuous fruiting', these have smaller berries with a slightly raspberry tang – some people actually prefer them to strawberries. The variety 'Baron Solemacher', which can be grown from seed, makes an outstandingly attractive edging plant for the ordinary garden and can be set 4–6in (10–15cm) apart as it does not produce runners. 'Tumbleberries' are rather untidy, but do reasonably well on a rockery.

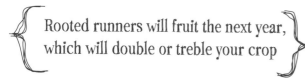

Rooted runners will fruit the next year, which will double or treble your crop

Other berries
There are a host of other berries you could try growing – blueberries, which are best suited to acidic soils and are particularly good in containers; gooseberries, which are easy to grow either as bushes or cordons and can cope with a wide range of soil conditions and partial shade; and goji berries which hail from the mountainous regions in the Himalayas and so thrive in poor soil.

Growing

17. Fertilisers and feeding

Plants need several nutrients in order to grow well – the main ones being nitrogen, phosphorous and potassium. These nutrients are present in the soil but the amount is not static. For example, rain washes out soluble nutrient salts from the earth and carries them, via the rivers, to fertilise seaweed. Phosphates react with lime or acids also present in the soil and become so insoluble that the plant roots cannot assimilate them. Denitrifying bacteria break down the nitrates that have been laboriously built up by the nitrifying bacteria. Once you start to take crops away from the growing area these losses become even greater – for example, every ton of wheat harvested removes from the soil about 65lb (30kg) of nitrogen, 55lb (25kg) of potash, and 30lb (14kg) of phosphates; and other plants have similar appetites.

In order for your plants to thrive you will need to be sure that the nutrients they need are present and available each year. The starting point should be ensuring your soil is as fertile as possible which can be done in a variety of ways:

ADDING COMPOST AND/OR MANURE

Compost provides humus, an essential ingredient for good soil which is difficult to put a price to. Humus is the generic name for the mass of fibres left after the softer parts of vegetable materials have rotted away; the fibres themselves disappear in time but this process takes much longer, and meanwhile they fulfil several vital roles in the health of the soil.

First, the presence of this network of fibres helps to retain a controlled amount of moisture, just like a sponge, and holds together particles of soil in an elastic 'crumb' structure, so that the surface doesn't dry out very easily, and doesn't break down to dust in dry or windy weather.

Apart from this purely mechanical improvement of the soil, the fibres in humus also play a part in the natural processes of nitrogen provision. The bacteria that produce nitrates from more complex nitrogen compounds need oxygen to thrive, and humus fibres assist them by making air channels through the soil, and holding these open even when the earth is pressed flat. The deeper the penetration of humus, the more nitrate you will get in your soil, and working in humus will improve the fertility as well as the texture of heavy or clay soils. Straw and similar vegetable matter with hollow stems can help in the same way; and, of course, the tunnels made by earthworms are extremely useful for admitting air – the only trouble is that the worms will come only if there is already some nutrient in the soil.

Lastly, humus acts as a long-term food supply for the many kinds of bacteria that live in the soil and are essential for its health. Worms again help in this process by dragging bits of leaves and dead vegetation deep into the ground, where they act as a nucleus for colonies of bacteria.

Animal manures are another source of humus and can be fairly high in nutrients as well. It is likely to be hard to source manure from organic farms as, apart from some poultry farms, they will be recycling all their manure on the farm. But manure from 'free range' or low-input farms/smallholdings is the next best option. Check too whether manures are from factory farming systems or where animals have been fed genetically modified (GM) crops. Manure should also be well rotted when used; if it isn't, stack it for a year (perhaps making use of it meanwhile as a hot bed – see page 93).

One product that doesn't add much to the soil in terms of fertility (which is just as well given its environmental cost – see box page 81) is peat. It is low in nutrients and difficult to work into the soil.

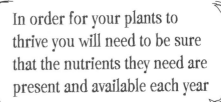

In order for your plants to thrive you will need to be sure that the nutrients they need are present and available each year

MULCHING

Mulches can be both organic and inorganic and are put on the surface of the soil for several reasons – not just to contribute to fertility. Covering the soil with carpet or plastic sheeting, for example, can stop weeds in their tracks, reduce water evaporating from your soil and prevent soil erosion from heavy rain or high winds. But organic mulches, such as compost, leafmould, lawn mowings, straw, bark chippings or manure will gradually biodegrade and help soil structure, as well as supplying nutrients and worm food. These mulches are usually applied on warmer spring soils when the soil is moist, since they will absorb a lot of water. For acid-loving plants, pine needles and composted heather and bracken can be used as mulches to increase the soil acidity.

GREEN MANURES

Some plants can be grown specifically as soil improvers – crimson clover or winter tares, for example, that add nitrogen to the soil by absorbing it from the air, storing it in their roots or leaves which are then dug into the soil, or grazing rye which has an extensive rooting system which helps loosen and aerate the soil. They are usually sown on areas of land which are going to be free of crops for six weeks or more, helping suppress weeds at the same time and preventing further nutrient loss through soil erosion, especially in the winter months.

Depending on the particular crop, they are usually left for around eight weeks before digging in, ideally before they flower if you want to avoid self-seeding, and left to decompose in the soil for around four weeks before your vegetables are planted. Check online for advice on the best green manure for your soil, the season and the time available for cultivation (see Useful websites guide, page 246).

CROP ROTATION

Crops can be divided into three main traditional groups – root crops, brassicas, and legumes – and these can be grown in different areas of your plot each year (getting back to their starting position on the fourth year, depending on whether you allow a year for green manures to grow on a bed). By rotating crops in this way, you not only avoid spreading diseases that single out particular groups – club-root in the case of brassicas, for instance – but you also ensure certain nutrients are replenished as peas and beans, for example, add nitrogen back into the soil if you leave their roots to break down after harvesting. Ideally, you should include a nitrogen-fixing green manure in a vegetable crop rotation, alternate fertility-building crops with those which deplete the soil and alternate weed suppressing plants with those that don't do so well when up against weeds.

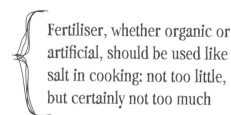

Fertiliser, whether organic or artificial, should be used like salt in cooking: not too little, but certainly not too much

It could be that despite all your efforts, some plants are still not flourishing and you will need to think about adding a fertiliser. This may involve having to buy-in specific products (whether approved for use in organic growing or not) but, although at times we must accept that strict self-sufficiency may not be possible, there is no need to go to the other extreme. Gardeners, smallholders and farmers buy and spread far too much fertiliser, most of which goes to waste (see box opposite). Encouraged by the advertisements of the large fertiliser companies, they seem to think that, if two bags of 'Phosphoblogy' doubles the crop yield, four bags will quadruple it. Plants do not work that way. Fertiliser, whether organic or artificial, should be used like salt in cooking: not too little, but certainly not too much.

The aim for the business-like grower should be to find out the optimum quantities of each nutrient for the particular crop and soil, to try to provide these using natural and on-site sources, and only then to shop around for the cheapest and most effective way of obtaining any extra nutrients that may be needed.

SPOTTING DEFICIENCIES

Deficiencies of certain nutrients can be detected by chemical analysis, but the behaviour of plants grown on the particular soil is a far more sensitive indicator of shortages – or, occasionally, excesses (some crops, like potatoes, cucurbits, and bush fruit, are greedy feeders that can take any amount of good stuff; most crops would lap it up, but go wrong on the proceeds, producing a lot of leaves and no fruit, or big forked and split roots).

Nitrogen deficiency
Leaves and stems yellowish instead of bright green, slow and dwarfed growth, drying up of leaves early in the season. In many plants this starts as a browning of the lower leaves and spreads upwards, long before leaves should start to wither.

Phosphate deficiency

Purple shades in leaves and stems, slow growth, thin stalks. Low yield of fruit and seed. Spindly roots in root-crops. Correct by applying phosphates.

Potassium deficiency

Mottling and curling of leaves, starting at the bottom of the plant. Scorching or browning of the tips and edges of leaves. Premature fall of leaves. Poor root development, often resulting in plants falling down in the wind.

Calcium deficiency

Young leaves in the terminal bud become hooked, and die back prematurely. Leaves have a wrinkled look. Roots are short and excessively branched.

Magnesium deficiency

General loss of colour, starting at the base of the plant and spreading upwards – the veins of the leaves often stay green. Brown patches on the leaves of potatoes, between the veins, but not starting at the edges – which is more often a sign of blight. A similar patching of the leaves of apple and cherry trees, and reddish borders to the leaves of gooseberries. Magnesium is vital for the production of chlorophyll, which controls the whole growth process plants, and, apart from the colour changes, the plants are usually stunted and have misshapen leaves, curling up at the edges. Magnesium deficiency is not common naturally except on chalky soils, where the chalk locks up magnesium in the form of insoluble dolomite, but the same thing can happen if you are over-enthusiastic with lime.

Sulphur deficiency

Young leaves are very light green, with the veins even paler. In some plants (potatoes, for example) the pallor appears as light spots or mottling on the leaves. Fruits appear prematurely and remain small and immature instead of ripening. Sulphur deficiency is fairly rare in the British Isles, largely because of dilute sulphuric acid in rain that results from air pollution. This starts in the big cities but drifts everywhere, so that even the most rural situation is not denied its share of sulphur.

ARTIFICIAL FERTILISER CONCERNS

Relying on artificial fertilisers exclusively and for many years (as has been the case in modern farming) can lead to the humus, present in the virgin soil, finally decomposing and not being replaced since no vegetable waste is returned to the ground. The result is erosion of the topsoil, either by water which washes away the loose powdery soil, or by the wind, as in a dust-bowl. The topsoil is literally blown away, leaving only the hard infertile subsoil. Once this has been allowed to happen, the land is ruined. Cash crops are out of the question and only years of careful planting and ploughing in of green manure crops can revive it – and, of course, this costs money.

You should also be aware that fertiliser manufacturing is a big contributor to greenhouse gases and resources in general. To produce just 1 ton of nitrogen fertiliser takes 1 ton of oil, 100 tons of water and releases 7 tons of greenhouse gases, according to organic certifier the Soil Association. The increasing use of nitrogen fertiliser worldwide has also contributed to higher levels of nitrous oxide (N_2O) in the air such that it has become the third most important greenhouse gas after carbon dioxide and methane – it is some 300 times more potent than carbon dioxide.

Fertilisers are also common pollutants; residues can leach into water supplies costing water companies dearly – many in the UK are now having to consider investing millions in nitrate removal plants, for example. They also upset the ecosystem of rivers, lakes and oceans – nitrogen-rich fertiliser run-off is the main cause of a serious depletion of oxygen in many parts of the ocean, leading to 'dead zones'.

Boron deficiency

Boron is one of the 'micro-nutrients' required in minute amounts by some plants; deficiency signs include brown cracks at the base of celery stalks; brown rot in cauliflowers; rotting in the hearts of swedes, beet and other root crops; and yellow tops on some leafy plants.

Iron deficiency

When nitrogen and magnesium needs are adequately met, yellow tips to leaf shoots, particularly on fruit trees such as plums and cherries, are probably caused by iron deficiency.

It is unfortunate that many of these deficiencies can be spotted only by partial or complete failure of the crop, but at least this enables the grower to be ready for next season. Some deficiencies show up in the early growth – nitrogen, magnesium and iron shortages can all be spotted quite early if you are paying the right amount of attention to your young plants – and in these cases it is often quite possible to save the crop by emergency action.

In the long term, the best strategy against deficiencies is to build up plenty of compost which will conserve the trace elements and – when taking in fertiliser from outside – use the organic materials, like farmyard manure, rather than chemical fertilisers.

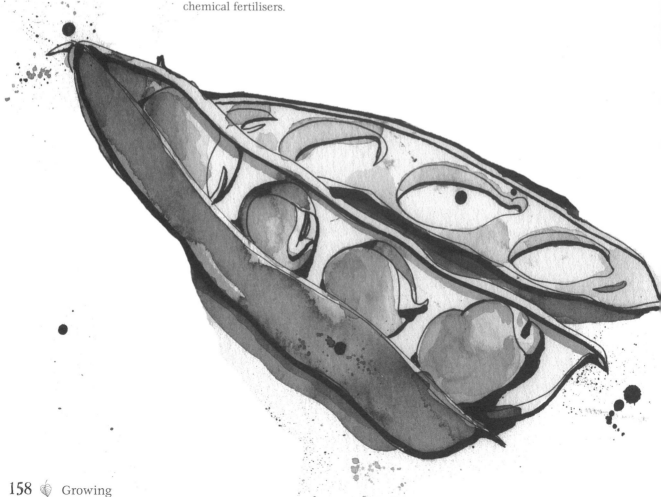

SPECIFIC SOLUTIONS

Nitrogen sources

Nitrogen compounds play a key role in the nucleus of every plant cell, so a certain amount of nitrogen is essential for every crop. However, leaves and stems need more than the rest of the plant, so it follows that produce grown specifically for the leaves – such as lettuce, cabbages, brussels sprouts, globe artichokes and, of course, grass – needs more nitrogen than those plants grown for edible stalks, such as celery, asparagus and rhubarb.

Plants grown for their fruit, seeds or pods, and roots do not need as much nitrogen, and indeed may give poor results if over-fed with nitrogenous fertilisers. Root crops like carrots and beet, for example, tend to produce luxuriant foliage and tiny twisted roots if their soil is too rich in nitrogen.

Plants live in an atmosphere that is roughly four-fifths nitrogen gas but unfortunately they cannot absorb the gas itself. They can only take up the necessary nutrient in the form of soluble nitrates or ammonium salts in the soil. Some nitrates – annually about 11lb per acre (12kg per ha) – are formed by lightning flashes; the nitrogen and oxygen in the air are united by the electrical arc, and a very dilute solution of nitric acid comes down in the rain during thunderstorms.

Nitrifying bacteria that live in the soil, and more particularly in the root-nodules of peas, beans, and other pulses, can absorb nitrogen gas from the air and turn it into usable plant food – hence the importance of beans in most systems of crop rotation. Their roots, left in the ground, serve as a reservoir of nitrogenous material for the next crop. Unfortunately, the work of the nitrifying bacteria tends to be undermined by a busy little tribe of denitrifying bacteria that can convert nitrates back into nitrogen gas. This is why the nitrifying bacteria dispersed generally through the soil do not in fact have much effect on the nitrogen content; it is only when they are concentrated in colonies, as on bean roots, that they manage to keep ahead in the nitrate race.

The other main natural source of nitrogen is any plant or animal that has died on the land. Various groups of bacteria break down the complex nitrogen compounds in proteins, cell nuclei and so on, and eventually release these as simple nitrates that can be assimilated by plant roots.

Where plants need more nitrogen than is provided by these natural processes, you can choose from a wide choice of supplementary sources, including a large range of chemical fertilisers. But before you rush out and buy hundredweights of urea or ammonium nitrate, consider carefully where and when you might need additional nitrogen, if at all, and how much.

Taking, for example, vegetables such as cabbage, brussels sprouts and kale, grown exclusively for leaf production, these obviously need more nitrogen than most other plants. Yet if you lift a 4lb (1.8kg) cabbage, you are only removing from the soil about 1/3oz (9g) of nitrogen; allowing for losses from denitrifying bacteria and nutrients leached away by the rain, the total nitrogen loss per plant is about 2/3oz (19g). You could obviously provide this necessary replacement with

> Plants grown for their fruit, seeds or pods, and roots do not need as much nitrogen, and indeed may give poor results if over-fed with nitrogenous fertilisers

4oz (113g) of ammonium nitrate or 8oz (226g) of nitro-chalk, but 8lb (3.6kg) of ordinary compost – a bucketful – will make up the loss just as well, and costs practically nothing. Even in a small garden, you can easily accumulate a ton or so of excellent compost just by processing vegetable waste, weeds, grass cuttings and fallen leaves. A ton of compost may only contain as much nutrient material as a hundredweight of branded fertiliser, but it costs a lot less.

If your plot needs nitrogen in a hurry, do not be too proud to buy artificial manures – but if you are seeking to avoid chemical fertilisers then look on organic gardening sites online for alternatives. They may well spell the difference between success and failure in the early years, before you have had a chance to build up a stock of good compost. Just try to work towards a system that provides not only nutrients, but humus.

Phosphorus sources

Phosphates play a part in almost every chemical reaction in the plant cell and are therefore essential for growth. They are particularly important in root formation and root crops should always be provided with ample phosphate nutrients. Fruits and seeds also benefit from phosphates.

The phosphorus cycle in the soil is far less complicated than that of nitrogen, because there is no reservoir of phosphorus corresponding to the nitrogen in the air. Plants remove phosphates, sometimes in large quantities – a 100lb (45kg) crop of potatoes, for example, means a loss of phosphate equivalent to about 8oz (226g) of calcium superphosphate, and these phosphates have to be replaced. Ideally this should be done by returning to the soil all the vegetable and animal materials that originated from it, but there must inevitably be losses. In addition, phosphates have an unpleasant habit of reacting with other soil ingredients to form insoluble and practically useless compounds, so there are losses from this process as well.

Phosphate minerals are fairly widely distributed, but mainly in the form of calcium phosphate – phosphorite, apatite – which is almost insoluble in water and therefore not assimilated by plants. If phosphate rock of this kind is ground up finely and buried in the soil for a long time, the natural acids will release phosphate in soluble form but this is a very slow process that may take years. The most common 'organic' forms of phosphorus – bones and bird droppings (guano) – also contain calcium phosphate, so they are no better than the rock.

In 1842, John Bennet Lawes of Rothamsted discovered that if phosphate rock was heated with sulphuric acid, quite a lot of the phosphate appeared in a soluble form and the resulting calcium superphosphate was in fact the first artificial

PLANTS THAT FEED

Some plants can provide valuable minerals to the rest in your plot. Comfrey, for example, is a useful source of potassium and can be cut four times a year and then spread as mulch – useful around fruit bushes. Other fertiliser plants include dandelion and nettles.

Liquid feeds made from these plants can provide concentrated sources of nutrients. For a comfrey tea take a tub, fill it with 6lb 8oz (3kg) comfrey leaves and 10 gallons (45 litres) of water then leave for three to five weeks – it won't smell good so keep a lid on it. Strain or use a ladle to remove the resulting liquid (which should be diluted to the colour of weak tea if using directly on plants including leaves) – it is great as a feed for tomatoes, runner or dwarf beans and potatoes.

Nettles also make a good liquid feed, especially young nettles cut in spring as this is when they have the highest levels of major nutrients. Leave 2lb 4oz (1kg) to steep in 2 gallons (10 litres) of water, cover with a lid, and use after two weeks – diluted to one part nettle liquid to ten parts water.

manure ever to be used in agriculture. When you are using phosphate materials, whether bought from a chemical company or in the form of compost, it is important to know what proportion of the phosphate is soluble and how much is still insoluble calcium phosphate.

Phosphates are particularly important in root formation and root crops should always be provided with ample phosphate nutrients

When selecting a phosphate fertiliser, exactly the same arguments apply as for nitrogen. Once you have lifted, for example, your 100lb (45kg) of potatoes, you need to replace the phosphate they have incorporated in themselves. You can do this with 8oz (226g)

of superphosphate, but you will get just as much phosphorus by adding 18lb (8kg) of compost or horse manure, and improve the condition of your soil at the same time.

One minor complication of all phosphate application is that soluble phosphate tends to get locked up in various insoluble forms. In limy soil, for example, superphosphate and organic phosphates are gradually converted to calcium phosphate. The process usually takes about six months, which means that if you are going in for intensive growing, with the soil in use all the year round, you should boost your phosphate levels twice a year, and in any case add fresh phosphate at the beginning of each spring.

In acid soils, another process locks away soluble phosphate: under these conditions aluminium and iron react with the phosphate to make insoluble salts. So when you are starting to cultivate a new garden or plot you may need extra phosphates until the soil is brought to the right pH balance.

Potassium sources
Potassium – the third of the elements that play a vital part in cell processes – is particularly important for the production of fruit (including tomatoes, melons, cucumbers, marrows, and similar cucurbits); seed and seed pods (peas and beans); tubers (potatoes and artichokes); and leaf bulbs (leeks, onions, garlic and shallots). It is thus important for almost all vegetables except the purely leafy ones.

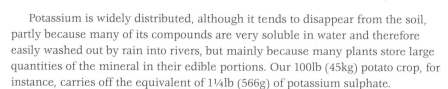

Potassium tends to disappear from the soil partly as it is easily washed out by rain into rivers, but mainly because many plants store large quantities in their edible portions

Potassium is widely distributed, although it tends to disappear from the soil, partly because many of its compounds are very soluble in water and therefore easily washed out by rain into rivers, but mainly because many plants store large quantities of the mineral in their edible portions. Our 100lb (45kg) potato crop, for instance, carries off the equivalent of 1¼lb (566g) of potassium sulphate.

On some soils, particularly the clay type, there is often a lot of potassium tied up in the form of insoluble complex compounds. These can be decomposed by liming, which thus releases the mineral for plants – and, as lime is far cheaper than any of the commercial potassium salts, this is good economics if you work on a clay soil.

As wood and coal (the fossil remains of prehistoric forests) contain a good deal of potassium, ash from fires is a useful source (ideally the wood ash would be from wood not chemically treated after felling).The main active ingredient in ash is potassium carbonate (the original 'pot-ash') which is rather alkaline, so it should not be allowed to come into direct contact with plants, nor mixed with materials like ammonium sulphate which cannot tolerate alkali. Coal ash is quite safe to use in the garden or smallholding but it is probably better to let it 'mature' in the compost heap for a month or two before it is applied to the soil.

Some gardeners burn other vegetable waste under the impression that the potassium is somehow only obtainable through ash; this is, of course, a mistake. The potassium is there all the time and burning the waste merely destroys other valuable materials, such as nitrogenous fertiliser and humus.

TRACE ELEMENTS

Calcium: Correct by applying lime, or by using a calcium-based fertiliser, spent mushroom compost, or similar materials. In cases where the soil is already rather alkaline, and would not therefore benefit from lime or chalk, another useful source of calcium is gypsum which is neutral. Such a condition is rare in untouched soil, but sometimes occurs on an old plot if it has been overdosed with wood ashes. Very sticky clay soils can often be improved by digging in gypsum at about 8oz to the sq yd (250g per sq m).

Magnesium: If acute deficiency is identified, correct by adding Epsom salts (magnesium sulphate) at about 1oz per sq yd (35g per sq m); this may be necessary as an annual treatment for chalky soils. In the long term, farmyard manure can be used to build up a reserve of magnesium.

> In the long term, farmyard manure can be used to build up a reserve of magnesium

Sulphur: In cases where the element is short, the simplest strategy is to add a small amount of gypsum to the soil. A very small amount will suffice, as sulphur is only required in trace quantities by plants.

Boron: The textbook way to add boron to a deficient soil – usually chalky as boron gets locked up as insoluble calcium borate – is to water it with a solution of borax at the rate of 1oz of borax in 1 gallon of water per 2 sq yds (20g in 4 litres of water per sq m). It may be necessary to carry out the borax treatment annually on chalky soils. Be careful not to overdo the application; many plants are sensitive to overdoses of boron. Don't use borax on soft fruit, like raspberries, strawberries and blackcurrants, or near tree fruit, such as apples, pears, plums and cherries. Peas, radishes, tomatoes and potatoes are fairly tolerant to boron – but it is better to apply it at the beginning of the growing season, not over the plants themselves – while lettuce, cabbage and other brassica, onions, beans, beetroot and asparagus seem quite tolerant to the dressing.

Iron: A couple of ounces of ferrous sulphate (sulphate of iron) crystals dissolved in water and applied to the foot of the tree may actually do some good, if you have spotted the tell-tale pale shoots quickly enough. In the long term, bury a handful of rusty nails among the roots of the tree. Soils that are chalky or very rich in manganese may suffer from a permanent shortage of iron, in which case you may have to treat your fruit trees with ferrous sulphate every year or two.

18. Pests and Diseases

The witch-hunters of the 17th century saw themselves as beleaguered in a world permeated by evil, where the agents of the devil could assume a thousand different and confusing shapes, fly through the air, creep under the earth, sidle into houses through cracks in locked doors and shutters, and cause mysterious and fatal pestilences.

You have only to look through the advertisements in *Farmers Weekly* and gardening magazines to get exactly the same feeling. The modern agents of the devil have names like Gummosis, Botrytis, Anbury, Tortrix – or, more simply, scab, rust, and smut – and the only protection against them is a constant repetition of the magic brand names given to pesticides, herbicides, etc.

Farmers and intensive growers of one crop may be forgiven for their responses to this haunted feeling. They know that one outbreak of rust or eyespot can spell the difference between profit and loss in cereals and that some diseases like potato wart can wipe out a whole crop, or even a complete potato-growing area, so they may feel they have little option but to pray and spray. However, many farmers even now admit that the cost of these chemicals, on top of seed, fertiliser, and labour, can itself wipe out the profit on the produce, and one feels that only a belief in magic, rather than economics or science, could persuade fruit growers to spray up to 20 times a season, as some do.

The smaller grower with a reasonably mixed range of crops is very unlikely to have a catastrophically bad attack of any of these pests or diseases and, in any case, the loss of one crop does not mean economic disaster. So before you go into your plot and blast everything in sight with a spray, think carefully about the economics of the process, and then think just as carefully about the long-term effects.

Some insecticides have undoubtedly done an almost miraculous job in making habitable parts of the world that were once completely overrun by dangerous insects: tsetse fly, malaria-carrying mosquitoes, lice that carry typhus, etc. On the other hand, in the more delicately balanced world of the average farm or garden, they tend to have much the same effect as a sawn-off shotgun in a crowded room. They wipe out not only insects that are pests, but also bees, ladybirds, earthworms and other beneficial insects, and even reduce the numbers of insectivorous birds, hedgehogs and moles because these absorb the poison with their prey.

The systemic insecticides have been thought of as a little better from this point of view, as they are absorbed by the plants and are meant to kill only those insects unsporting enough to bite into the produce. But there is growing concern that bees and other needed pollinators are being poisoned by the pollen and nectar in the flowers of treated plants. Unfortunately, human beings also bite into the vegetables and fruit eventually.

Some of the systemics – the organo-phosphorus group – are related chemically to the so-called 'nerve gases', of which a few milligrams of vapour or a drop absorbed through the skin can be fatal. Agricultural workers using some of these chemicals are obliged to wear gloves, overalls, leggings, helmets and respirators. Again, despite assurances that they are quite safe after a period, putting such a deadly substance on food at all seems an unacceptable risk compared with any possible advantages it might possess. Many of the more modern insecticides are less dangerous but their long-term effects on our health have still to be discovered.

The indiscriminate use of insecticides is also counter-productive because it interferes with the natural balance of predators and prey. Apart from birds, moles, hedgehogs and other

Some insecticides have much the same effect as a sawn-off shotgun in a crowded room

useful pest eaters, a whole range of insects live on aphids, mites and similar pests. Spraying often kills these beneficial insects while sparing the destructive ones. Red spider mite, for example, used to be confined almost entirely to greenhouses and similar closed situations, but is now spreading to orchards, fruit plantations and other outdoor sites because its natural enemies have been decimated by spraying.

Having said all this, what is the grower actually to do when blackfly are nibbling the tops of the broad beans, eelworms are making subway systems in the carrots, and the apple trees seem to have been struck by Poe's 'red death'?

The thing not to do is dash out and buy expensive back-pack spray apparatus and some even more expensive branded insecticide and blast everything in sight. This is not only costly but usually completely ineffective, and the long-term effects of the sprays may be worse than the disease.

Don't dash out and buy expensive back-pack spray apparatus and even more expensive branded insecticide and blast everything in sight

First, make sure that your troubles really are due to outside agencies. Many deficiency diseases, caused by minor shortages in the soil, can look very much like the work of insects or fungi. Yellowing leaves and falling fruit in apples and pears, for example, are more likely to be caused by dryness in the subsoil than anything above ground. Strange tints in leaves – brown edges, yellow stripes, etc – need not be blight. They are far more often symptoms of a deficiency of nitrogen, potassium, or calcium (see page 156). Critical shortages of boron can cause brown and hollow centres in swedes and beetroot, with all the appearance of sabotage by millipedes or eelworms. Even such a common event as frost can seem wildly dramatic if it happens at an unusual time of year. We vividly remember coming back after a weekend visit to find our plot ravaged as if by a rain of weedkiller: potatoes and tomatoes were black and dying, and even hardy shrubs like laurels had scorched brown leaves. It turned out to be an unseasonable frost, right at the end of May.

Next, if the trouble is definitely due to insects, fungi or bacteria, try to identify the exact cause. Some like greenfly and blackfly are obvious, but underground pests and fungus diseases may take a little more time. There are many excellent books or online guides which will help here; try to find one with illustrations or photos of the type of damage – second-hand gardening books can be great for this, even if the recommendations for treatment are a little savage and involve chemicals of doubtful safety, hints for diagnosing the causes of damage can be excellent.

PEST CONTROL

When you know your enemy, try to select a weapon that will do the maximum damage to it, and the minimum to yourself and the friendly creatures that share your garden. The following is a rough guide to the various techniques for getting rid of pests without using dangerous materials, and at the least cost. You may occasionally need something more drastic, but if you try to spot troubles as they develop, these homely methods will keep you out of difficulties most of the time.

SLUGS

Often cited as public enemy Number One amongst the nation's home growers, slugs can break the will-power of even the most fervent chemical pesticide hater. But there are many other ways of tackling them:

Clear the area: clear out any dark damp areas that are close to your crops, such as stones, logs, debris, and the compost heap.

Create a blockage: protecting really vulnerable crops such as seedlings can be done by covering with a cloche at night.

Traps: lure slugs away from your crops – they like an upturned pot, wet sacking, empty grapefruit and melon skins, yoghurt pots submerged in the soil with a little cheap beer in them. They will drown in the latter, but make sure the rim of the container is above the level of the soil so other, friendly insects don't go the same way.

Sacrifices: you could plant a few sacrificial lettuces next to vulnerable but more valuable crops – pick the slugs off at night.

Attract enemies: do what you can to encourage the enemies of slugs into your garden – hedgehogs are particularly useful, as are frogs, toads, chickens and ducks.

Go microscopic: naturally occurring microscopic nematodes seek and out and kill slugs in the ground – you can buy them in packs that are mixed with water and watered onto your patch (precise measurements are supplied with the packs). They only work in warm, moist soils and you need to start the first treatment two to three weeks before planting, repeating every six weeks as required.

Ground deterrents: slugs prefer smooth moist surfaces, so put them off by surrounding your crops with sharp sand, spiky twigs, broken egg shells, gravel, ash, pine needles, dried brambles, coffee grounds, etc. Some herbs – rosemary, lemon balm, wormwood, mints – are also said to deter slugs.

Shock treatment: a more expensive solution could come in the form of a copper strip or rings which causes a small electric current to flow when the slug touches it – not enough to kill them, but a definitely a deterrent.

Salty sprinkles: you can kill slugs by sprinkling salt on them, although it is not good for the soil or your crops.

Clear an empty bed: place a heap of cut comfrey leaves on an empty bed – clear the leaves and the feeding slugs a few days later at night.

BITING PESTS

The easiest pests to spot are those that actually eat holes in the leaves, stems and fruit of plants: caterpillars and maggots of all kinds, beetles, flies and so on.

• Sometimes, if the infestation has not gone too far, you can pick or brush most of the pests off the plants by hand, dropping them into a basin of salt and water to kill them.

• Traps can be used for earwigs, woodlice, chafers, and other similar scavengers, which mainly live on dead vegetation but are not averse to the occasional seedling. Flower pots stuffed with straw or newspaper and inverted on the ground or on short sticks or canes will catch a lot of these pests in dry weather. Shake out the straw or paper over a hard surface so that you can tread on the insects before they escape.

• Vine weevils – dull black beetle-like creatures with long snouts – can be caught with rolls of paper or sacking placed at the foot of vines.

• Borax powder will discourage ants and cockroaches: a mixture of borax with sugar or old beer as bait can be used as a poisonous trap. Ants not only loosen the earth around seedlings but, through their intensive farming of aphids, increase the numbers of these pests. If cockroaches become a pest in the greenhouse or frames (you may have to go out with a torch to spot them moving), sink a number of jam jars in the ground up to their rims and pour a little beer or molasses in each one. The creatures fall for this simple trick, literally.

• Fresh sage, penny royal, rue or tansy are also said to deter ants

SUCKING PESTS

Aphids, mealy bugs, and so on, may be a little more difficult to spot because they creep under leaves, and are often protectively coloured to match the plants they are destroying.

{ If the infestation has not gone too far, you can pick or brush most of the pests off the plants by hand }

• The ideal weapon against them is the ladybird, so any treatment should do no harm to this useful insect.

• Soap or washing-up detergent will induce many suckers to loosen their hold on plants, and can be used against blackfly, greenfly, mealy bugs, red spider mite and whitefly. Either use washing-up water or make up a solution of similar strength. More concentrated solutions may interfere with the respiration of the plant leaves, leaving brown or black 'scorch' marks.

• Blackfly on broad beans, a very common infestation, can often be prevented altogether by pinching out the growing tops of the beans as soon as the lower pods have started to form.

• Woolly aphids, which attack the woody parts of apple trees, can be killed off by brushing the white woolly covering of the insects with methylated spirit on a paintbrush – treatment not suitable for more fleshy plants. Treat this pest as soon as it is observed, otherwise the wood of the tree will crack at the attacked areas and fungal diseases can get a hold.

CREEPING PESTS

Those that attack roots and tubers, or the base of stems, may not be noticed at all until the crop is lifted and found holey, or a plant falls over.

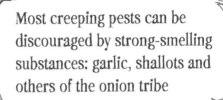

Most creeping pests can be discouraged by strong-smelling substances: garlic, shallots and others of the onion tribe

• Most of these pests can be discouraged by strong-smelling substances: garlic, shallots and others of the onion tribe can be planted in between root vegetables for this purpose. Various members of the spurge family also have this effect, although they are not so useful as food, of course. Some people say that spurges have such a strong smell underground that they deter moles, but we have not been able to confirm this. It would be rather a pity to drive moles away as they are great eaters of creeping insects, and only rarely knock over a plant by clumsy digging.

• Cabbage root fly, and similar insects that lay their eggs near their target plant, can be frustrated by cutting circles of roofing felt or similar bituminised material and placing these around the stems of the plants.

DISEASES

Plants can be afflicted with a wide range of diseases:

Fungal diseases

These affect a good many varieties of plant, which is not surprising, as thousands of fungi exist and are widely spread.

• Some can be avoided simply by setting up conditions which are good for the plants and bad for fungi: mildew, for example, will never develop in a well-ventilated greenhouse or frame, but in a neglected one it may get all over plants.

• Ring spot, which makes brown spots in brassica leaves and eventually kills them, can be avoided if the soil is not over-treated with nitrogenous fertiliser – a good thing anyway for most brassicas.

Bacterial diseases

Such diseases in plants are rare, but are seen mainly as soft rots. They affect root crops like carrots and potatoes, and sometimes the centres of cauliflowers and broccoli, usually where previous damage has occurred because of careless handling or holes made by slugs, snails or leatherjackets. The best answer is to avoid the initial damage.

Viral diseases

In plants, as in humans, viruses tend to be blamed whenever the experts are baffled. Potatoes and tomatoes seem to suffer most, becoming weakened rather than killed, but most other plants have been reported as suffering from viral diseases at some time or other. Nobody knows what to do about any of them except to breed resistant varieties – such as the well-known Scottish seed potatoes. But there is little doubt that they are spread by sucking insects, like thrips, aphids, capsid bugs and mites of various kinds, so the more you can do to discourage these the better your chances of avoiding viruses.

These lists of pests and plant ills may give the impression that every garden is a seething mass of corruption, but with luck and good management your plot will never know half of them. If you keep your eyes open for any odd colours in leaves, lumps and bumps in stalks, and bits missing from plants generally, you can usually catch those that do occur before they have done much damage.

One area that encourages pests and moulds, however, is that under glass: your greenhouse and frames. The combination of warmth, damp atmosphere, and plenty of dim holes and corners in which to hide, especially in wooden structures, tends to attract unwelcome visitors. The best way to overcome future problems is to give the entire area – including the glass and frame – a good scrub with hot soapy water. But the only way to deal with creeping pests in the soil itself is to change the soil regularly.

WEEDS

The harassed farmer, short of labour, and under pressure to produce a 'clean' crop that can be harvested mechanically, may be forgiven for his dependence on weedkillers, but the smaller grower will find that they have several disadvantages, apart from their considerable cost.

 In plants, as in humans, viruses tend to be blamed whenever the experts are baffled

First, the ideal commercial weedkiller is one that does not affect the actual crop but kills everything else. While this is rarely achieved in practice, selective weedkillers have been developed that can at least kill all the broad-leaved weeds in a field of cereals, or even wild oats in among wheat and barley. The trouble comes the following year. Most of these herbicides are quite long-lived in the soil, so rotation of crops becomes impossible. Many gardeners use products of this kind to kill plantains and so on in their lawns, but even this can be dangerous – the lawn cuttings cannot be used in compost or for mulching for months afterwards, because they would kill off broad-leaved plants near them.

There are, of course, the general herbicides, used to clear paths and so on. Of these, the simple ones tend to spread through the soil to places where they are not wanted, and the more sophisticated ones are very expensive.

The real weedkillers for any cost-conscious gardener or grower must be the hoe and the fingers. Regular hoeing will catch the young weeds almost as soon as they appear, and really takes no longer than the fiddly job of sprinkling weedkillers around each plant in a row. If you compost any weeds that get beyond the baby stage, you will get back most of the nutrients they have taken from the soil – although not the water, a point to consider in times of drought – and with none of the risk of side-reactions that can occur with chemical herbicides. Some weeds even make great liquid feeds for other plants – nettle and dandelion for example (see page 160).

If you are faced with a patch that has really got out of hand, or has to be cleared from scratch then consider covering it with thick plastic, carpets or tarpaulins – leaving it covered for a year should kill most of the weeds, although this may be too long to keep the land out of production. Covering for less time will definitely help and you can consider planting through a permeable membrane or mulching regularly to keep up the good work.

COMPANION PLANTING

Get to know which plants can help others by being cultivated near to each other. Some examples to try are as follows:

• Plant French marigolds with tomatoes to repel greenfly and blackfly

• Sow mustard seeds around brassicas to prevent flea beetle damage

• Garlic planted around roses can deter aphids

• Interplant rows of carrots with onions or leeks to disguise the smell that attracts carrot fly plus carrots repel onion fly and leek moth

• Grow sage with carrots or plants in the cabbage family – their strong scents will deter each other's pests

• Plant nasturtium with cabbages – caterpillars will prefer the former over the latter

• Plant asparagus next to tomatoes as asparagus roots produce a substance that is toxic to tomato eelworms

There are loads more combinations to learn – look online or in good gardening books for suggestions – and keep an eye out for what works in your plot.

Harvesting

19. Natural storage

When autumn comes, the average idle person feels depressed by the chill in the air, the certainty of winter to come and the equal certainty of bills to follow, and has only a wasted year to look back on. Virtuous gardeners, on the other hand, now reap the reward of their labours throughout the summer and have tangible evidence of their virtue. They collect and pile up gathered crops, and know they will stand them in good stead for months to come.

To stand the cold and storms of winter, all the produce must be stored carefully in a well-chosen place, by the best method for that crop, and in the best possible condition. As you gather your crops, look them over carefully for any slight sign of damage or insect attack. Any affected article will have to be used up as soon as possible or processed before storing.

STORING VEGETABLES

Leave in the ground: The bulkier, hardier crops can sometimes be left in the ground until required. When the cold weather comes, they cease to grow to any noticeable extent, are held in a kind of natural refrigerator in the dark, and can be lifted when they are wanted for use. This applies to root crops – like carrots, turnips, parsnips; beet brassicas tough enough for winter – like brussels sprouts, broccoli, kale, winter cabbage; and stem crops – like celery and chicory which are earthed over for blanching (pages 109–112).

This is fine for the brassicas, which have their edible bits above ground. It is not so good for root crops since, when the weather is frosty, they are held fast in the ground and cannot be dug without great demands on time and temper. They are also attacked by the ground-borne pests, which welcome your thoughtfulness in providing food stores for them. As time goes on, root crops become hard and woody and eventually start shooting again, producing new leaves at the expense of the root.

BLANCHERS

The whole class of plants which are blanched before use – chicory, celery, cardoons, etc – can be left in trenches in the garden, but the same problems apply as to roots left in the ground. Frost makes it difficult to lift them, and they are attacked by pests and frost. They can be moved into boxes and covered in the same way as roots, or transported with their own earth and slates to a site in a yard or shed and left to finish their blanching (see page 109).

Clamps: On the whole, it is best to raise at least half your root crop and store it in clamps. Dig up the individual plants cautiously, taking care not to break the tip or spear the side with your fork. Reject anything with broken skins and then twist off the tops for composting, using a screw action to prevent tearing any of the root itself. This is especially important with beetroot, which should be left with a couple of inches of stem, otherwise they bleed to death.

Leave the crop out for a day or two to dry – if the ground is already damp, spread them on wire or nylon netting to get both sides dry. Some of the dirt will fall away as it dries, but don't be tempted to wash off the rest to make the vegetables look nice – this will make them go wizened and shrivel up, if they haven't rotted first.

> On the whole, it is best to raise at least half your root crop and store it in clamps

The crudest form of storage is the simple clamp. Straw or dried grass is spread on the ground or in the yard, and the vegetables are piled on it in a pyramid or ridge, steadily decreasing in size. The pyramid is covered with more straw and then topped and sided with a thick layer of earth, smacked hard and smooth with the back of a spade. Stick a few upright straws in the earth to let a little air get to the crop. The finished clamp should be like a low-thatched house. The thick covering keeps the frost off the crop and the rammed earth 'roof' lets most of the rain run down the side (see illustration below).

There are, however, a couple of snags. First, if there is even one secretly diseased or damaged vegetable in the clamp, the whole lot may catch the ailment and go bad.

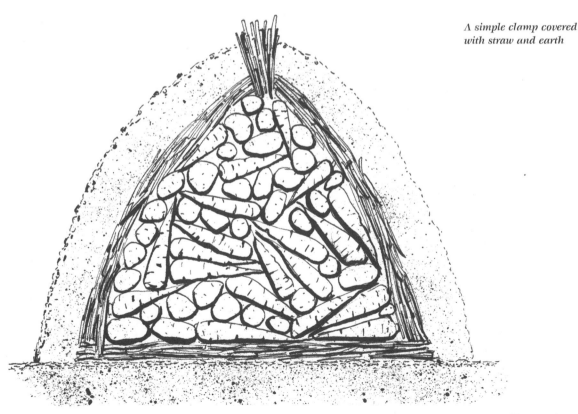

A simple clamp covered with straw and earth

Potatoes and carrots which have turned rotten smell really disgusting. In Lincolnshire, a clamp is called a 'grave', hence such doom-laden remarks as: 'When I opened the grave, 'twas naught but black slime to be seen'. Secondly, it is very hard to take a few potatoes or carrots out without letting moisture in, and a re-made clamp is never quite as weatherproof as it was at first. You can allow for this by making the clamp in sections divided by internal straw walls, but this is rather fiddly.

An improved method of clamping is to isolate each vegetable as far as possible. Either divide each layer of an ordinary clamp with straw, and extract one layer at a time, re-earthing the rest, or store the whole crop in a box, barrel or other container. The vegetables are stacked individually, with sand or vermiculite between each one. Carrots of the stumpy sort stack upright, and triangular carrots or parsnips flat, with every other one reversed (see illustration below). The container can be lined with straw or polystyrene for frost protection and the top should be well covered in the same material. It is easy to move the cover and fish out as many vegetables as are required without disturbing the rest, and as long as the stored vegetables are dry and dark, at a temperature of between 0–4°C (32–39°F), they will keep. The containers can be ordinary boxes (banana boxes from the supermarket are good for

> An improved method of clamping is to isolate each vegetable as far as possible

A barrel or box type clamp with all the vegetables fully separated by straw or sand

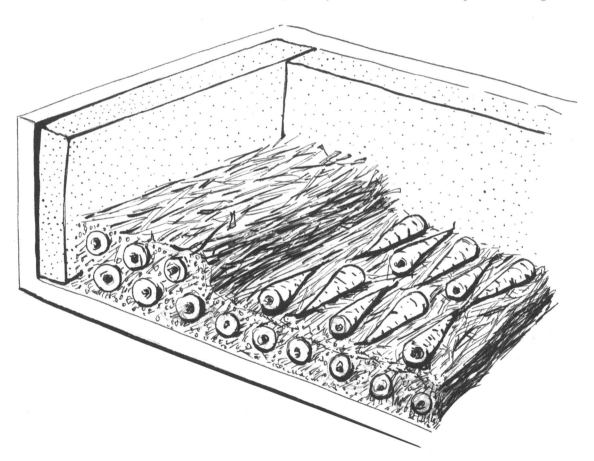

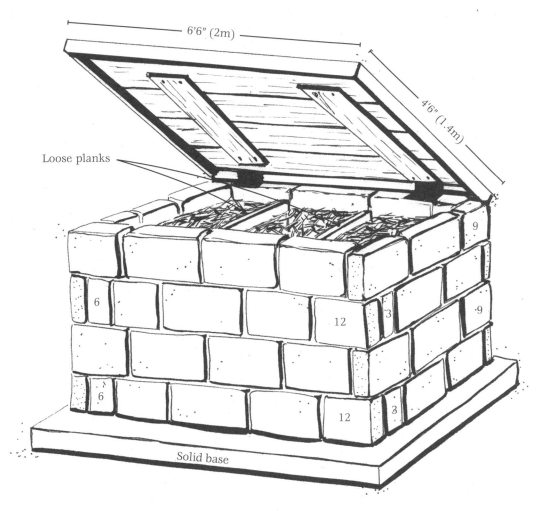

6'6" (2m)

4'6" (1.4m)

Loose planks

9

6

12

3

9

6

12

3

Solid base

this), barrels, a bottomless frame of four bits of wood resting on the yard, or they can be purpose-built.

An old coal bunker, or a similarly shaped container built of blocks, stationed just outside the kitchen door will be frost-free, handy and rain-proof. It is very simple to build, and good practice for anyone contemplating construction work around the house. The inside can be divided with loose bits of plank as required (see illustration above). This is a lot easier than storing your boxes in a shed full of other junk.

Heeling in: Other plants – like Jerusalem artichokes, roots, leeks – can be moved nearer the house and inserted into a slit trench in a convenient part of the garden. (Make the trench by inserting a spade into the ground and levering to one side.) Some of the same problems will apply, but a site near the house is likely to be more sheltered than in the

Clamp: building a bunker, made of 3in (75mm) concrete blocks. All blocks are full size except as indicated. 3 = 3in (75mm); 6 = 6in (150mm); 9 = 9in (225mm); 12 = 12in (300m). Cover and separate every vegetable and divide types with loose planks

It is simple to build a clamp and good practice for anyone contemplating construction work around the house

POTATOES

Unlike other root crops, potatoes need to be stored between 5–10°C (41–50°F). Any lower than this and the starch turns into sugars which can give them a sweet taste and any higher and you risk them sprouting. A good site would be a stone outhouse or back porch – an unused chest freezer would be ideal as long as you layer them with clean straw and leave the lid open a crack to let air circulate. You can also store potatoes in hessian sacks or paper bags – but leave the neck slightly open to allow excess moisture to escape.

They also must be kept away from light since prolonged exposure will lead to greening which is actually a sign that a poisonous alkaloid – solanine – has been formed (potatoes are part of the same family, as Deadly Nightshade – *solanaceae*).

A good tip is to empty your sacks or bags after about a month or so and re-check the potatoes for signs of rot and the odd missed slug!

open garden, so they shouldn't freeze in the ground. Parsnips, incidentally, are supposed to taste better when they have felt their first frost, although this is a matter of opinion.

String them up: Onions and garlic are traditionally kept hanging in strings from the ceiling, but both onions and garlic are prone to sprouting if the storage conditions are wrong, resulting in seed-heads at the top of the bulb stem and softening of the bulb.

First keep back any onions which are soft at the neck, or any onions or garlic that had flowering shoots. Eat them first, as they will not store very well. The rest you must dry off in warm sun before bringing them in. Sit them on a length of wire netting to dry (with a roof propped over it if it is wet and chilly) – this will take a few days in good weather.

Collect them with plenty of stem for stringing (see illustration below for stringing tips). Hang the string in a cool but frost-free place and pull as required. Kept in the kitchen, they look impressive, but they will sprout and rot.

Hang them up: The tough-skinned cucurbits – pumpkin and marrows – will keep for some months if they are stored in a cool, frost-free place, but they must be able to get to the air on all sides. Sling them in a strong net from a sturdy beam and check for pressure marks from time to time. Don't hang a pumpkin by its curved stem since this dries up and drops the fruit like a small bomb. Ridge cucumbers keep a while but are best pickled. Melons have a limited store life. Onions without stems and shallots can also be hung in nets, though shallots are mostly pickled.

How to string onions

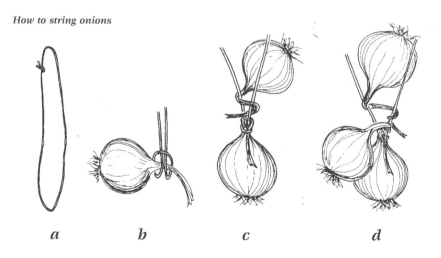

a   *b*   *c*   *d*

Any onions that you don't string can also be stored in net bags. Make your own by cutting old pairs of tights into individual 'legs'. Separate each onion from the other with an elastic band or knot, then you can just snip off an onion as necessary.

STORING FRUIT

Only hard top fruits like apples and, to a lesser degree, pears will store well without processing, and only the very best of the crop should be selected for this purpose.

Pick the fruit from the tree by hand – don't shake the branch to accelerate the process or the whole lot will be bruised. The fruit is ripe and ready to come when a gentle twist of the stem will detach it. If it fights back, leave it for a few days. Set the fruit down carefully in a bowl or bucket – don't throw it in or, again, it will bruise.

> Don't hang a pumpkin by its curved stem since this dries up and drops the fruit like a small bomb

Inspect every fruit closely after it is picked, and sort into heaps – perfect, very slightly bruised or specked, rather bruised or specked, and half-way gone. These are respectively for dry storage, process and store, use right away, and wine. Anything worse goes straight on to the compost heap.

Each perfect fruit should be individually wrapped in paper – newspaper or tissues, not plastic – and stacked on a slatted tray, preferably in a single layer, but two if you are short of space. The wooden trays with little projections at the corners, made for tomatoes, are ideal; they can double as apple trays and potato chitting trays at different seasons.

Apples will usually keep until spring, and individual wrapping means that even if one goes bad it won't get at the others, provided you check the trays occasionally and shift any rotten ones before they ooze out of their paper. When apples are stored unwrapped, the skin wizens and the taste changes. They are then very mellow, which some people prefer.

Apple trays: wrap fruit in newspaper or tissues, not plastic, and inspect them regularly

Pears don't store as well as apples, and you will be lucky to keep any past Christmas.

Conference and russet pears, which have a tougher skin, keep the best. Soft-skinned types, like Williams, have no lasting power at all, so you might as well make a complete pig of yourself and preserve the rest. Rotting of the juicy types of pear can be retarded for a while by wrapping them in greaseproof paper or aluminium foil, but check them every day. The moment they feel soft, they must be eaten or the next day they will go sleepy – like rotten cotton wool. Then they are only fit for compost.

{ Individual wrapping means that even if one goes bad it won't get at the others, provided you regularly check the trays

Any apples which are less than perfect must be eaten or processed as soon as possible, to arrest their slide into the next category down. The majority of the pear crop and all the stone and soft fruits need processing. Many of them will freeze and retain most of their fresh characteristics. Most will bottle, jam or puree, and some are regularly used in pickles or chutneys. Nothing of the whole harvest which can be caught in time need be wasted.

20. Food processing

Apart from storing produce more or less as it comes from the plant, there is a whole repertoire of traditional tricks for keeping food through the winter in a reasonably palatable and nutritious form.

By processing your food your fear of gluts will be a thing of the past as you preserve any excess and save yourself money and time in the months to come.

PRESERVED GOODNESS?

Of the main diet factors, there is usually no difficulty in storing carbohydrates and fats – the calorie foods. Grain, honey, sugared preserves, butter, cheese and nuts all retain their energy value for long periods, and the usual trouble is that we tend to stuff ourselves with high-calorie food in the winter, to the detriment of our health and waistline.

Proteins are also easy to store: meat can be frozen; dried beans and peas keep for months; bacon, cheese and eggs can all be kept for a reasonable time in a cool place.

The main shortages arise, as they have for centuries, in providing the essential vitamins during the winter months. A variety of vegetables is, on the whole, the best safeguard against vitamin deficiency. Preserved, and particularly frozen, vegetables can fill the gap when fresh vegetables are harder to come by. This is the real argument for the trouble of preserving produce and the cost of running a freezer – one week's loss of time through illness or lethargy due to diet deficiency can easily cost you more than running a couple of freezers throughout the year.

Vitamin A is destroyed by drying and, for that matter, by any high-temperature treatment like roasting, but it is usually easy to get enough from carrots, green vegetables (brassicas go on through the winter), and butter or margarine (and full-cream cheeses). Freezing does not affect the vitamin, neither does pickling in salt or vinegar.

Vitamin B1 is rather more delicate, and is lost to a large extent during high-temperature cooking, such as baking and bottling. It is also soluble in water, so if you cook your food in a lot of water and then throw this away, you throw away the vitamin as well. Blanching of vegetables before freezing reduces the B1 content – although, if you have a lot of produce to freeze, you can save some loss by using the same water over and over again; this also saves fuel, as you don't have to heat up every batch from cold. Fortunately, bread and potatoes, as well as fresh vegetables, contain thiamin, so you are unlikely to contract beri-beri, the deficiency disease, in Britain even in the winter.

> Grain, honey, sugared preserves, butter, cheese and nuts all retain their energy value for long periods of time

Vitamin B2 occurs in bread, cheese and other milk products, and most vegetables – including pulses, like peas and lentils, green vegetables, and mushrooms (a good source). It is hardly affected by processing, except that it can be dissolved in water; so dried, bottled, pickled or frozen foods retain their riboflavin. Light destroys it, however, so don't leave your bottled foods in the open or your milk on the doorstep.

Vitamin B3 is one of the most stable vitamins and stands up well to drying, boiling, pickling and freezing. The most serious losses are invariably due to boiling food in too much water, so use conservative cooking methods. Meat, grains and most vegetables contain fair amounts of this vitamin.

Vitamin C is the most difficult vitamin to get throughout the winter, and many people actually show signs of a shortage. Scurvy, the major deficiency disease, is fortunately rare, but minor symptoms are common: bad skin, broken blood vessels, minor wounds that will not heal, and soreness or bleeding of the gums. The trouble is that vitamin C is destroyed by heat, light and exposure to air, so not only most methods of preserving, but even cutting up fresh food for cooking, causes losses. Freezing does the least damage and you can ensure your winter vitamin C by storing frozen (not bottled) fruit; frozen vegetables, especially green-leafed ones; and some roots – swedes and turnips are quite a reasonable source. Potatoes are also a source of vitamin C but old potatoes from clamps have lost a lot of the vitamin by the time you get them.

Vitamin D is necessary for bone formation, so a shortage causes rickets. It is normally formed naturally in the skin by exposure to sunlight, so inevitably it tends to disappear in winter – and may be slightly lacking all the time if you live and work in a very dark area, or wear very concealing clothes. Fortunately, the main food sources – butter, margarine, eggs, cheese and so on – are all easy to store throughout the winter. Once the vitamin is in a food, it is hardly affected at all by processing.

A solar dryer – the flap at the bottom of the collector can be opened or closed to control air flow. The roof should not fit too closely to the walls, as air has to escape under the eaves

DIY SOLAR DRYING

If you get two days of sunshine in a row with some regularity, solar food drying is worth a try. (For cloudier days, consider installing a backup heating system such as 200-watt light bulbs as heating elements).

The drying chamber is basically a box with perforated shelves, to let the hot air through – peg-board would be suitable, if you give it a couple of coats of gloss paint – while the solar collector is made like a drawer, except that it has a flap at the lower end which can be opened to let air in, and is covered with glass. The inner surface should be painted black with a matt surface – water based, poster paint, or soot mixed with a little vegetable oil (if you use spray paint or other toxic paints, let the collector bake in the sun for a day or two before use). Line the bottom of the collector box with a black plastic rubbish bag or paint the bottom black as well.

In action, the flap at the bottom is set to control the flow of air, to allow for the strength of the sun and the temperature that you require for drying. You could, if you wanted to be more elaborate, fit a small cylindrical fan – as used in fan heaters – at the lower end, and control this with a thermostat in the drying chamber. This does mean, however, that you have to be able to get electricity to your dryer.

Place the dryer in a sunny spot facing south and for faster drying reposition to face the sun as it moves across the sky. For some foods it will only take one day of sunshine to dry; wet foods such as tomatoes or pears will probably need a second day.

Incidentally, when your dryer is not in use for food, it is the ideal arrangement for sterilising soil for the greenhouse.

Vitamin B12 is the only other vitamin that is likely to be deficient in even the most processed diet; ironically enough, shortages are normally confined to enthusiastic food reformers. Lack of B12 leads to pernicious anaemia. Unfortunately, while the vitamin is fairly widely distributed in animal products such as meat, liver, eggs and cheese, it is almost entirely absent in most vegetable foods, so vegans suffer more than meat-eaters. Now for the good news: it is hardly affected by any kind of processing.

DRYING

Bacteria and moulds need moisture to grow so, if you can deprive them of it, your food stays safe from attack. Unfortunately, some foods are made so brittle or leathery by drying that they are hardly worth keeping – biltong, for instance, is a sun-dried meat that is no doubt better than starvation, but not much.

Still, drying keeps a high level of flavour and nutrients, and home-dried food has the additional advantage of being free of sulfites (a sulfur-based preservative) and other additives found in commercial dried foods, while providing a convenient, compact, easy-to-store supply of your favorite produce.

There are several methods of drying. One of the fastest and most reliable is to use a food dehydrator (commonly available online ranging from around £70 to over £500) although this requires an initial outlay and the ongoing costs of electricity which adds to the overall cost of storage.

> Drying keeps a high level of flavour and nutrients and home-dried food has the additional advantage of being free of additives found in commercial dried foods

The cheapest option is to air dry or use the sun's energy to dry (see 'Solar drying' box opposite). Or you can use your oven, which is at least already present in your kitchen. The following are some common foods that can be dried successfully:

Apples
The kinds of apple that do not store well in trays can be dried to apple rings. Peel and core the fruit (save the scraps for making pectin stock, see page 194); cut them into slices about ¼in (6mm) thick and spread out on baking trays or a piece of board.

You can dry them either in a cooling oven, after baking, or in a solar-heated dryer. In either case, try not to let the temperature go over about 80°C (176°F) or the rings will be leathery when dry and mushy when reconstituted. It should take about four days to get enough moisture out – you can check on progress if you weigh a few of the rings first and use these particular ones to follow the process. When they have reached a quarter of their fresh-sliced weight they are dry enough.

Pack the fruit in wooden or cardboard boxes lined with greaseproof paper or, alternatively, airtight jars or containers and store in a very dry place. Apple rings made this way are useful for pies, apple sauce, curries, and so on, and are really quite nutritious. They retain a little of their vitamins B1 and C, although most of the C disappears during subsequent re-cooking.

Mushrooms

These and other edible fungi can be dried in the same way as apples or you can air dry them by stringing them onto a strong piece of thread using a darning needle and hanging them in a warm airy room (try an airing cupboard or suspended over a radiator) for a couple of weeks, or until they feel dry. Then keep them in a paper bag for a week or so to ensure that all moisture has gone and then keep them in an airtight box until you need them. If the mushrooms start to go mouldy in the airtight container they have not been dried enough so throw them away. Be sure to select firm mushrooms only and wipe the tops, with either a soft cloth or brush, before drying.

They make a useful source of protein for winter soups and stews, but lose a lot of flavour. Many people prefer salted or pickled mushrooms, chanterelles, etc.

Hot peppers

As with mushrooms, hot peppers can be strung together using heavy thread, piercing the peppers near the stem end with the needle. Rotate them so they point out in different directions as you add them, then hang them up in a warm, dry, place until completely dry.

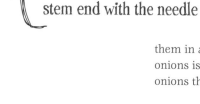

Hot peppers can be strung together using heavy thread, piercing the peppers near the stem end with the needle

Onions

Cut onions into slices and dry them like apples. As they contain a lot of natural moisture you will need to wait until they have shrunk to one-eighth of their original weight, otherwise they could rot in storage. Don't dry them in a closed oven or solar dryer with other foods. The food value of dried onions is not very great, but they are useful for flavouring. Sometimes strung onions that are going slightly soft can be salvaged by slicing and drying them.

Plums

These can be dried to prunes for storage. Pack the fruit neatly in a shallow wooden box or deep baking tray, with the stalks uppermost. Put aside any with insect bites or gummy spots for immediate eating or cooking. Be careful not to bruise the others; cover them with a sheet of kitchen paper or aluminium foil and put them into the solar dryer, or pop them in an oven which has just been used for baking. As they shrink, pack them closer together; if you have more than one tray full at first, transfer from one to another as the fruit shrink, so that you keep one tray completely occupied.

The prunes are ready when they have shrunk to just over a quarter of their original weight. Keep them in tins with tight lids, or well-stoppered jars in a dark place. Prunes are mostly sources of sugar (about 40 per cent), but also contain useful amounts of iron, vitamin A and nicotinamide (niacin, one of the B2 vitamins).

Apricots can be dried in the same way.

Sweet corn

The cobs can be dried in the sun until the grains peel off with a fairly blunt knife. Store these in a dry place until you need them, then boil for about 20 minutes in the minimum amount of water. Corn stored in this way is a stop-gap food – the grains never regain the plumpness or taste of fresh corn and are inferior to deep-frozen corn.

You can make the grains a little more exciting by wetting fresh-stripped corn with milk, rolling the grains in sugar, and drying these in a cool oven. This makes 'corn flakes' with the same texture as sugared popcorn, and was a traditional American snack food for children.

Tomatoes

There are a couple of options for drying tomatoes. For the first, halve every tomato and place them on a baking sheet in an oven set to its lowest temperature. Check after two hours to see if they're dried to your liking and, when ready, pack them straight into a sterilised jar, and pour in enough olive oil to fully cover them. Seal and keep in the fridge.

Alternatively, tomatoes can be concentrated in the form of puree, a traditional ingredient in Italian cooking. Dry the tomatoes, in an oven or solar dryer, on a piece of smooth board and scrape the pulp off every day, spreading it afresh until it is quite thick. The acid in tomatoes helps to preserve this pulp, although it is not nearly as dehydrated as most dried foods. The puree contains some vitamin C and traces of B1 and other useful nutrients, but its main value is as a livener for dull winter menus.

Green tomatoes can be treated the same way, but the puree is rather acrid to some tastes. It is probably better to save surplus green tomatoes for chutneys and sauces, where they will add an edge to ingredients with a blander taste.

Raspberries and strawberries

You can dry berries in the same way as tomatoes. Wash them (large strawberries will need thinly slicing) and then place on baking trays in your oven with the temperature at its lowest. Leave for a few hours until dry.

Raspberries can take a long time to dry in this way so you could try another method – puree the fruits, sieve out the seeds, and spread thinly over a tray before drying in the oven. Break up the resulting 'leather' to make raspberry chips which can be used in cereal and cookie recipes.

Peas and beans

Beans – such as flagelot, borlotti and fava beans – and peas can be dried very successfully. Allow the beans to ripen fully by leaving them on the plant. When the pods are brown, dry and rattling, remove the beans or peas and spread them out for some time in an airy place until all moisture has evaporated (squeeze a bean between thumb and fingernail to test if thoroughly dry – there should be no imprint left). Then store them in covered jars or pots, to keep them clean and safe from mice.

Herbs

Gather herbs for drying early in the morning on a warm dry day in order to preserve their essential oils. You should also try to pick herbs just before they flower to avoid tough leaves. Pick as sprays or handfuls of leaves, remove any dead or withered ones, and hang up in an airy place (over a cooker or in an airing cupboard) to dry naturally in a week or so – the process can be accelerated by putting them on trays in a cooling oven after baking but remember to turn them over halfway through to ensure they are dried evenly.

You can also use a microwave to dry herbs. Start with two sheets of kitchen paper and then layer the herbs on top, separating each layer with another sheet of kitchen paper. Heat on 'high' for one minute, then in bursts of 30 seconds, moving the herbs and checking them at regular intervals. They should be dry in around three minutes.

When ready the leaves will be dry and brittle and can be powdered or fragmented between thumb and finger, over a plate, or using a rolling pin. Store them in airtight jars and keep in a dark cupboard. Label the drying herbs as you go, since several tend to look alike when powdered.

Herbs that suit drying include: parsley, mint, sage and marjoram.

SALTING

Salting is really another method of drying, except that salt is used instead of heat to remove the water. Some traditional foods – bacon, for example – depend on the salt for their taste. Others need to have it boiled out before they become palatable.

Beans

A crock or bucket can be used for salting beans. Most people prefer earthenware, but a plastic bucket with a lid is just as good – if you can get over the psychological block of using such a thing for a folksy recipe.

Pick runner or French beans on a dry day and put aside any bitten or bruised ones for immediate cooking. Dust the bottom of the crock with salt (cooking salt is cheaper but table salt will do just as well); add a layer of beans, one bean deep, then more salt, and so on until the beans have run out or the

{ Gather herbs for drying early in the morning on a warm dry day in order to preserve their essential oils }

crock is full – finish with a layer of salt, put a lid on it and store in a dry place.

To cook the beans, take out as many as you need (with dry hands), wash off the salt with cold water, dunk them in boiling water for about five minutes, then drain, and finally cook them in fresh boiling water. This should get rid of enough salt to make them edible. Beans stored in this way do not lose any protein but most of their vitamins B1 and C are lost either in storage or in the successive washing and boilings.

CURING

Curing commonly uses salt and sugar to both preserve and flavour foods – mostly meat and fish – and smoking is also used to cure foods. Historically, the curing of meat and fish has been taking place for centuries, saving valuable food for use in winter and as insurance against poor hunting seasons. Salted meat and fish are still staples in North Africa, Southern China and the Arctic.

Bacon and ham
Many people prefer home-cured bacon and ham, even if they have to buy the pork from outside. The necessities are salt to preserve the meat, and sugar of some kind – molasses, even honey in some recipes – to make it soft and moist. Bacon can be made with salt alone but it has the consistency of old shoe-soles. Saltpetre – potassium nitrate – is added in most curing recipes because it gives the bacon or ham a good colour. Bacon cured with just salt and sugar is quite tasty but greenish-grey instead of pink. The pink colour of commercial cured meat is due to substances called 'nitrosamines' which are produced by the saltpetre. Some researchers believe that these can cause cancer (see 'Health risks' box, page 192). If you therefore decide to leave out the saltpetre, replace it with an equal weight of salt.

Wet (brine) curing: For a 10lb (4.5kg) ham or flitch, rub the meat well with ordinary salt and leave it to sit in the curing tub for 24 hours. Wipe away any blood or moisture that has exuded after this time and then cover it with the curing brine. The basic recipe for this is:

> The curing of meat and fish has been taking place for centuries, saving valuable food for use in winter and as insurance against poor hunting seasons

2lb (0.9kg) salt
1lb (454g) sugar
¼oz (7g) saltpetre
1 gallon (4.5 litres) water

Bring the mixture to the boil and pour it, hot, over the meat in the tub, making sure that there is enough to cover it completely. Put a piece of board with a stone on it to hold the meat under the surface of the curing brine – don't use an iron weight, as it will rust and discolour the brine.

There are dozens of minor variations on this: you can use brown sugar (the same weight), or treacle or honey (twice the weight), instead of ordinary sugar; old beer instead of some of the water (as in Derbyshire ham); and sea salt instead of common salt – if you don't mind bromides in your ham.

Whatever cure you use, leave the meat in for at least two weeks, preferably three days per pound (454g), turning it every day to make sure it is thoroughly impregnated by the brine.

Look out for bacterial attack which is revealed by sliminess or 'stringiness' of the brine – it actually hangs from your fingers like thin jelly. If this starts, pour away the brine, wash the meat under the tap until all the slime has gone, and make up some fresh brine with a little more salt in it than usual. The ham or bacon should be alright if replaced in fresh brine promptly.

When the meat is cured, wash it and hang it up in a cool dark place for about a week – and make sure that flies cannot get at it. You can eat it green (unsmoked), but if you prefer the smoked flavour, as most people do, smoking is quite easy to arrange.

Dry curing: This is achieved by rubbing a curing mix into the meat and leaving it for several days (although you usually remove water that has leached out each day). A curing mix usually includes some sugar or molasses to add flavour, assuming the meat is not going to be smoked afterwards – a classic mix being 4lb 8oz (2kg) of salt, ½oz (15g) of saltpetre, 7oz (200g) of sugar and 2 tbsp black peppercorns (which will be sufficient to get you started for a whole pork belly).

Smoking: You will need twigs or chips of hardwood – oak is traditional in Britain, hickory in America, but any hardwood seems to work. Don't use softwood, or your meat will taste of turpentine. Get an old, but clean, galvanised dustbin, the sort with corrugations in the lid and knock a few holes in the bottom to let the smoke in. Stand it in a secluded part of the garden, with enough bricks or stones under it to keep it about 12in (30cm) off the ground. Invert the lid, and hang your cured meat from the handle, so that it is clear of the sides and bottom of the bin.

Nearby, start a small fire with your hardwood scraps. Don't use a paraffin firelighter, or the smell will get into the meat; if necessary, ignite the wood with a blowlamp. When it is smouldering well, but not actually burning, shovel it under the bin, so that the smoke goes up through the holes and out under the lid. Keep the fire fed with occasional bits of wood, for about three days if possible. When ready, wrap the meat in greaseproof paper or preferably cooking foil to exclude light, which makes cured meat turn rancid.

A quicker alternative, but one that relies on having an electrical supply, is to fit an electric hot plate inside a galvanised bin (running the electrical lead out through a drilled hole towards the bottom of the bin with the edges smoothed to prevent cutting of the cable). Place a cast-iron skillet filled with wood chips and covered tightly with foil on the hot plate which should be set to medium heat. Place the food to be smoked on a metal grate on top of the bin and cover with a lid.

You should also remember to drill a small hole in the top for a thermometer probe to check that the temperature is correct. Always check the temperature inside your smoker and that of the food you are smoking. The temperature inside the smoker should be maintained at 120–150°C (250–300°F) for safety. The temperature should also be used to determine when the meat is ready, rather than the time spent smoking it. Use a digital probe meat thermometer to monitor the temperature of the meat while it smokes.

You can find guides to temperatures online (see Useful websites guide, page 246) but as an example, beef ribs will take approximately three hours at a temperature of 107°C (225°F) and are ready when the meat reaches 80°C (176°F), while chicken thighs need to be smoked at 120°C (250°F) for around one-and-a-half hours and reach 75°C (167°F) when ready.

> Oak is traditionally used for smoking food in Britain, hickory is used in America

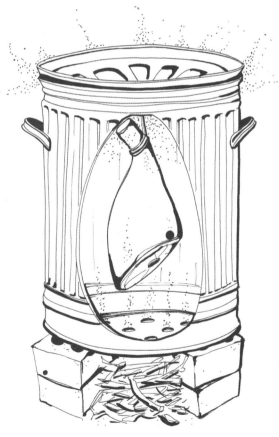

A galvanised dustbin converted to a smoker

Research continues to show links between processed meats, ie. meats that are salted, cured, smoked or preserved with nitrate, and a greater risk of developing certain cancers, most particularly bowel cancer. Reducing your intake of these kinds of meats is recommended by many health professionals and the World Cancer Research Forum suggests people should ideally eat no processed meat at all in order to minimise their cancer risk. The Food Standards Agency also suggests people 'avoid eating too much of highly salted, cured or smoked foods such as meat and fish' in its advice on reducing the risks of developing cancer. However, the cured meat industry has made changes in the past few decades, reducing the use of nitrite and adding other substances which further help reduce nitrite and nitrosamine production.

If curing at home it is important to only use the quantity of nitrates or nitrites specified in the recipes as they are toxic to humans in higher concentrations and there is evidence that meat cured with excess nitrates or nitrites can be carcinogenic when cooked at high temperatures. Having said that, they provide protection against the growth of botulism-producing organisms in the meat.

There are also risks associated with the salt content of cured foods since high salt consumption is linked to raised blood pressure and therefore higher risks of heart diseases, strokes, etc. Again the Food Standards Agency recommends cutting down on heavily-salted foods, such as bacon and smoked fish.

Any type of meat can be cured this way. Leg of pork makes ham; gammon or back makes lean bacon; belly of pork makes streaky bacon. Lean beef can be salted for traditional salt beef, or salted and smoked for pastrami. Even joints of mutton can be cured – 'macon' isn't very exciting but it keeps well.

You can use similar brine for curing fish, but omit the saltpetre as this makes very little difference to its colour. Fillet and gut fresh fish, spreading out the two halves of herrings and similar small fish, or cutting up larger ones into chunks of about 1lb (454g). Put them in the brine for 24 hours – using it cold, not boiling. Then get two heavy pieces of clean plank; lay the fish out on one and sprinkle coarse salt thickly over them, then press them down with the other plank.

Put the fish to dry in the open air for three days – keeping cats away – then brush off loose salt and either wrap the fish in cooking foil for storage, or smoke them.

A simple wooden or basketwork rack, or a wire cake tray, will serve for your smoker. About 24 hours of smoking is usually enough. You will find that the fish have far more flavour than most commercial 'smoked' fish – these are sometimes only brined and then painted with a solution of 'smoke flavour' and brown dye.

Preserving with sugar
Sugar is another way of baffling bacteria and moulds – when the sugar concentration is over 70 per cent they cannot grow. This is one of the oldest treatments for preserving food, for even before cane sugar was readily available people preserved meat and other foods in jars of honey. You can use sugar in particular to preserve fruits, either in syrup or in crystallised form.

Black- and redcurrants
These can be stored simply by surrounding them with sugar. Put aside any broken or squashy fruit for immediate cooking or wine-making; drop a few cloves into the bottom of a jar, then alternate layers of currants and sugar – use equal weights of each – until the jar is full. Tie a paper cover over it and the currants should keep for at least six months.

Candied fruit

This will keep almost indefinitely; the idea is to impregnate the produce with a sugar syrup so strong that it crystallises. Hard produce, such as orange or lemon peel, chestnuts, walnuts and the herb angelica should be pre-cooked in plain water until they just begin to soften. Then boil them with the sugar syrup as described below. Early May is a good time to cut the angelica, as it is then firm but not too tough.

Peel chestnuts and shelled walnuts first by dropping them into boiling water, then cold water. Soft fruit (pears, plums, greengages, peaches, cherries) need only be cored or stoned and added directly to the syrup.

> Sugar is another way of baffling bacteria and moulds – when the sugar concentration is over 70 per cent they cannot grow

You can treat tomatoes the same way – select them red but not squashy, and be prepared for a shock when you taste the finished result. A few very delicate things, like crystallised violets and candied rose petals, should be made by completing the sugar boiling first, then adding the flowers at the last possible moment before it crystallises.

In every case, start with a syrup in the proportions 1lb (454g) sugar to 1pt (0.5 litre) water. Add the fruit, nuts, etc – pre-cook if necessary – and bring to the boil for about 20 minutes. Then leave for at least 12 hours for the sugar to impregnate

the produce. Then add another 4oz (113g) sugar for every 1lb (454g) you originally used and bring to the boil again. This time carry on with the process until the syrup temperature reaches 115-120°C (240–250°F). It is at this point that flower petals are added for making these confections.

If you have no sugar-boiling thermometer, boil to 'soft-ball' – when a spoonful of the syrup dropped into a saucer of cold water can be rolled up into a soft ball like toffee; brittle strings, or a hard ball like a marble, show that the process has gone too far.

Drain off the syrup, put the fruit, etc, on to a baking tray, and finish drying it in a cool oven. When cold, store the produce in a stoppered jar, or wrap chestnuts (marrons glaces) individually in kitchen foil.

JAM MAKING

A useful way of preserving the flavour, at least, of summer fruits, this is basically a jelly of fruit and pectin – a natural thickener that occurs in many fruits (but not all, see box) – and enough sugar to preserve the mixture, usually about 70 per cent of the total. There are countless recipes for jam making, but all of them – if they are going to work – reduce to a very few simple principles:

> A useful way of preserving the flavour, at least, of summer fruits, jam making is basically a jelly of fruit and pectin

The principles of jam making

1. You will need: a preserving pan or heavy-based large saucepan, a long-handled wooden spoon for stirring, wax-coated paper discs for covering the surface of the preserve, cellophane covers to seal the jars if not sealing with jam jar lids, labels, and a preserving thermometer (optional).

2. Use approximately equal weights of fruit and sugar – 1lb (450g) sugar to 1lb (450g) fruit. The best sugar to use is coarse-grain white granulated sugar as the coarse grains dissolve more slowly and evenly but fine caster sugar can also be used.

3. Adjust the water used to boil the fruit so that you have approximately 1pt (0.5 litre) cooked fruit for every 1lb (454g) sugar. By always using the same wooden spoon and saucepan for your jam making, you can save a lot of time – measure out 1pt (0.5 litre), 2pt (1 litre), 3pt (1.7 litres) and so on of water into the saucepan, and make a notch in the spoon when it is held upright. In that way you will easily know the volume of liquid.

4. Pectin and acid help to make jam set, so fruits with plenty of both never need help in setting (see box for a guide to pectin content in fruits). Medium-pectin fruit may need to be mixed with one of the high-pectin kind or dosed with extra pectin or acid. Low-pectin fruits and marrow or swede, which are often used to add bulk to jam, always need assistance to set. Use slightly under-ripe fruit as this is when the pectin content will be at its highest. Over-ripe or damaged fruit will not set as well and can deteriorate rapidly.

5. You can make up for lack of pectin or acid by adding any of the following: 2 tbsp of lemon juice or ½ tsp of citric or tartaric acids per 4lb (1.8kg) fruit; 2oz (56g) powdered commercial pectin to 4lb (1.8kg) fruit; ¼pt (142ml) pectin stock (see page 194) to 4lb (1.8kg) fruit. Don't overdo these measures, or add any of these things to jam made from high-pectin fruit, or you will have to cut your jam up with the breadknife. If you are adding pectin, always do so before the sugar.

6. If you have a sugar thermometer, boil until the temperature of the jam is about 104°C (220°F). Otherwise test for the setting point by spooning a little of the jam on to a cold plate (put it in the fridge or freezer first) to see whether it solidifies – the surface should go wrinkly.

7. Always use sterilised jars to store jam – to sterilise wash in hot, soapy water, rinse well and then place upside-down on a rack to dry in a cool oven at 140°C (284°F) for at least half an hour. Warm the jars before pouring in the jam, otherwise they will crack. Seal them well, but first put a disc of greaseproof paper on top of the jam so that condensed moisture inside the lid does not dilute the surface – if the sugar concentration is reduced below about 70 per cent, mould can grow. As long as you scrape it before eating the jam, it does no harm but it can spoil the flavour a long way down the jar.

Bottling and canning

One of the simplest ways to preserve food it to shut it in jars, sterilise it by heat and then seal the containers. Home bottling – Americans call it 'canning' – necessitates a supply of Kilner or similar heat-proof jars with lids that can be screwed down, rubber rings to make the seal under the lid, and a saucepan deep enough to immerse the jars up to their shoulders in water.

Fruits

All types of fruit can be preserved in this way. For berries and currants, simply clean the fruit and pack it straight into the jars, trying not to bruise it. Apricots, plums, greengages and cherries can be packed as they come, or stoned. Peaches, unless they are very small, are best halved and stoned. Apples and pears should be cored and halved or quartered, according to size.

Make up a syrup with 1lb (454g) of sugar in 2 pints (1 litre) of water. Pour it warm, not boiling, over the fruit to immerse it. Dip the rubber sealing rings in boiling water to sterilise them and fit them to the lids. Screw the lids down – then unscrew a quarter-turn to let steam out during the sterilising so that your jars don't burst.

Put two or three pieces of wood or a coiled-rope mat at the bottom of the saucepan to keep the jars from contact with the hot metal – these will do just as well as the special racks and trivets sold for

BOTTLING SAFETY

Botulism and other microorganisms can be a problem in food that is improperly bottled so it is vital that the jars and food are properly heated in the process and the seals are effective.

The spores that lead to botulism prefer a low-acid environment, which is why high-acid foods such as: apples, apricots, berries, jams, and tomatoes, can be bottled using boiling water as described. Low-acid foods such as: asparagus, beans, carrots, corn, mushrooms, peas and pumpkin, can be bottled using a pressure canner (available online) since they need to be bottled at a constant temperature of 115°C (240°F).

Signs that your bottling process has failed include: a bulge in the lid, mould growing on the surface, odd colours or cloudiness in the liquid surrounding the food. If you see any of these then throw the food away as re-heating will not make it safe.

Store bottled goods in dark, cool places to help preserve vitamins and reduce the chances of decay. Home-bottled food can last for several years but ideally eat within one year as over time, food preserved in this way lose some of their crispness and nutritional value.

this purpose. Stand the jars in place; stuff some bits of folded paper down beside them to stop them rattling against the side of the saucepan, and cover them to the shoulders with warm water. Now bring the water to the boil, turn down the heat, and simmer for about 20 minutes at around 88°C (190°F). This temperature need not be exact, just make sure the jars stay near boiling point without actually being battered about by the bubbling water.

When this is done, turn off the heat and, with a cloth or oven glove, screw down the lids tightly. It is important that you do this before the jars have cooled appreciably, otherwise they will suck in air and fresh bacteria from outside. Stand them on a wooden surface, or an old towel spread out, and let them cool.

Next day, unscrew the rings and hold up each jar by the edges of the lid. If the lid comes away, the seal is inadequate; you should either eat the contents straight away or repeat the sterilising process with a new rubber ring, as this is probably the cause of the leak. If all is well, pack away your jars until needed.

Vegetables:
Acid vegetables, like tomatoes, can be treated the same way as fruits above. You can cut down on the sugar, if you like, but add a little vinegar to the water to aid preservation. However, this method should not be used for other vegetables or meat, because the temperature is not nearly high enough to kill all the bacteria and there is a risk of botulism – a particularly nasty form of food poisoning.

You can also sterilise your jars in a pressure-cooker, if it is deep enough to take them plus a wooden or rope spacer at the bottom. Put about 2in (5cm) of water in the cooker; place the jars in position, remembering to unscrew the lids that crucial quarter-turn; put the 5lb per sq in (0.024kg/sq cm) weight on the valve and, as soon as the cooker is up to pressure, lower the heat, maintaining the pressure for two minutes for soft fruits, like berries and currants, and four minutes for larger fruit, rhubarb and tomatoes. You can pack pectin stock (see above) for jam-making: give it five minutes, as it contains hardly any sugar to preserve it.

Turn off the heat and leave the cooker to cool for ten minutes. Take the valve off cautiously, open up and, as soon as you can, screw down the lids of the jars. Test them the next day as above.

> To brine the vegetables properly at least two weeks will be needed, and more for some

When bottling vegetables, clean them thoroughly, pack them in jars and cover them with 2 per cent brine (1oz of salt in 2½ pints of water or 20g per litre). Sterilise them for ten minutes in the pressure cooker using the 15lb per sq in (0.070kg per sq cm) weight – this will give you a temperature of 121°C (250°F); at least 115°C (240°F) is needed to sterilise vegetables properly. Make sure that your cooker is not leaking, even slightly, or the pressure, and therefore the temperature, will be lower.

Pickling
Acids are far more effective than sugar in stopping mould and bacterial attack. Ordinary vinegar, which is 5 to 6 per cent acetic acid, will preserve most food. Lactic acid is a similar material, produced in many traditional preserving processes, and often the two are used together.

Vinegars can be used, with or without flavourings added, to preserve:
• red or white cabbage: rub the slices of cabbage with salt, leave them for about two days under a cloth, and pack them in jars with hot vinegar;
• mushrooms and other fungi: boil them for about 20 minutes and then pack them, not too tightly, in jars and cover with hot vinegar;
• boiled beetroot, either in the form of baby beets or slices;
• nasturtium seed pods, which make a very pleasant substitute for capers;
• small sweet-corn cobs: you often find some left on the stalk at the end of the season – they cannot grow any more, but are quite a delicacy if pickled;
• apples cut into chunks, and cherries.

Other vegetables and fruit can be packed in vinegar if you only want to keep them for a short time, but they may turn soggy if left for more than a month or two. To get over this, you need to brine them before putting them in vinegar. This salt treatment is not just to extract water or improve the flavour, but helps to encourage lactic acid bacteria to develop in the produce, so that it is pickled 'from the inside'.

To preserve beans (French or runner, use only the young ones), cauliflower, cucumber (especially the small outdoor type, for gherkins), marrow, and onions or shallots, make up a brine with 10 per cent salt (1lb per gallon, or 100g per litre) sufficient to immerse all the produce you have.

Cooking salt or coarse preserving salt is better than table salt for this. Use only wooden or plastic containers – not metal (and particularly not copper, which may dissolve in the lactic acid and actually make the vegetables rather poisonous); stir with a wooden or plastic spoon, and have an effective insect-proof cover.

Prepare your vegetables – cut beans and cauliflower into conveniently sized pieces, peel onions, and so on – weigh them, and put them in the brine. Now weigh out more salt corresponding to one-tenth of the weight of produce, and add this as well, stirring it in. Cover the vessel and leave it in a cool dark place, stirring every day.

To brine the vegetables properly at least two weeks will be needed, and more for some: with marrow and gherkins you can tell how well the process is going, because the lactic acid production turns the flesh from white or cream to a translucent green.

When the vegetables are thoroughly brined, wash them in several changes of warm water to remove excess salt, and leave them to soak overnight in water to extract some from the inside. Then pack them in jars and cover them with hot spiced vinegar. Your own tastes will tell you what spices to use – the traditional

CHUTNEYS

Vinegar is also the main preserving agent for chutneys – often a combination of vegetables and fruits which are chopped and simmered with vinegar, sugar and spices before being transferred to sterilised jars and stored for up to a year. There are hundreds of recipes out there including spiced courgette chutney, rhubarb and date chutney and classic apple chutney. The huge advantage with them is that, unlike in jams, windfall apples, green tomatoes and other end-of-season fruit, such as rhubarb, can be used as you do not have to worry about their ability to set.

As with pickles, most chutneys need to mature for about three months before eating – before this they can be very vinegary and harsh to taste. To test if a chutney's ready, run a spoon gently across the top of the chutney – if it leaves a trail and no excess vinegar runs into it then it's ready. They improve with age and, if properly stored, will remain in good condition for years.

Vinegars can be used, with or without flavourings added, to preserve

If the product from the first run does not seem as sour as wine vinegar should be, pour that lot through again and slow down the rate a little by controlling the tap on the wine barrel

ones are chillis, garlic, pimento, black peppercorns, cloves and allspice.

Dill pickles are made with gherkins brined in 10 per cent salt solution, as above, but with about 4oz of sugar added to each gallon (25g per litre), and the dill, allspice, coriander, bay leaves and so on added to the brine, so that the flavour penetrates right from the beginning. You need to watch this preparation very carefully, as it can easily develop mould if you do not stir regularly.

Home-made vinegar

Vinegar, as most home wine-makers know, is the final product when wine, cider, or beer goes sour, and you can in fact make your own vinegar quite easily by disregarding all the precautions given in the brewing section (see Chapter 21, page 206).

For wine vinegar, select a bottle of wine that is already a little sharp to the taste, and let it go sour by deliberately exposing it to the air in a jug. Put some muslin or similar material over the top to let air in but keep insects out. Now get a small cask or barrel – preferably wooden – and make holes in the ends so that air can circulate above the level of the liquid. Pour your sour wine in, put the barrel on its side, and fill up to just below the level of the holes with more wine. Plug the holes lightly with muslin so that air can circulate, but insects cannot.

Keep it in a warm place, and you should find that a thick mat of bacteria – called 'the mother' – will form on the surface of the liquid. You should be able to run off wine vinegar after about six weeks and, if you are careful to retain most of the mother of vinegar in the barrel, it will make further quantities every time you fill the barrel with wine.

This is a slow and rather tricky process but, if you can get hold of beech shavings, there is a quicker and more reliable method. Use a cask with a detachable lid and three-quarters fill it with the shavings – beech is best as most other woods give the vinegar an odd taste. Put the lid back on and arrange so the wine from the barrel or jar can trickle in at the top of the cask, over the shavings and out through the tap at the bottom.

Sour a little wine as before; pour it into the cask so that it soaks well into the shavings; leave it for a couple of days for the acetic acid bacteria to start multiplying, and then allow a thin trickle of wine to pass through. Try not to get the shavings wine-logged, or air will not be able to penetrate to complete the process. If the product from the first run does not seem as sour as wine vinegar should be, pour that lot through again and slow down the rate a little by controlling the tap on the wine barrel. It does no harm if you put the vinegar through several times. When you have made a batch or

FLAVOURED VINEGARS

Vinegars can also be used for flavouring. If you boil them with herbs, such as tarragon, onions or shallots, spices and so on, you can make a whole range of exotic vinegars that are ideal for marinating food or simply to serve at table. The amount you use is obviously a matter of taste, but if in doubt try 1oz of spice or herbs per 1pt vinegar (50g per 1 litre) and go up or down from there.

two, the mother of vinegar will have become established and the process can be speeded up. This method works for cider vinegar also.

With this home-made equipment you can produce malt vinegar. Make up a brew, as described on page 211 for beer but without hops; let it ferment to the stage of bottling, then use either of the methods above. Hops not only give a bitter flavour to the vinegar, but may slow down the process by their preservative effect.

If sourcing barrels and finding space is a problem, there is another simpler method of vinegar making. First create your mother of vinegar by pouring 18fl oz (500ml) vinegar and 18fl oz (500ml) wine, cider or fruit juice into a medium-to large-sized jar (it is best to use organic, preservative-free wine or juice as chemicals can slow or stop the vinegar-making process). Again, cover with muslin or similar material to let air in but keep insects out, then store in a warm place such as an airing cupboard for roughly two weeks. After this time the layer on top will have formed – the mother of vinegar.

Pour four times as much wine/organic juice as you have mother of vinegar into a second jar – the mother of vinegar should still float on top of the liquid as it did before (it needs to be able to get oxygen). Cover and store this jar in the same way as before but for a month. Taste every now and then to check flavour – once you have the taste you arc after filter it and store in a sterile glass bottle, sealed with a cork.

Sauerkraut

Sauerkraut is made with firm white cabbage pickled entirely in naturally-formed lactic acid. The white cabbage must be really firm and you will need a vessel with a well-fitting heavy lid that rests inside it. The lid is there to hold the cabbage under the surface of the pickling liquid; some commercial manufacturers actually use chunks of solid concrete with handles set in for this purpose. A large round stoneware dish would do very well, as long as it can move up and down in the crock or bin. Never use metal containers or utensils.

Sauerkraut making – cover with muslin and weight lid

Slice your cabbage thinly with a sharp knife; weigh it, and then weigh out salt at the rate of 4oz for every 10lb of cabbage (25g per kilo) — cooking or coarse salt is best. Pack the cabbage tightly into your crock, with salt dusted in between the layers; cover it with a piece of cheesecloth tucked down the sides and put your weighty lid on, pressing the cabbage down well.

Try to keep the temperature of storage between 15–25°C (60–80°F). After a day or two, the salt will have extracted enough juice for it to be visible just under the lid; make sure that all the cabbage is held under the surface, or it can go mouldy.

After about four weeks, your sauerkraut is ready. You can keep it in the crock, if you remember to put the lid on and push the cabbage down every time you remove some. Ideally keep it in an airtight container at or below 15°C (60°F) for up to several months, or you can pack it into Kilner jars and sterilise it when it will keep almost indefinitely.

Cheese

Cheese is another food preserved by lactic acid and it is well worth making if you have your own supplies of milk, or can buy it in bulk direct from the producer or the dairy. It is not economic to make cheese from milk delivered to the door because of the dairy overheads, but you might conceivably make a profit if you could master the art of making, for example, Stilton or Camembert to professional standards.

The starting-point for all the various types of cheese is the same. Milk consists of a mixture of casein, lactose (milk sugar), fat, and a few other ingredients, in water. You need to separate the casein (curds) from the rest (whey). This happens naturally as milk goes sour, when lactic acid bacteria work on the lactose and the acid precipitates the casein. Other acids, such as fruit juice or vinegar, will do the same. Natural digestive enzymes, like rennet or pepsin, also have this effect: you can buy rennet, which is also used for making junkets, and pepsin is sometimes sold as a meat tenderiser.

Let the curds settle; pour off as much of the whey as you can, then strain the curds in muslin or a fine-mesh wire strainer. Curds made in this way and lightly salted become cottage cheese; if you press them in the cheesecloth to get out more whey, then salt them, you have farm cheese. These cheeses will keep for several days in a cool place but should not be left too long.

To make hard cheese that will keep well, you need to press out a lot more whey and this necessitates some kind of mechanical help. You can make a very primitive press from an old saucepan, using stones as weights to get the pressure. If you can turn a wooden screw on a lathe, or get hold of some heavy-duty threaded rod from some machine, you can contrive a really effective screw-press. An old-type mangle might give you the screws – we use iron screws from an inherited embroidery frame.

Take about five gallons (22.5 litres) of milk – it is not really worth using less for hard cheese; if you have a small quantity to use up, make cottage cheese – and let about one gallon (4.5 litres) stand in a warm place until it is just on the turn: not smelly, but ready to separate. Warm the rest of the milk to body temperature 37°C (98°F), add your ripened gallon, then rennet (follow the manufacturer's instructions for quantities), and hold the temperature until the curds begin to separate throughout the milk.

Heavy stones
Board
Curd in cheesecloth
Drainage holes

A simple cheese press made from a saucepan

If you cannot get rennet, use lemon juice or vinegar, at about 1 tbsp to the gallon (4.5 litres), though the cheese may not mature quite as well. An extract of the leaves of nettles, or lady's bedstraw (*Galium verum*), is supposed to act like rennet, but we have never tried this. Any slightly acid plant should work, if it is not poisonous and does not interfere with the lactic acid bacteria.

Strain off the whey from the curds; add salt – try about ¾oz (20g) with the quantities above, but adjust more or less to taste when you have the system working regularly; chop the curd well to mix in the salt and allow whey to escape, and wrap it in two layers of cheesecloth.

Put it in your press and squeeze it until no more whey appears – you can spread this process over a few days, pressing a little more each day. Then put your cheese, in its inner cloth, in a cool dark place to mature for about two months minimum. If you notice signs of mould on the surface, peel off the cloth and rub the cheese with salt. You should get about 1lb of cheese, resembling Cheddar, from each gallon of milk (1kg from every ten litres).

Yoghurt

This is milk partially fermented with *Lactobacillus bulgaricus*, a particular variety of lactic acid bacteria. For an easy and cheap method of making yoghurt buy a sample of 'live' yoghurt – not pasteurised and not fruit-flavoured – and stir about 1 tbsp of this into 2 pints (about 1 litre) of ordinary milk (the spoon needs to be plastic or metal so it can be sterilised).

First heat milk to 85°C (185°F) using two pots that fit inside one another which will prevent the milk from burning, then cool the milk to 43°C (110°F) – put the pan into a bowl of ice water to quickly lower the temperature. Then add the spoonful of starter yoghurt which should be at room temperature.

Keep the mixture as close to 38°C (100°F) as possible for about eight hours – in a warm cupboard or a wide-mouthed vacuum flask. Your yogurt should be ready for you to put in your fridge for several hours before serving. It will keep for one to two weeks.

Once you have successfully made a batch of yoghurt, some of this can be used to start off the next. You will find, however, that after a while an off-flavour begins to develop, due to 'wild' bacteria getting in. By keeping everything clean and sterilising all your utensils, this can be staved off for a while; if it does happen, get rid of your culture and buy another pot of yoghurt.

Most of the costs of food storage, where they are quantifiable at all, are very low compared with the value of the produce. By collecting every bottle and jar you can lay your hands on – especially glass ones with well-fitting lids or caps – you can keep your dried food, jams, pickles properly packed for almost no outlay.

Wooden barrels are sometimes available second-hand from importers of fruit juice and similar commodities – use these for wine or cut them in half to make sauerkraut tubs or salting vats. Wash them out carefully with several changes of hot water – you can usually tell by the smell whether you have got rid of all the sour juice – and, when used for wine or sauerkraut, rinse them with sodium metabisulphite solution as a final precaution.

Stoneware crocks and jars tend to be collectors' items now, and very overpriced. You can occasionally pick them up in out-of-the-way junk shops, and they are well worth having.

There are additional costs to factor in such as the running costs of a freezer. Unless your garden is very small or you are very unlucky with your crops, about 20 cu ft (570 litre) of freezer capacity will be needed for the average family living on its own produce. You may be lucky and find a second-hand commercial model, and there are some domestic freezers around at this size. Alternatively you could buy two chest freezers, each of 12–14 cu ft (340–400l) capacity which will hold upwards of 700lb (320kg) of assorted food.

You can get second-hand and reconditioned models, and these are usually a good buy, because freezers are among the more reliable of domestic electrical appliances. If you buy a new one, it should give you about 20 years' active service. Don't add unnecessary costs by entering into an annual servicing agreement. If you keep your freezer in a cool, dry area you should not really anticipate much trouble – damp surroundings can cause corrosion, which means expensive repairs.

Insurance of the contents may be worth your while if you store a lot of expensive cuts of meat, but most insurance policies specifically exclude losses due to deliberate power cuts.

Freezing

Preserving food in ice has been practised for a very long time. Freezing slows down the growth of bacteria, although it never quite stops it; but it is certainly one of the best methods of retaining the taste and nutritional value of food. Running a modern deep-freeze successfully is quite easy, if you follow a few general guidelines:

1. Don't put in too much food at a time. Food at room temperature is 'hot' compared with that of the freezer and the machine can only cool it at a certain rate. Your freezer should have a rating – quoted in the instructions or specification – that tells you what weight of food you can freeze in 24 hours. If you put in more, or try to freeze hot food, stocks already in the freezer may be warmed up and spoiled.

> Preserving food in ice has been practised for a very long time. Freezing slows down the growth of bacteria and is one of the best methods of retaining the taste and nutritional value of food

2. Freeze everything as quickly as you can. Slow cooling makes large crystals of ice and the food becomes broken up and soggy when thawed. You may also lose vitamins during a slow freeze. All appliances have a quick-freeze compartment near the cooling coils and many have a booster switch to enable you to get more power when you put food in.

3. Don't let food stay in the freezer indefinitely. A year or 18 months is as long as you can reasonably expect anything to keep, and many foods go off sooner than this (see tables on page 204-205). Try to code or date every packet of your own produce so that you always know what to use first.

4. Pack food in air- and moisture-tight material. This stops one food tainting another – fish and ice-cream, for example; and it helps prevent drying out and 'freezer burn', which is the effect of combined low temperatures and oxygen getting at the produce. Choose plastic boxes with tight-fitting lids or use heavy-duty freezer bags to store the food.

5. Pack food in meal-size portions, then you will not have the bother of having to break up a pack and re-freeze part of it.

6. Do not let the freezer temperature rise above -18°C (-0.4°F); ideally it should run at -21°C (-5.8°F). If there is a power failure or other emergency, resist the temptation to open the freezer, kept tight shut and undisturbed, and with luck it will stay cold for at least three days, unless you have recently put in fresh supplies.

> Coarse herbs, such as rosemary, sage and thyme, can be dry-frozen by removing the leaves from the stalk and packing into small plastic bags

7. All your home-grown vegetables, except herbs, need to be blanched (treated with boiling water or steam) before they are packed – unless, of course, you cook them completely before freezing, as with beetroot. This hot-water treatment destroys enzymes in the plants which can spoil the flavour, texture and food value in quite a short time. To blanch: cut or otherwise prepare your vegetables, and drop them into ready-boiling water for the set period (see table on page 205). Drain off the water rapidly through a colander; wash the produce with cold water, then leave it to drain thoroughly. Pack it when cold. If you have a steamer, get the water boiling rapidly before you put the vegetables to steam and, again, cool rapidly as soon as the blanching period is complete.

8. You can save yourself a lot of trouble by freezing your vegetables on flat trays covered with polythene; then, when they are quite hard, pack them into freezer bags (remove as much air as possible from the bag by using a straw). This stops them from freezing together into a large lump, and you can take out part of a bag without having to repack or re-freeze the rest.

9. Fruit is best frozen either in dry sugar (allow half the weight of the fruit, and sprinkle it so that each fruit is surrounded completely); or in syrup – 40 per cent sugar in water (8oz to a pint or 400g to a litre). The sugar will absorb juice that runs from the fruit and will become syrupy on defrosting – ideal for fruit to be used in cooking or making jam.

10. Other fruits – apples, pears, plums – can be stewed, lightly mashed and frozen in tubs or heavy-duty bags once cool. Use the defrosted fruits for sauces, puddings and jams.

11. Coarse herbs, such as rosemary, sage and thyme, can be dry-frozen by removing the leaves from the stalk and packing into small plastic bags. Extract the air and freeze. Soft herbs, such as parsley, basil, tarragon and chives, can be finely chopped and frozen with water in ice-cube trays. Bag them up once frozen and you can remove a cube at a time as you need them. They will discolour during freezing.

12. Always defrost food thoroughly and avoid re-freezing. Defrost food in the refrigerator, not at room temperature or submerged in water – this prevents loss of moisture.

Freezing guide for your produce

Fruit	Method	Storage life (weeks)
Apples	Peel, core, slice into slightly salted water, drain, dry sugar pack	12
Apricots	Skin, stone, dry sugar pack	12
Blackberries	Dry sugar pack or tray freeze	12
Cherries	Stone if required, 40 per cent syrup or tray freeze	15
Currants (black, red, white)	Dry sugar pack	15
Gooseberries	Dry sugar pack	15
Greengages	Halve, stone, 40 per cent syrup	15
Loganberries	Dry sugar pack	15
Peaches	Skin, halve, stone, 40 per cent syrup	12
Pears	Not really suitable for freezing	12
Plums	Halve, stone, 40 per cent syrup	15
Raspberries	Dry sugar pack	15
Rhubarb	Remove leaves, boil, 40 per cent syrup	18
Strawberries	Dry sugar pack	12

Vegetables	Method	Storage life (weeks)
Asparagus	Blanch 3 min water, 5 min steam	12
Aubergines	Slice, blanch 3 min water, 5 min steam	8
Beans, broad	Pod, blanch $2\frac{1}{2}$ min water, $4\frac{1}{2}$ min steam	8
Beans, runner	Cut, blanch 2 min water, 3 min steam	12
Beans, runner	Slice, blanch 1 min water, 2 min steam	12
Bean sprouts	Seal loosely in polythene	3
Beetroot	Boil completely; slice large beets	18
Broccoli	Separate florets, blanch 4 min water, 6 min steam	15
Brussels sprouts	Trim, blanch 3 min water, $4\frac{1}{2}$ min steam, freeze on flat before packing	15
Cabbage	Trim, slice, blanch $1\frac{1}{2}$ min water, 3 min steam	12
Carrots	Trim, slice large carrots, blanch 3 min water, 5 min steam	15
Cauliflower	Trim, separate florets, blanch 4 min water, 6 min steam	15
Mushrooms	Use buttons only, blanch 2 min water, 4 min steam	8
Parsnips	Trim, slice large parsnips, blanch water 2 min, steam 4 min	18
Peas	Pod, blanch 1 min water, $1\frac{1}{2}$ min steam, freeze on flat	12
Peppers	Use green only, slice and remove heads and seeds (do not blanch)	6
Potatoes	Peel, chip, blanch 1 min water, 12 min steam, freeze on flat	6
Spinach	Wash, separate, blanch 2 min water, 4 min steam	8
Swedes	Peel, dice, blanch 2 min water, 4 min steam	12
Sweetcorn	Trim cobs, blanch 6 min water, 8 min steam	12
Sweetcorn	Boil, strip grains, freeze on flat	12
Turnips	Peel, dice or slice, blanch 2 min water, 4 min steam	2

21. Home-grown Hooch

From the true economic point of view brewing liquor from fruits and grains is not efficient. True, the alcohol has some energy value, but rather less than you could obtain from the sugar or starch it is made from. Many wines and beers contain valuable vitamins and minerals, but again only things that you could absorb more efficiently by eating the raw materials.

As the retail costs of alcohol have plummeted, it is also the case that you might be better off buying your beer and wine from the local supermarket as opposed to making your own. But, making your own can provide numerous other benefits. Knowing that your wine hasn't been made with grapes sprayed with pesticides is one of them, the same goes for beer – hops are often sprayed with up to 15 types of pesticides. Equally, you will be reducing your carbon footprint (think of the saving compared to buying a wine that's travelled from Australia or Argentina, for example). Then there's the great feeling of satisfaction that comes with uncorking your very own bottle of plonk – and just think what fun you'll have with the label design.

RAW MATERIALS

All brewing operations depend on yeast breaking down sugars to alcohol. The sugar may be glucose or fructose naturally present in fruit or vegetable juice; lactose in milk (as in the Eastern European drink koumiss, made from mares' milk); glucose made by breaking down starches in potatoes, grain, etc; extracts from sugary plants, such as molasses, used for rum; or refined sugar or honey added deliberately to the brew to increase the alcohol content.

There are several plants in the tropics that produce very sweet juices – the sugar cane itself, of course, and the toddy palm, used to make palm wine or arrack – but only one European plant, the grapevine, regularly makes enough sugar for a decent wine of full strength. Cherries, apples, and so on, make weaker wines, which sometimes do not keep. Most other products need help from added sugar, or the conversion of starch to sugar by malting (see page 210).

However, it is worth looking at the available resources of starch and sugar in a number of fruits and vegetables (see table opposite).

So, for example, if you were making a gallon (5 litres) of parsnip wine, and have 4lb (2kg) of parsnips, this provides 7½oz (230g) of fermentable material (the

Fruit	Sugar	Starch %	Vegetables/foods	Sugar	Starch %
Apples (eating)	11	0.3	Plums (eating, Victorias)	9	-
Apples (cooking)	9	0.4	Plums (cooking)	6	-
Apricots	7	-	Raisins (dried)	64	-
Bananas (peeled)	16	-	Raspberries	6	-
Blackberries	6	-	Beetroot (boiled)	6	-
Cherries (eating)	12	-	Carrots (raw)	5	-
Currants (black)	6	-	Parsnips (raw)	9	2.5
Currants (red)	4	-	Potatoes (old)	0.5	20.3
Currants (white)	6	-	Swedes (raw)	4	0.1
Damsons	10	-	Turnips (raw)	4	-
Gooseberries	9	-	Barley	-	70
Grapes (black)	13	-	Maize	1	68
Grapes (white)	16	-	Oats	-	60
Greengages	11	-	Rice (polished)	-	79
Loganberries	3	-	Rye	-	72
Medlars	9	-	Wheat	-	71
Peaches	8	-	Golden syrup	79	-
Pears (eating)	11	-	Honey	76	-
Pears (cooking)	9	-	Molasses (blackstrap)	67	-
Pineapple	12	-			

sugar and starch added together – as it all ends up the same way, it is quite sound to add them together). A further 1lb (454g) of raisins will give 10½oz (320g) more. If you need a total of 2½lb (1.25kg) of sugar/starch, you must add a further 1lb 6oz of sugar per gallon (700g of sugar to your 5 litre batch).

YEAST

This is a living organism, and the requirements of its lifestyle account for much of the complication and mystery in fermenting. You will usually find that it behaves if you note the following points:

1. Yeast dies if it gets too hot, and gets sluggish when it is cold. Try to keep your brews in the 15–25°C (60–80°F) range. In any case, when the temperature gets over 25°C (80°F), alcohol starts to evaporate at a serious rate and bacterial attack is encouraged. A warm cupboard can easily be fitted up for fermenting, with a small lamp or heater worked by a thermostat if you want to get really organised.

BASIC WINE RECIPE

Taking into account all these requirements, it is possible to make up a general method for wine which should give a drinkable product and you can then go on to adapt it to your own tastes and raw materials.

• Take 3lb (1.4kg) of fruit or vegetables of the sugary kind, and 2 pints (1 litre) of water.

• Crush or pulp the fruit in the water, and boil the vegetables until soft. Heat the fruit to about 80°C (180°F). Put your pulp in a bucket or tub (plastic or wooden, never metal) with a cover to keep out fruit flies.

• Calculate how much sugar your raw material contains (see table on page 207). Weigh out enough sugar to make this up to 2lb (1kg) total, dissolve this in 6 pints (3.4 litres) of warm water, and add it to the stock in the bucket.

• Add about 1oz (30g) of yeast and 1oz (30g) of ammonium phosphate (and either the juice of two lemons or ⅛oz (4g) of tartaric acid, if you are working with vegetables).

• Cover the vessel, and let the mixture ferment at about 15°C (60°F) for eight to ten days.

• Then strain off the solids, squeeze out any liquid trapped in the mass, clean out the fermentation vessel, and put the liquid back in it.

• For a medium to dry wine, add a further 1lb (454g) of sugar; for a sweet wine use 1½lb (750g).

• Leave the mixture to ferment again for about four days, then strain it into a gallon jar fitted with a fermentation lock.

• Put it in a warm place (around 15-17°C or 60-65°F) and leave it until all signs of bubbling have ceased.

• Pour it carefully, or siphon, into another bottle to collect the clear(ish) wine and leave the sediment. You may have to 'rack off' like this several times.

• Leave the wine for at least four months, longer if possible, before drinking any.

You can scale up these quantities as much as you like – you may have fruit and sugar to spare.

Many batches seem to work better on the large scale and, of course, you lose less, proportionately, in straining, racking off and similar separations. A 20 gallon plastic water butt with a lid makes a good vat.

2. Yeast needs organic material to grow on just like a plant. Most fruits and vegetables provide this, but if you have rather a 'thin' brew with a lot of plain sugar, add ammonium phosphate as a 'fertiliser'. You can buy this as yeast nutrient.

3. Yeast needs air to multiply, so there is a first stage in fermenting where you leave the wine in an accessible tub or bin so that you can stir it and work air in. Once you have enough yeast, you can let it work in the absence of air (anaerobically, the second stage) in bottles or barrels.

4. Yeast is eventually killed off by the alcohol it produces. Some yeasts, such as ordinary baker's yeast, may be killed by alcohol at 8 per cent or even lower, but special wine yeasts have been developed that struggle on until the alcohol level is around 15 per cent. Your own yeast will gradually adapt itself by natural selection to take higher concentrations of alcohol. The 15 per cent level is about the top for any yeast, and as this will be produced from roughly 30 per cent sugar or starch (3lb to the gallon, 300g per litre), any sugar over this concentration will never be fermented and will stay in the wine as sweetener. If you come across a home-made wine that is sickly sweet, it is often because the maker did not realise this limitation and just bunged in sugar in the hope of making stronger wine.

This is a living organism, and the requirements of its lifestyle account for much of the complication and mystery in fermenting

OTHER ORGANISMS

There are other organisms just as interested in yeast in your sugar solution and they will try any tricks to get into it. Unfortunately, the most common ones are the acetic acid bacteria that turn wine to vinegar (see page 196). Fruit flies – tiny things that will be depressingly familiar to any winemaker – carry large numbers of these bacteria and can thus infect the wine. You should therefore cover all vessels carefully; wash everything that has had fruit or juice in it, and treat all bottles, funnels, corks and so on with a solution of sodium metabisulphite* (1oz per pint of water, 50g per litre). You can also put this solution in a fermentation lock to make sure that bacteria do not sneak in through this.

Metabisulphite is also used to kill bacteria naturally present on the fruit; it is fairly harmless to yeast. This is a tricky job on the small scale and some people prefer to sterilise the fruit by bringing it almost to the boil, then cooling before fermenting. You can buy measured amounts of metabisulphite in the form of Campden tablets from wine-makers' suppliers; follow the manufacturers' instructions.

* Some people are allergic to sulfites – symptoms include rashes, hives and wheezing – which are present in most wines as it is used as both a steriliser and an antioxidant in the process of brewing beer or fermenting wine.

CARBON DIOXIDE

When yeast works on sugar solutions, it converts about half the weight of sugar into alcohol and the rest into carbon dioxide gas. You can see and hear the bubbles when fermentation is going well, and in fact a gallon of wine of average strength produces about 12 cu ft of the gas during making (5 litres of wine give 380 litres of gas). Obviously, if you bottle up wine in a closed container before this process has finished, a build-up of pressure will blow out the cork or perhaps burst the bottle. Yet you need to keep air and bacteria out of the wine, so you must have protection of some kind.

The most efficient way to do this is to fit a fermentation lock to the top of the container. This has a little pool of liquid – preferably bisulphite solution – which allows gas to bubble out from the wine but stops anything getting in. If you don't want to go to this trouble, close your bottles with corks very lightly pushed in, or tie paper or parchment over the top, until you are quite sure that fermentation has stopped.

The exception to this is making bottled beer, with some gas in it. Here you let the fermentation go to completion, taking care that the alcohol content is not above 8 per cent, then put the beer into bottles with a spoonful of sugar in each bottle. This gives the yeast something to work on and a small amount of gas is produced. Sparkling wines are made the same way.

CLEARING WINE

Apart from alcohol and the flavouring compounds from your fruit or vegetables, your wine will contain residues of fruit, dead and living yeast cells, and other debris. The large bits you can strain off before you put the wine into bottles or barrels; the rest has to settle naturally – you can filter wine, but it is a long and usually unsatisfactory job on the small scale. When the debris has settled, carefully pour or siphon the clear wine into another container. This is known as racking.

Tannin, which is present in most fruits – in the skins of grapes, for example, and very obviously in damsons and sloes – helps to speed up the settling process. Some fruits contain very little tannin; there is none at all in vegetables or flowers, so recipes for, say, parsnip or elderflower wine may specify cold tea as one of the ingredients. You can try this yourself if your wines do not clear properly.

Acid is necessary for the most efficient fermentation. Most fresh fruit contains enough, but dried fruit, vegetables, and honey need some added. Lemon juice can be used, or you can buy powdered citric or tartaric acid from a chemist or wine-makers' supplier. Go easy with it, unless you like alcoholic vinegar.

MALT

You can ferment starchy things with yeast, but it is rather slow, because it has to break down the starch to sugar before it can make alcohol. A centuries-old way of speeding up this process is to let grain sprout, which naturally produces sugar by enzyme activity. Barley does this particularly easily and the process is called malting. You can malt barley on the small scale by an adaptation of the method for making mung bean sprouts:

• Get a large food can or similar container of about ½ gallon (2.25 litre) capacity, and punch a few holes in the lid to drain off water without letting the barley grains through.

• Half fill it with clean dry barley, soak the grain in warm water for 12 hours, then drain off the surplus water and leave the barley to sprout at about 21–23°C (70-75°F). Moisten it with warm water from time to time.

• When the sprouts are about half the length of the grains (after around four days), the malt is ready for drying.

The intensity of the drying makes a lot of difference to the taste and colour of the malt and the liquor you produce from it. If you bake it very lightly so that its colour does not change appreciably, the malt will contain a lot of sugar but will not develop the characteristic 'malty' taste.

If you put your sprouted barley in the oven on a baking tray, or in your solar dryer, and dry it until it is only just browning, you can produce such a light malt. This can be used for pale beers of the lager or American style, or even for wine, as an extra source of sugar.

Purists may shudder at the thought of mixing grain and fruit, but in fact a light malt gives no 'beery' taste to the brew. This is one way to get over the problem of sugar supplies for wine, if you do not want to use commercial sources. You can also add malt to other starchy materials, like potatoes or wheat, to speed up their breakdown to sugar.

If you roast the malt until it is golden brown – in an oven (your solar heater will not get hot enough) – you get the normal malty taste and a beer that is amber. Further roasting makes 'black malt' and dark beers like porter or stout, with a taste of burnt sugar from the caramelised malt.

> The intensity of the drying makes a lot of difference to the taste and colour of the malt and the liquor you produce from it

HOPS

Traditionally used to flavour beer, hops have no effect on the alcohol. Apart from the bitterness, they help to preserve the beer. You can grow your own hops (see page 126), or buy them ready-dried from suppliers online. While the quantity used is a matter of taste, for a start try 2oz of dried hops per gallon of beer (65g per 5 litres).

BASIC BEER RECIPE

Beer is usually less alcoholic than wine, except barley wines that can be up to 15 per cent alcohol. If you are going to drink the stuff by the pint, far better to work at 6 to 8 per cent – even this is stronger than some commercial brews.

• Take 5lb of malt, roasted to the colour you fancy; beat it with a mallet to crack the grains, and soak it in a gallon of water (2.5kg of malt to 5 litres of water), warming the water to 60°C (140°F) and maintaining this temperature for several hours. The idea is to let the enzymes in the malt work on the starch and convert it to sugar; if you use cold water the process is very slow, but if you steep at more than about 60°C (140°F) you run the risk of destroying the enzymes by heat.

• After about 12 hours, or whatever you can manage in the way of steeping, strain off the liquor ('wort'), squeezing out as much as possible from the malt residues, and boil the wort with 2oz (65g) of dried hops. You can just dunk the hops in and strain them off again, but it saves time and trouble to put the hops in a cotton or muslin bag and tie or sew it up; then you can simply lift it out when the boiling (about 20 minutes is enough) is over.

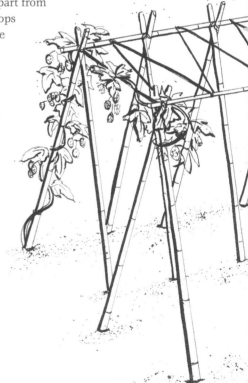

MEAD

If you have only tasted commercial mead, which is usually imported grape juice flavoured with a little honey, you can have no idea of the distinction of real mead made entirely with honey. It is a luxury well worth indulging in if you can get hold of honey in bulk.

Honey usually contains about 75 per cent sugar, to obtain maximum alcoholic strength make up 4lb of honey to a gallon of water (2kg to 5 litres). Very tolerable mead can be made with lower strength, and 2lb per gallon (1kg per 5 litres) is more appropriate for quaffing from goblets. For best results add the juice of two lemons or 1/8oz (4g) of tartaric or citric acid for each gallon (5 litres). Some people add cold tea for tannin, but nothing much needs to be cleared from mead so this is an unnecessary addition and may spoil the delicate flavour of the honey. Try to keep your mead – it really improves with time.

• If you want stronger beer, start off with more malt, or add sugar – up to 1½lb per gallon (750g per 5 litres) – at the wort stage, but the quantities given will make quite a strong brew without additions.

• Let the wort cool to about 37°C (98°F), add yeast, and ferment as for the wine recipe, except that you will not have to add extra sugar half way through.

This beer should be ready for drinking in about a week or two. If you want a bottled beer of the gassy sort, wait until the fermentation has completely stopped, then take some clean beer bottles with good screw stoppers, put a teaspoonful of brown sugar into the bottom of each one, fill them with your beer, and screw them down. Don't be tempted to put in more sugar to make the beer stronger – you will just burst the bottles. If you want it stronger, start the whole fermentation process with more malt or sugar.

CIDER

Cider is difficult to make in the traditional style – by fermenting pure apple juice – because not many varieties of apple produce enough juice or enough sugar. Most people are more naturally interested in cider as a way of using up surplus apples as they come. Incidentally, make sure you only use fully-ripe apples that are undamaged and not heavily bruised (also keep in a cool place for several weeks to soften the skins).

The best solution is to use the basic wine recipe (see page 208), with 3lb of apples per gallon (1.5kg per 5 litres) and added sugar to make up the total. With cider, as with beer, don't overdo the strength if you intend to drink pints – a total of 1½lb of sugar per gallon (750g per 5 litres) is plenty, taking the apple sugar and added sugar together.

We find it best to boil most varieties of apple – partly because apples are usually earmarked for cider when they are scarcely fit for eating or cooking, and the boiling at least helps to sterilise them; and partly because it releases the juice from the hard, crisp type of eating apple. The only disadvantage is that this also releases pectin, which can make the cider slow to settle.

Such cider looks, and tastes, quite drinkable after about two months, but if you aim for crystal clarity you can buy a commercial enzyme, pectinase, that breaks down the last cloudy specks of pectin. This can be used in other fruit wines, for the same purpose.

Harvesting

22. Making it pay

Having worked hard at your garden in a reasonable year, planting a few extra crops here and there to allow for failure, there will probably come a time when you have far more produce than you will need in the next year. Even when you have squirrelled away what you can and given some to a deserving cause or to the friend who showed you how to prune, there may still be a surplus.

The good news is that there are now many options out there for a grower keen to make this surplus pay. But be prepared to wise up on legislation – trading standards, environmental health, food safety, etc – if you go down the retail route.

EXCHANGE AND COOPERATIVE GROWING

If you do not fancy getting involved in the commercial side of gardening, try advertising your surplus produce in the local paper or on a newsagent's noticeboard, and pass the word around among your friends and people at work. You may be able to arrange the exchange or barter of surpluses between a group of neighbours. Do this in advance of planting, and agree who will grow a possible surplus of which crop; otherwise everybody will have lettuces, or apples, and consumer resistance develops. Decide on a fair basis for exchange – by weight or by value of produce – and keep an acurate record of debits and credits. If one person is forever popping raound for the odd half kilo of tomatoes, you must be sure how much in produce they owe, otherwise things can get nasty and local feuds build up.

You don't even have to arrange the exchange network yourself anymore – online exchange groups are increasingly springing up (see Useful websites guide, page 246).

You could also take a look online at the LETS (Local Exchange Trading Systems or Schemes) Link UK website (see Useful websites guide, page 246) which directs people to local community-based mutual-aid networks in which people exchange all kinds of goods and services with one another, without the need for money.

There might be a local group that you can link in with – there is a real push in many of our major towns and cities to encourage people to grow their own food such as the Capital Growth initiative in London and, as a result, all kinds of projects are springing up. In Hackney, London for example, the 'Growing

Communities' project is seeking to increase the amount of organic produce grown in the borough by setting up urban market gardens and it has run some 'The Good Food Swap' events. These events, described as an 'inner city version of the village show' provide growers with an opportunity to show off produce and swap with fellow producers.

SELLING YOUR PRODUCE

A stall outside your home: If you are keen to make a pound or two from your surplus produce you could just take a table down to the gate, set up a stall and hopefully clear the lot in a couple of hours. But your first customer could be a policeman asking if you have a Street Trader's Licence. If you are trading on private land and you are within seven metres from the public highway you will need a Street Trader's Licence (which you obtain from your local council), unless you are a shop and the display of goods forms part of the main business.

> Online exchange groups are increasingly springing up and there might be a local group that you can link in with

Door-to-door sales: If you sell from a car moving about, or go from door-to-door, you will need a Pedlar's Certificate which allows a person to sell goods whilst on foot. Pedlars can travel from: door-to-door, place-to-place, or town-to-town and once a certificate has been issued it can be used anywhere in the UK*. But the 'pedlar' cannot remain in one place and sell items, pedlars go to their customers to sell items rather than allow customers to come to them. A Pedlar's Certificate is obtained from the Chief of Police from the area where you live.

   * Note than in London, in those areas where a Street Trader's Licence is required, there has been an amendment to this general definition of a pedlar in that they can only sell door-to-door and not direct to customers in the street.

A roadside stall: Often the best sales from wayside stalls are made on main or busy roads. If people can pull off the road into your own driveway, this is all right provided again you have a Street Trader's Licence; but you must not encourage them to stop or wait on double yellow lines or a clearway, or cause an obstruction anywhere. The general point to note here is that if you use the public highway to sell goods or services you must have a Street Trader's Licence.

Summer fairs/car boot sales: These can be very busy events so it's worth investigating on local websites and in local papers to see when they are on. Check also if they allow food to be sold and whether you will need a licence to sell.

A market stall: Food markets are as popular as ever in Britain, especially since the advent of farmers' markets in the past ten years – there are over 500 farmers' markets in the UK. You can find a list of them on the National Farmers' Retail & Markets Association website (see Useful websites guide, page 246).

   Most insist that the stallholder must have produced the food they are selling and they often have a distance rule only allowing produce to be sold that has been produced perhaps within a 30–40 mile radius from the market, or in certain counties. Some also require that the stall must be attended by the principal producer, or a representative directly involved in the production process, such as a close relative or a member of staff.

Individual market operators or managers usually have the final say about what can be sold at their market, so start by approaching them. Remember, if you produce something different, you are more likely to be able to get a stall (see 'Growing for sale' box, page 218). You should also consider the size, timing and mix of stalls at the market and the practicalities such as hours, access, parking and other facilities.

The rent for a stall or pitch is usually quite reasonable, if you have plenty to sell. Fees are sometimes based on sales, with a set minimum, or there is a fixed fee. Other costs might include the hire of a canopy or umbrella, a table, and perhaps electricity supply.

For selling, you will want paper bags, which might be created out of twisted cornets of newspaper; boxes for display and carrying the goods to and fro; price labels; a secure tin for money and a float of small change to start you off; and a pair of gloves for handling the food.

Find out what rules apply to vehicles delivering to the market in the morning and where you can park safely during the day without incurring a fine which would dent your profits. If there is no easy access to the stall, enquire about use of trolleys or bring a pram. If your stall or pitch is in a good position, try to book the same one each time so customers can easily find you again.

THE ALL-IMPORTANT RED-TAPE

If you are serious about growing enough to sell (including perhaps processed foods such as jams and chutneys) then you must look into registering your premises with the Environmental Health department at your local authority at least 28 days before opening (registration is free). Registration applies to most types of food business, including catering businesses run from home and mobile or temporary premises, such as stalls and vans. If you use two or more premises, you will need to register all of them and if the food premises are used by several catering businesses – your village hall, for example – then the person who allows the premises to be used for this purpose is responsible for registering them.

All food businesses must also have a Hazard Analysis and Critical Control Points (HACCP) manual – a food safety management system which identifies what could go wrong in your processes, how to prevent it and how to address it. It could also be a good idea to get a basic food hygiene certificate (about six hours of training, usually run by local colleges), especially if you are handling ready-to-eat food products.

Further advice should be forthcoming from you local authority's Environmental Health department and from the Food Standards Agency (see Useful websites guide, page 246).

Other requirements for retailing your own food include a product and public liability insurance (several insurance companies have policies specifically designed for market stallholders that are good value) and compliance with Trading Standards. Contact your local authority's Trading Standards department for advice on weights, measures and labelling – often leaflets are produced to guide those that are specifically interested in selling at farmers' markets for example.

Be aware also that setting up in business brings other administrative requirements: VAT, income tax, accounts, as well as licences. The odd casual sale may be neither here nor there, but when done regularly, especially if you make a success of it, you will need to be in touch with the authorities.

Remember, when working out your profits, to deduct the cost of seeds, pots, packaging, compost, soil, nutrients and labour from any income you have received from sales.

GROWING FOR SALE

An unplanned surplus is most likely to occur at the end of the season, when it has no scarcity value – unless you grow nectarines or Chinese cabbage. If you are really keen to sell, perhaps you should set out from the start to grow something marketable. Sound out your markets first: make sure that your ideas are acceptable and fix a tentative date. To keep that deadline, you may have to protect your crops with glass; the purchase of this will dent your profits in the first year, but be re-usable afterwards.

The crops most likely to sell on a small scale and a casual basis are earlies, exotics and certain 'old-fashioned' varieties. You will certainly need glass and a favourable growing area if your earlies are to live up to their name. You may be able, without impoverishing yourself, to undercut a distant commercial grower sufficiently for the local shopkeeper to consider it worth their while to take your produce – since transport costs add a lot to central-market prices.

Exotics and vintage varieties are probably easier to grow competitively. Most commercial growers go for the big markets and don't bother with items for which there is not a large guaranteed sale all over the country.

Some of the popular varieties of apples, plums, tomatoes, lettuces, etc are no longer grown commercially because they don't yield huge crops or uniform sizes. In certain areas, there will be the potential to sell these vintage varieties among people who value good flavour.

Wash or brush the worst of the mud off all the produce and trim off stems. Pack it securely to withstand the journey and humping to the stall. Small fruit is best pre-weighed and sold in containers, especially if it won't take much handling. Cost this bit of the operation very carefully. Unless you have adequate packaging material to re-cycle, the boxes could cost more than the fruit.

Pricing is obviously important – it has to reflect costs of production but must not be too cheap and not too expensive, especially if a similar product is available in the area.

> Unless you have adequate packaging material to re-cycle, the boxes could cost more than the fruit

Don't try to work a stall alone for a whole day. It is astonishingly hard on the feet, if you aren't used to it, and even the most iron-bladdered will need to go to the loo some time. On the other hand, get help from a volunteer if possible because if you have anyone working for you, you'll need employer's liability insurance cover and may need to meet other employment regulations.

Unless you have enough produce of your own to fill a stall, the operation won't be economic. Even though the stock comes 'free', there are still the overheads to consider: rent, packaging, transport, equipment and any extra costs, like babysitters or loss of wages.

Check first before bulking out the produce with home-made cakes, cheese or wine. Some markets don't allow prepared foods; others do, but you will have to comply with all kinds of food and hygiene regulations. You can't sell home-made wine without an alcohol beverage licence, for example, and a good many other commodities are affected by some bit of legislation or another (see 'Red tape' box, page 217).

Selling to a shop: You could try selling through local shops. The local greengrocer will have regular contracts with commercial growers, but if you offer them produce which is very early, out of the ordinary, or especially fine, they might buy it from you so they can display it as 'locally grown'. A general shop of the more enterprising sort might accept your produce, even if it does not normally sell fresh vegetables.

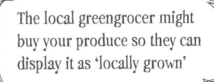

The local greengrocer might buy your produce so they can display it as 'locally grown'

Take a sample of your wares, well presented in a box, to see if the owner is interested. The owner will expect strawberries or raspberries to be in punnets, to save them being damaged by handling; these cost money and will reduce your profit. The price you are offered could bear very little resemblance to the price they will charge their customers, and the more perishable your goods, the less you are in a position to haggle.

Selling to restaurants: It could be that a local restaurant or café might consider buying your produce, but before you beat a path to their door note the following:
• Many restaurants need large volumes, so start with the smaller operations unless you can be sure of big surpluses.
• Pay the chef a visit and provide samples.
• Chefs will need reassurance that you can supply a certain amount of something over a given period of time in order to plan their menus – if you can't live up to this promise then don't bother.
• The restaurant business is fickle and uncertain – be prepared for demand to suddenly cease or even for the business to close (so ensure payments are made regularly and on time).
• Looks count – many chefs are looking at the aesthetics of the produce as well as the taste so find out what they are looking for, including the look they are trying to achieve.
• Keep it fresh by focusing on local businesses so you can deliver on the day of harvest, ideally first thing in the morning so you don't have to store the produce at all.
• As with markets or shop sales, focus on unusual crops that no one else is growing – vintage varieties and so on.

Keeping animals

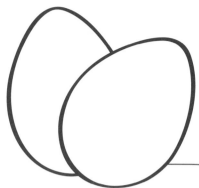

23. Livestock

If you are considering keeping livestock then you should truly weigh up the pros and cons. Of course it feels great to collect your own fresh eggs for breakfast and, if you like goats milk, then a ready supply from your own goats could contribute a great deal to your self-sufficiency, but there are some pretty crucial aspects that you will need to ponder:

Do you have the space?
Most animals require room to roam. The amount obviously depends on the animal in question but nonetheless, a minimum amount of outdoor space is going to be required – apart perhaps from a bee hive which can fit in quite small areas, even rooftops.

Are you ready for the responsibility?
Animals and birds are a tie. You must deal with them at least twice a day – letting them out, shutting them in, preparing food and feeding, mucking out, providing cages and bedding, coping with breeding and birth, checking on their welfare in the worst of weather and being alert to the first sound of fox attack in the night.

Making arrangements to cover a garden's needs, if you are away for a few days or a long holiday, is not too difficult. But for stock, you must have experienced care. An inexperienced neighbour or a casual teenage friend of a friend won't do. Animals left unattended or treated wrongly, die. This isn't just upsetting for the owner, it could lead to legal prosecution. So, unless you are able to give your stock 365-day care, don't keep any.

You must also be ready to deal with bureaucracy. There may be local bylaws preventing anyone from keeping poultry, for example, and many properties have covenants to prevent you keeping poultry and other livestock (if you rent your property you will need to check with your landlord). Depending on the size of the shelter and/or run you may also need planning permission – contact your local planning department to find out.

You may end up having more contact with your local Environmental Health (EH) department than you would like. If rats and mice are attracted to the site they can take action against you to eradicate any infestation, and if neighbours complain about any odours or noise you might also get a visit from EH.

Be prepared to purchase public liability insurance cover, especially if you have animals that like to roam – escapees can cause damage to people or property and you will be legally liable no matter how well you have tried to contain them.

National policy must also be adhered to. Under the Animal Welfare Act 2006 it is against the law to be cruel to an animal and you must ensure that the welfare needs of your animals are met, including the need: for a suitable environment and diet; to be housed with, or apart from, other animals; to be protected from pain, injury, suffering and disease; and to be able to exhibit normal behaviour patterns. Anyone who is cruel to an animal, or does not provide for its welfare needs, may be banned from owning animals, fined up to £20,000 and/or sent to prison.

There are numerous other rules and regulations that will necessitate action on your part – whether it is tagging cattle or registering your poultry under the Great Britain Poultry Register (voluntary if you keep under 50 birds). For a good guide to these for businesses (large or small ... and this includes the amateur smallholder) check Government advice online (see Useful websites guide, page 246). Be sure to check regularly as these regulations are constantly changing, especially when they concern disease control.

ANIMALS AND ALLOTMENTS

If you are considering keeping chickens perhaps, or a bee hive on your allotment make sure you are aware of the legal situation. According to the National Society of Allotment and Leisure Gardeners Limited a local authority can make rules governing the conditions on which plots will be let and this might include a prohibition on bees. It also states that, generally speaking, any animal can be kept on an allotment with the express permission of the Landlord Paramount (the municipal authority), but domestic chickens (not cockerels), and/or rabbits, can be kept and housed on an allotment plot as of right. Although it advises that it is only 'courteous for a plot holder to inform the municipal authority of an intention to keep and house domestic chickens and/or rabbits, to inform the authority of the number of creatures it is intended to keep, and to supply a contact telephone number in case of any problem with creatures'.

For more see Useful websites guide, page 246.

Can you cope with the brutal reality?

The question of what happens when they reach the end of their useful lives needs to be thought through. You keep hens for their eggs and when they stop laying they will do for the pot. Goats give milk but, when they are old, they are meat – so are all billy kids. Ducks, geese and turkeys are mostly destined for the table, pigs completely so. But before they can be eaten, they must be killed. Some animals must be slaughtered by licensed persons anyway – this adds to the cost of rearing pigs. Can you see yourself killing the rest? It would look odd taking rabbits or chickens to the butcher or farmer to be killed, apart from the cost. The alternative is physically picking up a creature and breaking its neck or cutting its throat – and seeing it jerk about after you have done that.

Even if you are sure you could carry out this necessary task quite unemotionally, will you feel the same after you have got to know an animal over weeks or months of protecting it from danger? Your children certainly won't. A daddy who slays Henrietta Hen or Benjamin Bunny is a loathsome creature not fit to be spoken to for at least a week and the more sensitive child will refuse to eat the cooked corpse.

> Some animals must be slaughtered by licensed persons but can you see yourself killing the rest?

One way around this is to arrange with another animal-keeping family that you eat theirs and they eat yours. Your Henrietta becomes their *poule au pot*, and their Mary Ann is your *pollo diavolo*. But if your children are bosom friends of the other children, or even attend the same school, you might end up with double trouble.

A better alternative is to depersonalise any animals destined for the pot. Number them for statistical purposes and from time to time harp on about the quantity of meals they represent. This is rather difficult with pigs, who are bright, affectionate creatures, but you could give the children one of the litter to keep as a pet – with a promise that it will never be killed.

What's the impact on your carbon footprint?
It is true that the commerical production of meat and dairy is linked to high greenhouse gas emissions – partly due to the methane cows produce and also due to the fossil fuels used to manufacture the feed given to livestock (not to mention the deforestation that occurs in order to grow more crops to feed more cows ... and so on). To ensure your livestock keeping is low in carbon emissions, the majority of feed should come from your own patch and source additional feed locally and sustainably. The same goes for bedding and other inputs.

Can you afford them?
Beyond the initial outlay of buying in your animals, you will also have the associated set-up costs such as the provision of housing, fencing and possibly a trailer for moving the livestock. Then there's the ongoing costs of feedstuffs, bedding, vets bills and so on. You will need to factor in all possible costs – including the time that will be taken out of your day tending the animals and filling in the forms!

> Some animals and birds are extremely useful for clearing land of perennial weeds and the odd garden pest

But despite the many potential drawbacks of keeping livestock there are most definitely some good reasons to give it a go.
• If you have poor quality land that is unlikely to support fruit and vegetable production, then ruminants, such as sheep and cattle (and even geese which will fatten almost entirely on grass), could still make that land productive.
• Some animals and birds are extremely useful for clearing land of perennial weeds and the odd garden pest such as slugs and snails.
• You will be sure of the quality of your meat/milk/eggs.
• You are taking more steps towards self-sufficiency and cutting your costs as well (the cost of meat has risen by over 16 per cent recently, while milk, cheese and eggs have risen by 19 per cent – so having your own supply will really help your budget in the long run).
• You will be cutting your 'food miles' especially if you find an abbatoir that is local to you.
• If you select rare breeds you will be doing your bit towards conserving those that are no longer in favour as they are not so suited to intensive commercial farming (see Useful websites guide, page 246).
• The manure will be gold dust for your vegetable beds, increasing fertility, and ultimately saving you money on buying in this valuable soil improver.

• There are plenty of breeds out there to choose from, some of which will be more suitable for smaller plots – the Dexter, for example, which is a miniature cow that can give 16 pints of milk a day, produces 70 per cent of the steak of a cow twice its size and is happy eating grass on a couple of acres (0.8ha) of land. Look online for breed societies that can give you advice on what is out there.

The following is an introduction to some of the requirements of the main types of animal that are commonly kept:

COWS

There was a time when the ambition of all true Britons was to own three acres and a cow. This is no longer a practical proposition for many, with the rising price of land. You could, theoretically, run a cow on an acre (0.4ha) of land, devoting half of it to the animal and the other part its fodder. Even so, the cow would have to come inside in the winter – it would need a strong, weatherproof shed – and feed,

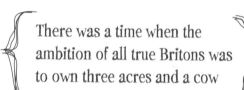

There was a time when the ambition of all true Britons was to own three acres and a cow

very expensive now, would have to be bought in. Cows are not cheap and need skilled care to remain healthy. They also require servicing (fee for bull) and some help with calving (fee for vet). Therefore, for the ordinary garden-owner, cows are definitely 'out'.

However, should the desire to have your own fresh, unpasteurised milk prove too strong but you still don't have the space for a cow then consider other options. You might find a local farmer or landowner has land you could rent – a corner of a field that could be fenced and your cow moved around it for grazing.

SHEEP

Sheep, which need to be in multiples, can require the same area as a cow. Very strong fencing is essential, for the urge to escape is born in them. They follow their chosen leader anywhere – into your garden, into the neighbour's garden, out into traffic. They eat roots and brassicas and dance on cloches and frames. They give you meat and wool – and a lot of headaches.

If you have the space then consider first what you want them for – do you want lambs to fatten and eat? Use them for their wool? Or maybe just need the grass dealt with in a large area of fallow land? The answer will determine both the breed of sheep you need and whether to buy a lamb or ewe/ram.

The amount of land you need depends on the numbers of sheep you are keeping. You can expect to have a maximum of ten ewes to an acre (0.4ha) but you will need to move them to another acre or so in order to allow the first area to recover and prevent a build up worms. If you only have an acre of land then divide it up into three, reduce the flock size and rotate the sheep between the three areas.

Lastly, be prepared for hard work if you opt for lambs. Orphaned lambs can often be bought quite cheaply from local farmers but you will need to invest a great deal of time, energy and money, bottle feeding them and keeping them alive. A two to three year old ewe might be a better bet.

PIGS

Pigs were traditionally kept in cottage gardens, where they fattened up happily on left-overs, with a bit of grain thrown in at gleaning time. They will eat anything, but need a lot of it, which means that, unless you have a large garden and a wasteful family to match, you will have to buy in food (but it is illegal to feed them any meat at all).

They need grazing space in summer, and unless securely fenced off, they will graze on, and dig up completely, any garden plot and its produce. They must have a sty to live in, and sows want a low hutch to farrow in, when you have paid to have them mated. You could build a sty of any old sturdy scrap, but this would look a mess – and a messy sty in a back garden attracts unfavourable attention from the neighbours. Pigs are, in fact, as clean as their owners let them be. They have a very rapid throughput and must be mucked out frequently. Their manure is rich, and stinks after about six hours. Unless it is shifted, they slip around in it and get plastered from top to toe.

An earth-floored sty cannot be cleaned out properly, so you must either build a floor of proper concrete or indented tile, which can be raked out and swilled down with water, or learn to live with an increasing aroma. This is when your neighbours will call in the Environmental Health department. Either way, pigs aren't going to be easy to live with unless you have a fair bit of land and either tolerant or distant neighbours.

> { Pigs aren't going to be easy to live with unless you have a fair bit of land and either tolerant or distant neighbours }

GOATS

Goats are not so piggish about food. They eat rough vegetation which no cow would even look at and so are great for ground clearance. Theoretically, goats could exist on wayside verges and common land but, in practice, verges tend to be sprayed with herbicides and commons can contain litter and broken glass. Goats cannot be run in an orchard, because they strip every bit of growth from the trees. This means strong fencing but as they can jump incredibly high it is best to tether

them by long ropes. They need dry housing to sleep in, and feed must be bought in for nanny goats in milk. Mating, too, costs money.

They are, however, great company and thrive in the company of other animals and humans. Plus nanny goats produce a lot of milk which can be an alternative for people allergic to cow's milk (although not suitable for babies due to its low levels of vitamin B12 and folic acid). It is an acquired taste, so try some before you start keeping goats. You could also consider making cheese from it.

POULTRY

Geese, ducks and chickens are the most common in gardens and small holdings. Ducks need fresh, running water to root around in and soon get distressed if they have no access to it. If you can provide a duck pond with fresh water running through it then they might be worth keeping – especially given the benefits they bring in keeping slug and snail populations under control. Khaki Campbells and Indian Runner breeds are good for gardens and small spaces and are good egg layers – but you will need to provide a safe house for them to lay in.

> Geese are admirable security guards and can be really useful in alerting you to the presence of foxes

Geese are admirable security guards – even against their owner's family – and can be really useful in alerting you to the presence of foxes. For this reason the odd goose is often kept with chickens. But they should not be kept where they can get into the road, because they attack passers-by and can injure children. Geese also cover any grass with their huge squashy droppings (guano) although they will definitely help keep your grass down.

You will need somewhere to house them at night and probably a good amount of land to let them roam and eat – an orchard would be ideal. Also remember they can live a long time – up to 20 years.

Hens are, with certain reservations, a practical proposition on a small scale. They need grass, but they are improvident and rip it to pieces with their claws. When they are laying, they must have grain – some of this can come from wheat straw. Check the cost of local straw and grain before you buy chickens. Both commodities are more easily and cheaply found in the country than in town.

A chicken house, preferably of wood, will be needed, with nesting boxes accessible from outside and a food hopper for expectant hens; also a wire run of small mesh, so that baby chicks can't get out or strangle themselves in the attempt. A second-hand chicken house can often be bought locally or look out for advertisements in *Poultry World*. If you're really lucky you might find one on Freecycle or another online exchange forum.

In theory, chickens can run free around an orchard, picking up scraps hurled out there. In practice, they need to be fenced in, because they are incredibly stupid and will wander off for miles and forget their way home. They are totally vulnerable to attack by foxes – even (perhaps especially, given the rise in urban foxes) in the suburbs; they often don't run to safety, even if the house is a few feet away, but sit there squawking until they are eaten.

Half a dozen birds is about the smallest number to maintain a reasonable supply of eggs. Hens don't need a cockerel to produce eggs, although they do to

BEE-KEEPING

Bees provide honey, which was our natural sweetener long before this new-fangled stuff, sugar, came to Europe, and many folk claim that eating honey has far fewer attendant health risks. It certainly tastes delightful and, when you get tired of it, you can use it to make mead (see page 212).

Bees take up very little room and can be kept in quite a small garden. They look after themselves, feeding from your plants and flowers or any others in the neighbourhood. In doing so, they help pollinate fruits in the garden and orchard and are tremendously valuable because of it.

They need very little attention and can be left alone while you are away on holiday without any worries (although once you are hooked on bee keeping you could find it takes more and more of your time). You might be able to acquire them free of charge – a fellow bee-keeper may have some bees or a swarm available (but make sure they are actually honeybees and not bumblebees or wasps). Once you have them – provided you don't take all their honey in summer – they stay with you for years, recreating colonies all the time.

If they are not interfered with, bees are not normally dangerous. Only when you disturb the hives for honey gathering will they get upset, and maybe sting; you should therefore wear impervious garments and a face veil for the purpose, and use a smoker. Just a few people are allergic to bee-stings, so it might be sensible for the whole family to experience being stung before you start – if anyone is more than mildly irritated, consult a doctor to check if this is an allergic reaction.

Although bees can be kept in any old box or rough hive, it is a lot simpler to use a purpose-built sectional hive, in which the honey layer can be separated from the bee-grub layer, without killing the bees or going through a rather messy process. Second-hand ones may be available but be careful as they might be infected with disease, such as Foul Brood disease. You should also be aware of the risk of varoa mite which is a parasite that thrives if husbandry is poor – ensuring the hive is not overcrowded and removing dead bees and other debris from the hive will help avoid the mite, which necessitates chemical treatment if present.

Before starting, take the opportunity to spend time with existing bee-keepers and get experience of handling bees. Visit the British Bee Keepers' Association website where you will find leaflets, advice and the details of local groups around the country that you can join or visit to find out more (see Useful websites guide, page 246).

fertilise them, if you want to increase your stocks. But don't keep a rooster in the suburbs; it will wake up early – and so will everyone else within earshot.

Birds can be bought very cheaply as day-old chicks, which are pretty but fragile; as eight-week pullets or at point-of-lay (18+ weeks when ready to lay eggs) – which are the most practical choice. Read up on the subject first – there are numerous websites and books and urban chicken keeping is becoming increasingly popular (with some chic but expensive coops and houses to match).

With all poultry, rats can be a big problem – both in stealing your eggs and causing you problems with neighbours and Environmental Health. They will often set up home under your hen house, so you will need to be alert and seek to eradicate them as soon as you spot them. Foxes too are also a threat – a dog, goose or rooster will help alert you to them, you might also smell them as they mark their territory with a strong scent. They often attack in the daylight so be vigilant and protect your poultry as well as you can.

Rabbits breed like rabbits – thirty days from mating to birth, then off again as soon as the buck sees the doe

RABBITS

Easy to keep in a garden, rabbits need strong cages of adequate size, with sleeping and living compartments. A suitable hutch can be adapted from an old orange box or the base drawer of an old-fashioned wardrobe. The dimensions vary according to the size of the rabbit, which must have room to stretch and turn without hitting the sides.

Rabbits like an outdoor run in summer, but must be confined in a netted cage, or they will eat every vegetable in sight. The cage will also protect them from predators, which they are not clever enough to do for themselves. They should be given hay or straw for sleeping and fed with vegetable scraps and ends, plus a daily meal of bought-in oats, bran or other cereal.

In return, rabbits provide you with a good supply of meat, which mixes well with vegetables in casseroles and stews. Their skins can be tanned and made into rugs or garments, with some sales potential. Flemish Giants are best for meat, Rexes and chinchillas for their skins. The Angora rabbit's long fur can be stripped and spun into wool; each produces about 1lb (450g) a year, but brushing and combing the coat regularly is essential so that it does not get matted.

Rabbits breed like rabbits – thirty days from mating to birth, then off again as soon as the buck sees the doe. This will necessitate a lot of cages and room to stack them. Rabbits need an awful lot of straw and hay to keep warm and dry, and they eat their bedding – which can be pricy so check your source of supply before you embark on the enterprise (farms being cheaper than a pet shop in town, for example).

Get a book on rabbit keeping and make the cages before you buy the stock. A good local breeder would be the best source of supply and could give advice on cage sizes and eating habits.

Alternative energy

24. Solar and wind power

If food is the main priority and expense for most families, energy runs it a close second. Fuel costs are rising all the time, and we have to pay an even heavier price because of the way we have squandered it – in uninsulated homes, thirsty car engines and an agriculture tied to mechanisation and oil-based chemicals.

But the costs are huge if you take climate change into account – over 40 per cent of the UK's man-made CO_2 emissions comes from the energy we use everyday. Plus there's the fact that global oil production will start to decline – once we are past the point of 'peak oil' – and that spells the end of cheap oil for most of us.

While we can reverse some of these trends and get back to more economical ways of living and working, it is clearly as important as ever to develop alternative sources for essential energy requirements. Few people want to return to a life-style of constant discomfort and back-breaking work, and there is no reason why we should have to. There is no real shortage of energy, it is simply that we have tied all our equipment to the wasting resources of the oil-well and the coal-mine, and largely ignored the almost limitless supplies of solar and wind power (in the UK, only around 5 per cent of our electricity comes from renewable sources).

When considering your energy requirements for growing – heating the greenhouse, powering an irrigation system, etc – it is certainly worth considering solar or wind power. There is plenty of advice online – the Energy Saving Trust, for example, provides an online Home Energy Generation Selector which will help you identify the technologies that might be suitable to generate heat or electricity for your home (see Useful websites guide, page 246). Plus, the price of renewable energy systems keeps getting lower and the availability greater. But for small-scale applications you can also have a go at making your own.

SOLAR ENERGY

The sun radiates a colossal amount of heat and light into space. Only a tiny fraction of it reaches the earth and, of this, only a fraction again actually penetrates to ground level, but this still provides around 1,000 watts per 10 sq ft (1 sq m) and enough solar energy falls on the earth's surface in twenty minutes to meet the planet's energy needs for a year.

So why do so few people actually use this energy? Apart from sheer lethargy, and the legacy of cheap fuel, there are two main reasons. One is that, while the average amount of solar power received is more than most people's requirements, the quantity we get in the winter is far lower. Unless you have a very large solar installation, you need some kind of conventional heating to back it up and this is expensive in capital equipment costs whichever way you do it.

The second reason for the neglect of solar power is that any obviously has to be set up where it can receive the most sun, usually on a south-facing roof of a house. This usually entails a lot more structural alteration than, for instance, putting in a conventional boiler. However, if you do most of the work yourself, the expense of the equipment and installation need not be crippling and you should reckon to get your money back, in terms of saved fuel bills, in a few years.

> Installing a solar collector usually entails a lot more structural alteration than, for instance, putting in a conventional boiler

SOLAR PANELS

A popular type of collector is a solar panel with circulated water. It works basically as a radiator in reverse, picking up heat from the sun and transferring this to water that circulates through the panel. To achieve maximum absorption, the surface is painted matt black.

There are several quite good solar panels on the market, made up complete with channels for the water, black finish, and plumbing outlets to connect to the

A typical solar panel design – the inlet and outlet pipes should be lagged

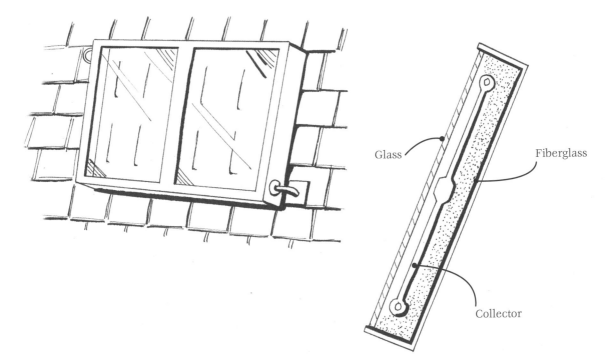

Glass

Fiberglass

Collector

It is not really worth while thinking about solar heating for the average house, at least in Britain, unless you have a minimum of 45 sq ft (4 sq m) of roof space which faces east to west through south and receives direct sunlight for the main part of the day.

According to the Energy Savings Trust the costs for a typical solar water heating system range from £3,000 to £5,000 and a solar water heating system can provide about a third of your hot water needs, reducing your water heating bill by between £50 and £85 per year. It will also save up to 1,300lb (580kg) of CO2 emissions, depending on what fuel you will be replacing.

There are plans to provide loans for homeowners who are keen to install solar panels and other renewable energy systems. The loans, from commercial companies, would be for between £10,000 and £15,000 and would be paid back over 20–25 years. A key difference from other loans though is that, if you move house before the loan is paid off, the new buyer would take over the payments.

The Government is also looking into 'feed-in-tariffs' where people who generate electricity via photovoltaic solar panels, wind turbines, hydro power or anaerobic digestion will receive up to £0.36 per kW/h of electricity, even if they use the power in their homes rather than feed it into the national grid. An extra £0.06 will be paid for every unit supplied to the grid.

water system. Alternatively, you could use some second-hand panel-type radiators – although it is fair to say that these are not really intended to be exposed to the weather and may corrode externally – or clip a labyrinth of ¼in (6mm) microbore copper piping to a metal backing plate, if you are good at handling this material and can make tidy bends.

Whatever the material of the panel, it should be mounted in an insulated box (fibreglass insulation is ideal), and covered with a sheet of glass tightly sealed to the box, so that there is no loss of heat through air escaping. If you are making your own panels, you can design the outer cases so that they fit horticultural glass which comes in standard sizes.

To get the heated water from the panel to your existing hot-water system, you will need connecting pipes running to a cylinder. If you have the space, you can fit another indirect cylinder next to your existing one. Alternatively, you can fit a dual-purpose cylinder in place of your existing one; water from the solar panel runs through one internal coil and your conventional heating boiler is connected to the other.

The main reasons for isolating your solar panel from the rest of the water in the system are: so that a leakage or burst in the panel will not empty your whole hot-water supply over the roof, and, to avoid such bursts, it is best to add anti-freeze to the water circulating through the panel and you don't want this mixed up with the rest of the water.

You should also have a pump, of the conventional central-heating type, so that water is circulated when you want it. There are gravity arrangements in use for some solar-heating systems, but they put severe restrictions on the placing of the panel and cylinder, and even the type of piping you can use for connections. The pump can be controlled by a thermostat that measures the temperature of the water in the main cylinder and that in the panel; it switches on the pump only when the water in the panel is hotter than the inside, thus ensuring that you do not circulate hot water from inside the house to warm the night air outside.

The panels have to go where they can catch most sun, which means facing south and at an angle to receive as much of the winter sun as possible. The best angle for this is given by the simple formula L + 13½° to the horizontal where L is the latitude of your site in degrees. Thus, at latitude 52°, you should set up your panels at 65½.

> There are plans to provide loans for homeowners who are keen to install solar panels and other renewable energy systems

Most solar water-heating systems don't need planning permission, but you should check with your local planning office before installing a system, particularly if you live in a listed building, a Conservation Area or a World Heritage Site.

An alternative to the roof might be a sunny site in the garden; here you will need to lag the pipe runs very thoroughly, but at least this does not need planning permission.

Solar panels in the garden can also be used very effectively to increase the heating in a greenhouse. Set up a line of panels, facing south, with a pump and thermostat control as for the house installation, and use these to supply hot water to a radiator under the staging in the greenhouse. If you have room to fit a well-lagged hot-water cylinder beside the house, this could conserve the heat overnight.

WIND POWER

We tend to associate wind power with two jobs: grinding corn and pumping water, but windmills can be used for any heavy work, and have successfully ground cement, broken stones, worked saw-benches and run electric generators.

Savonius rotor

A very simple type of windmill, useful for such purposes as pumping water around your plot, is the Savonius rotor. You can make one very easily and cheaply. Cut an old 50 gallon (225 litre) oil-drum down the middle so that you get two half cylinders, bolt these to two discs cut from ½in (12.5mm) plywood, 3ft (90cm) in diameter. Large washers will be needed to spread the load on the bolts, as the metal used for these drums is not very thick.

The discs will need bearings; the lower one can be made from a salvaged wheelbearing from a small car – you can pick one of these up very cheaply at a carbreaker's yard – using the wheel studs to bolt the bearing to the disc.

The upper bearing takes only a light load, so you should be able to use a medium-duty ball bearing from a scrap car, old lawnmower or some similar piece of machinery. Fix a pulley wheel to the upper disc so that you can run a belt drive to the pump or whatever it is you want to operate.

Now make a framework in 4in (10cm) sq timber. This may sound heavy, but there are many strains on the structure, particularly when the wind is high and the rotor is spinning well.

> Solar panels in the garden can also be used very effectively to increase the heating in a greenhouse

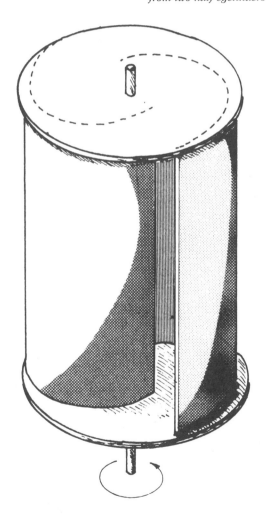

Savonius rotor – made from two half cyclinders

Wire guys, tightened by turnbuckles, are set at each corner and connected to iron stakes or heavy stones buried in the ground. This will help to ensure that the framework cannot lean out of true and get in the way of the rotor.

A Savonius rotor of these dimensions should give about 0.13hp (100 watts) in a wind of 20mph (32kmh); 0.45hp (335 watts) in a 30mph (48kmh) wind. This may not sound spectacular but it will pump a lot of water – perhaps from your rainwater butt to the greenhouse, or for a simple irrigation scheme. Built from scrap parts and second-hand timber, the rotor should cost less than a 'half-horse' electric motor, irrespective of the running costs.

A slat-mill

The conventional type of slat-mill is also simple to make on a small scale. It will provide a very useful source of power in the garden and looks a great deal more interesting than concrete gnomes. A 6ft (1.8m) diameter mill is quite a good size, as suitable pieces of timber can easily be found. Its output will be about 0.45hp (335 watts) in a 20mph (32kmh) wind; 1.5hp (1150watts) in a 30mph (48kmh) wind – so you could use it to drive a 10in (25cm) circular saw for example.

The sails are what are called warped sails; the sail-bars which cross the sail-stock – the centre spine of the sail – are set at an angle to the plane of the sail, and this, the weather-angle, decreases from about 18° near the centre of the sail to 7° at the outer end. This variation is to allow for the fact that the sail-tips have to travel much faster through the air than the portions near the centre, and therefore encounter more pressure.

The conventional slat-mill is simple to make on a small scale and will provide a very useful source of power in the garden

The main shaft – the sail-stock – takes a lot of strain and should, if possible, be made from hardwood, like ash or hickory, about 1½in (38mm) square. You can sometimes find suitable pieces of hardwood in the framing of old furniture or, if you are lucky, in an old house that is being demolished.

Finish off the sails by nailing the edge – the hemlath – to the sail-bars. You can cover the sails with canvas, as in the traditional windmill, or alternatively use marine plywood to make fixed slats to catch the wind.

Four sails like this have to be fitted into a large central boss – called the poll-head in real windmills – which carries the shaft. An iron rod is suitable for the shaft, which is best set back at an angle of about 15° rather than horizontal; this saves strain on the bearings. Fit a pulley to the shaft, and you have a power unit that will work very well when pointing into the wind.

The traditional mill has to be able to point into the wind from any direction, which means that it must be mounted on a rotatable platform – the mill and its shaft are set up on a round platform made from ½in (12.5mm) plywood; this itself is fixed to a salvaged wheel hub and bearing which can usually be obtained from a car-breaker's yard. The wheel studs serve to bolt the plywood to the hub, and the fixed part of the bearing is fastened to the pole or other mounting on which the mill is set up. All that needs to be added is a tail that will turn the mill into the wind.

One very useful occupation for such a wind-powered unit is to drive a small hammer-mill or compost shredder. When there is a good wind blowing, you can toss in all your awkward bits of garden waste that would otherwise take a long time to compost down – cabbage stalks, sweetcorn stems, tough weeds like cow-parsley and docks, hedge trimmings, even old newspapers – and they will be shredded to a compact mass that composts quickly.

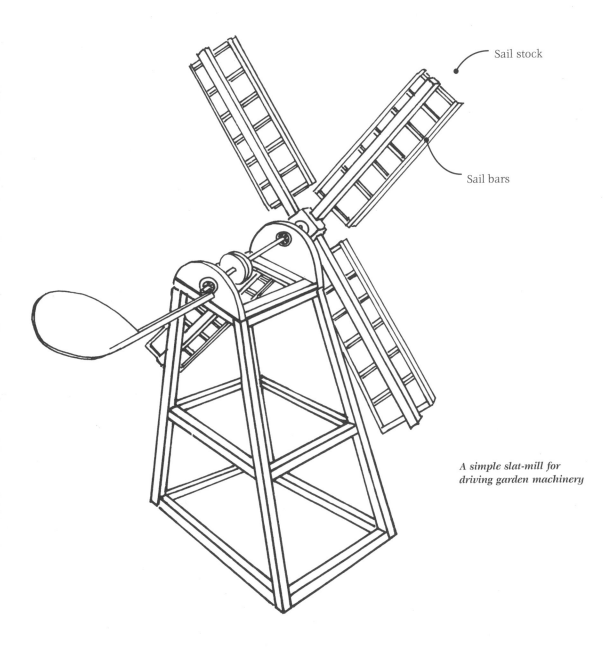

Sail stock

Sail bars

A simple slat-mill for driving garden machinery

Taking stock

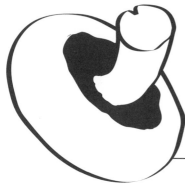

25. Is it worth it?

THE FINANCIAL BENEFITS

The whole enterprise of running a self-sufficient garden is intended to be cost effective. You will want to check if your personal effort is economically viable, if only to have an answer for idle friends and armchair critics. The only way to do this is to keep a detailed account of profit and loss, under various headings. The first year's expenditure is going to make the accounts look pretty silly if it includes the whole of the outlay on items which are going to last for years. The answer is to spread the costs in a logical way, as follows:

Running costs
First, extract the annual running expenses. These will be very similar every year and include the cost of the following:
- packets of seeds
- onion sets, seed potatoes, and any annual plants bought in
- sand, potting composts, growing bags
- any feeds/treatments/manure that need to be bought in
- plant pots, plant ties, natural fibre nets and anything else which doesn't last more than one season
- rent of allotment
- charge for metered water
- any paid labour for holiday periods
- cost of advertisements, hire of stall, packaging, etc, for selling surplus produce.

In later years, repairs and replacements will also figure in running costs – these are dealt with below.

Asset costs
Against the running costs, set the value of any assets in hand other than produce. You will have quite a lot of seeds and probably some compost which can be costed, for example.

Small equipment and accessories bought in the first year will last, with luck, for other years. In the case of single items, assess their life-span realistically: thick bendy polythene will probably last three years, hard plastic two; galvanised wire netting seven, and plastic-covered wire nine or ten years. Items which get a lot of handling, like seed trays, deteriorate faster than static equipment like water butts.

Having estimated the life expectation, divide the initial cost by two, three, eight, or whatever, and include it in your account each year, plus the whole cost of any item damaged during the period. In the case of an item intended to last three years which is smashed in the second, one-third of the cost has already been written off in the first year, so include the whole of the balance – two-thirds.

> The total outlay on your plastic greenhouse will work out over the years as the same as, or more than, a glass one would have cost, but with greater maintenance problems

Larger equipment is difficult to assess. It costs more, so in theory it should last longer, but some expensive plastic items are fragile. Judge the article on whether it can simply be repaired. When a one-piece, shaped, propagator top breaks, it is useless. Rate it at two years. A glass barn cloche, on the other hand, is made of several pieces of glass and a wire framework. The glass may break but can easily and cheaply be replaced to make the cloche as good as new. Rate it at about seven years – the probable life of the most durable component – and add in the whole cost of replacing panes of glass as and when they occur.

A glass and aluminium greenhouse ought to last 20 years or more, with no more than an occasional glass replacement; and a wooden one easily the same, if the wood is regularly treated (cost of this to be included in running expenses). The framework of a plastic house might last as long, depending on the metal used, but the plastic cover will need replacing at regular intervals. In the case of a soft-plastic-covered house costing, you might have to replace the cover every third year. This is such a high proportion of the initial outlay that you might prefer to assess the annual cost differently. Take the prime cost and add on the cost of the minimum six covers – assuming the price stays the same over the years, which is doubtful. Divide this by 20, for the expected frame life, and charge this amount each year. Incidentally, the total outlay on your plastic greenhouse will work out over the years as the same as, or more than, a glass one would have cost, but with greater maintenance problems.

Tools, which are a big expense at the beginning of your gardening career, will last an average of ten years, given reasonable care; so charge one-tenth of the cost each year, plus the total cost of anything damaged or rusted beyond repair. Add the total cost of repairs as running costs, but if you buy new tools as replacements or additions, include one-tenth of the cost from the year of purchase.

Perennial plants, like asparagus, fruit trees, etc, will last for many years and increase in value over most of the period. Fruit trees last 30-odd years (less for dwarf types); bushes for 20, asparagus for over 15, artichokes four and strawberries three years. However, it may be best to amortise them over half the expected life period, since they are liable to loss at any time, in theory. If they die, the whole balance must go down in that year and, if you move house, they count as fixtures and should be left behind, which means writing off the whole cost.

Any bulk-purchased goods, like a whole roll of wire, last for many years and the best way of costing is probably to measure the length used in any year, making an allowance for any part of it which is as good as new at the end of the season.

VALUE OF PRODUCE

Against all this expenditure, reduced to an annual figure, you should set the value of your produce. This can be worked out quite simply by weighing it as it is harvested and checking the current prices in local shops. Early produce is worth more than main crops, because you would have had to pay more for it at the time.

When you have a surplus of produce, don't include it in the normal accounts at its shop value if you mean to sell it. You won't get the shop price for it, unless you are a remarkable salesman. Regard what you make, less expenses, as profit since the produce would otherwise have gone to waste. Keep a record of the weight of this produce, and any you give away, so as to judge yields of any type of plant.

> Gardening is hard work when done consistently and conscientiously. Some economists insist that you should include in your accounts the cost of your labour

Where food is stored in its natural state, it would be strictly fair to deduct the price of anything which goes bad before use. When it is treated before storage, charge the cost of any materials – like salt, sugar, containers and fuel used in the treatment. Re-usable containers, bottles, crocks and boxes can be written down in value over a period of years – quite a long one in most cases.

When freezing produce, you should charge the cost of wrappings, boxes (reusable), salt, sugar and the small amounts of fuel used for blanching. Include the actual running costs for the freezer. The total cost of the operation will be more than wiped out by the amount you would have lost by almost any other method of storage. Include the amortised cost of the freezer over about 20 years and any amounts spent on repairs, servicing or insurance.

Food which you process should be valued at the equivalent commercial rate, rather than the cost of fresh food. Don't forget to deduct the same poundage from the unprocessed total, if you have included it already. Pricing frozen food is easy, but it may be hard to find a commercial comparison for your bottled fruit. If necessary, treat it as the equivalent weight of tinned food.

Sauces and pickles, sauerkraut, etc, can be costed from the nearest similar product. Jam is difficult, since your home-made product is usually all fruit and sugar, whereas some cheaper commercial grades include stretchers, like swede and other cheap vegetables. Compare yours with the best quality stuff in price, and allow a sum for fuel, since the long cooking process does cost more than the few minutes for freezer blanching.

Gardening is hard work when done consistently and conscientiously. Some economists insist that you should include in your accounts the cost of your labour. We think this would only be equitable if you were giving up other paid work to do the gardening. The vast majority of folk do it in their spare time – for which they would be covered financially by their monthly salary. Indeed, it might be fair to consider the alternative. If you were not gardening, what would you be doing? Driving around? Golfing? Drinking? All those activities cost money – perhaps the amount you save by not doing them should be added to the profit account?

THE OTHER BENEFITS

There are many other benefits to giving self-sufficiency a go – and you don't have to actually be entirely self-sufficient to realise most of them.

Health: You should enjoy better health, not only from working out of doors but from eating food which has not been doused in chemicals and is eaten fresh after harvest. There is a world of difference between the apple picked from your un-treated tree and the average industrially-produced apple which may have been sprayed up to 16 times with 30 different chemicals. There is also a big difference between the exhausted gardener and the exhausted commuter – the former usually sleeps far better, is fitter, and feels a sense of satisfaction that the latter can only dream of.

Environment: Self-sufficiency will entail working more closely with natural cycles and in that process you should see your natural environment thrive, with wildlife encouraged into your garden or allotment. This has been shown at the farm-scale with organic farms having on average 30 per cent more species and 50 per cent more wildlife like birds, butterflies and bees. (Plus the environment at large will also benefit – stopping the use of artificial nitrogen fertiliser, for example, will help reduce the run-off that cause algae blooms in coastal waters and creates a headache for water companies.)

> There is a big difference between the exhausted gardener and the exhausted commuter – the former usually sleeps far better is fitter, and feels a sense of satisfaction that the latter can only dream of

Carbon: Nitrogen fertiliser manufacturing for farming and food production, is one of the worst offenders for creating greenhouse gas emissions. By producing as much of your food yourself you will be reducing your 'food miles'. Aiming at true self-sufficiency should see you reduce the amount of 'extras' you need to buy-in such as fertilisers – both of which will reduce your carbon footprint.

Community contact: From exchanging seeds to sharing land, the potential for meeting people with shared interests and working together as a community is huge when you pursue the path to self-sufficiency. You will suddenly find you need each other more than you need the superstore up the road and, from that, all sorts of good things are likely to flow.

Hard work it may be, time consuming it certainly is – but the path to self-sufficiency can bring happiness, good health and the chance to break away from old routines and dependencies. Ultimately, it is a life-changing opportunity.

Useful websites guide

Getting started

SELF-SUFFICIENCY

An urban guide to becoming self sufficient: www.selfsufficientish.com

For practical advice and useful tips on becoming self-sufficient visit www. countrysmallholding.com or search for your local Smallholders Association

ALLOTMENTS AND COMMUNITY GARDENS

For information on allotments visit www.local.gov.uk/publications/growing-community-second-edition

National Trust: www.nationaltrust.org.uk/features/allotments-and-growing-spaces

Capital Growth: www.capitalgrowth.org

Lend and Tend: www.lendandtend.com

Social Farms & Gardens: www.farmgarden.org.uk

For the latest on national allotment legislation visit the National Society of Allotment and Leisure Gardeners Limited website at www.nsalg.org.uk

ORGANIC GARDENING BODIES

For advice on organic growing visit www.gardenorganic.org.uk

For the latest information about biodynamic growing techniques visit www.biodynamic.org.uk

GREEN ROOFS AND INTRODUCING WILDLIFE

For information on green roofs visit www.livingroofs.org or the European Federation of Green Roof Associations website at www.efb-greenroof.eu

You can find out more about wildlife from the following websites:

www.wildaboutgardens.org

www.rspb.org.uk/wildlife/wildlifegarden

SEEDS AND SEED EXCHANGES

Seed Sovereignty: www.seedsovereignty.info

Seedy Sunday: www.seedysunday.org

For green manure visit the Sow Seeds Limited website at www.greenmanure.co.uk

You can obtain heritage seeds from the following websites:

www.victoryseeds.com

www.gardenorganic.org.uk/hsl

HERBS

For general information about growing herbs visit www.herbsociety.org.uk

FRUIT TREES

For advice on growing fruit trees visit www.rhs.org.uk

Visit www.englandinparticular.info and www.theorchardproject.org.uk to find out more about orchards

EXCHANGING AND SELLING PRODUCE

Visit www.vegexchange.com to exchange home-grown vegetables in your local area

Another exchange site is www.letslinkuk.net

National Farmers' Retail and Markets Association: www.farmretail.co.uk

Open Food Network: www.openfoodnetwork.org.uk

Food Standards Agency: www.food.gov.uk

KEEPING ANIMALS

For advice on keeping livestock visit www.gov.uk/government/organisations/department-for-environment-food-rural-affairs and www.rspca.org.uk/adviceandwelfare/farm

Rare Breeds Survival Trust: www.rbst.org.uk

Visit www.smoking-meat.com for advice on processing meat at home

For advice on keeping chickens visit www.bhwt.org.uk/hen-keeping-starter-guide

For more information about keeping bees visit www.bbka.org.uk

ALTERNATIVE ENERGY

For advice on alternative energy visit www.energysavingtrust.org.uk

Visit The Centre for Alternative Technology website at www.cat.org.uk for information about solar and wind power

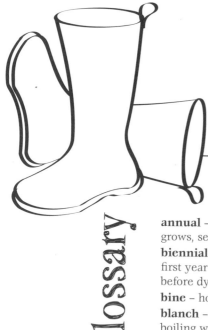

Glossary

annual – plant which germinates, grows, seeds, and dies in one year

biennial – plant which grows in the first year and seeds in the second before dying

bine – hop vine

blanch – to dip fruit/vegetables in boiling water briefly before freezing, or exclude light from vegetables (stems of celery and leeks) to maximise tenderness and flavour

bolting – plants that flower or seed prematurely before they have sufficiently grown and reached maturity, often caused by poor soil or lack of water

brassica – family of vigorous vegetables like cabbage, sprouts, turnips

cash-crop – crop produced for sale, not for own use

catch-crop – rapidly growing plant that can be intercropped between rows of the maincrop or between periods of regular crop production

clamp – pile of earth and straw which is built over a heap of vegetables to preserve them through winter

clean – term used to refer to land/soil which is free of weeds

cloche – low transparent cover put over young plants to protect them from cold

club-root – major disease of cabbage-family plants

cold frame – glass or plastic covered frame used to protect and acclimatise plants and seedlings

companion planting – practice of inter-planting different species to reduce pest problems or improve plant growth

concurbits – mostly climbing or trailing plants (courgettes, cucumbers, melons, pumpkins)

cordon – a particular way of training fruit trees so they are convenient to pick

cross-pollinating – transfer of pollen from the flower of one plant to the flower of another plant

crown – part of a herbaceous perennial that is just at soil level, from which roots and shoots grow (rhubarb, asparagus)

curing – the preservation of meat and fish using salt and/or smoke

cutting – small piece of wood/plant removed from a mature plant with the objective of being rooted to create a new plant

damping down – watering the floor and staging of a greenhouse or cold frame to increase the humidity and lower temperature in warm weather

dibber – a pointed stick used for making holes in soil when transplanting seedlings

division – teasing, pulling or cutting apart clumps of plants in order to produce more

dwarf – fruit trees propagated onto different rootstocks to produce trees far smaller than a standard variety

earthing up – piling soil up to bury the normally above-ground part of the plant to encourage growth of additional tubers (potatoes)

espalier – way of training a fruit tree along horizontal wires, making it easier to manage and pick fruit

fan – way of training a fruit tree into a fan shape for ease of management

forcing – encouraging plants to grow, flower or fruit before their natural time by placing in darkness or a heated greenhouse

furrowing – creating narrow trenches in preparation for sowing seeds, planting out

germinate – to begin to sprout or grow

graft – union of a detached shoot or bud with a growing plant by insertion or attachment

green manure – soil improver planted to add nitrogen by storing it in roots and leaves which are then dug in

growbags – plastic sacks of prepared compost, sometimes with added nutrients

harden off – gradually expose a plant to outdoor conditions after it has been kept in a greenhouse or indoors

hardy – term applied to plants that are able to survive outside in normal winter conditions

heeling in – putting plants in a trench so as to cover their roots whilst they are temporarily in storage

herbaceous – plant that does not form a woody stem, and usually dies down each winter and grows again in the spring

horticultural fleece – thin, unwoven, polypropylene fabric used as a floating mulch to protect early crops and other delicate plants

hot bed – glass-covered bed of soil heated with fermenting manure used for germinating seeds or protecting tender plants

humus – the largely decomposed masses of vegetable matter which make up a vital part of good soil structure

hungry gap – the period in spring when there is little or no fresh produce available

leafmould – a form of compost produced by the breakdown of shrub and tree leaves

legume – family of plants which create their own fertility through nitrogen-fixing bacteria in root nodules (clover, beans, peas)

light – the description of soil which contains a high proportion of sand and is therefore quick to dry out and easy to work

lime – mineral compound used to reduce soil acidity and supply calcium for plant growth

loam – ideal soil type containing an equal balance of sand, silt and clay

mash – the mixture of malt, hops, and water which is heated up and processed to make beer

mulch – a layer of reasonably inert material which is spread on to soil to keep down weeds and prevent loss of moisture

neutral – a soil that is neither acid nor alkaline and has a pH of about 7

nitrogen – a natural element occurring in the soil and air, which is absorbed by plants primarily to make leaves

nutrients – nitrogen, phosphorus, potassium, calcium, magnesium, sulphur, iron and other elements needed by growing plants and supplied by minerals and organic matter in soil and fertilisers

organic matter – plant and animal residues, such as leaves, trimmings and manure, in various stages of decomposition

perennial – plants which grow on from year to year without reseeding

pH – term used to measure acidity – acid or alkaline

pinching out – removal of a shoot tip, usually from a young plant, to encourage development of side shoots

pot bound – a plant that has outgrown its container such that its roots have no more room to grow

propagation – various techniques which are used to create small new plants from existing mature plants

rack – to siphon clear liquid from above sediment during the process of making beer or wine

rhizomes – underground runners of some types of plants that extend laterally to create new plants

roots – crops that yield a root which makes good food

rotation – technique of changing crops grown on a piece of land every year to create a pattern which minimises disease and boosts fertility

row crop – crops which are grown in rows for ease of hoeing, weeding, and harvesting

runner – vegetative shoot produced by 'walking' plants to propagate themselves

seedlings – young, recently germinated plant that has a single unbranched stem

self-fertile – plant which sets fruit and seed when fertilised with its own pollen

sets – what you call small onions which are planted as 'seeds'

solar dryer – a chamber enabling air drying by using the sun's energy

standard – the shape of a young tree where a single trunk extends at least 6 feet (1.8m) from the roots to the first branches

subsoil – light-coloured soil layer found beneath the topsoil, containing little or no humus

tender – what you call plants that are sensitive to frost damage

thinning – pulling out or cutting off some seedlings in a row, plot, or flat, for the benefit of those that remain

topsoil – the topmost layer of soil with the highest concentration of organic matter and mircroorganisms and where most biological soil activity occurs

weed – vigorous plants which unless removed swamp cultivated plants

About the authors

Eve McLaughlin wrote the original version of *Cost-Effective Self-Sufficiency* with her husband, Terence McLaughlin, a scientist, who is since deceased. Eve is a genealogist and has written a number of books and guides about family history. At the age of 82, Eve continues to be a keen gardener and propagator, and enjoys spending time in her farmhouse garden in Buckinghamshire.

Index

A DAVID AND CHARLES BOOK

© David and Charles, Ltd 2022

David and Charles is an imprint of David and Charles, Ltd

Suite A, Tourism House, Pynes Hill, Exeter, EX2 5WS

Text © Eve and Terence McLaughlin 2010
Revised and updated by Diane Millis
Illustrations by Lotte Oldfield

First published in the UK as *Cost-Effective Self-Sufficiency* or *The Middle-Class Peasant*, 1978
Revised edition published in 2010
This edition first published in 2022

Names of manufacturers and product ranges are provided for the information of readers, with no intention to infringe copyright or trademarks.

A catalogue record for this book is available from the British Library.

ISBN-13: 9781446309124 paperback

This book has been printed on paper from approved suppliers and made from pulp from sustainable sources.

Printed in the UK by Page Bros for:
David and Charles, Ltd
Suite A, Tourism House, Pynes Hill, Exeter, EX2 5WS

10 9 8 7 6 5 4 3 2 1

Editor: Sarah Callard
Art Editor: Prudence Rogers
Designer: Dawn Taylor

David and Charles publishes high-quality books on a wide range of subjects. For more information visit www.davidandcharles.com.

Layout of the digital edition of this book may vary depending on reader hardware and display settings.